RESTRUCTURING INDUSTRY AND TERRITORY

THE EXPERIENCE OF
EUROPE'S REGIONS

T0300018

REGIONS, CITIES AND PUBLIC POLICY SERIES

Series Editor: Ron Martin, Department of Geography, University of Cambridge

Throughout the industrialised world, economic transformation, rapid techno-logical change and increasing globalisation are giving greater prominence to the nature and performance of individual regional and urban economies. The patterns and processes of regional and urban development are being fundamentally redrawn. At the same time, regions and cities are assuming an increased importance as arenas of public policy innovation and implementation and as new loci of social and economic intervention and regulation. *Regions, Cities and Public Policy* is an international series which aims to provide authoritative analyses of the new significance of regions and cities for economic development and public policy. It aims to combine fresh theoretical and empirical insights with constructive policy evaluation and debate, to provide a definitive set of conceptual, practical and topical studies in the field of regional and urban public policy analysis.

RESTRUCTURING INDUSTRY AND TERRITORY

THE EXPERIENCE OF EUROPE'S REGIONS

edited by

Anna Giunta, Arnoud Lagendijk
and Andy Pike

Routledge
Taylor & Francis Group

LONDON AND NEW YORK

First published in 2000 by The Stationery Office

This edition published 2014 by Routledge
2 Park Square, Milton Park, Abingdon, Oxon OX14 4RN
711 Third Avenue, New York, NY 10017, USA

Routledge is an imprint of the Taylor & Francis Group, an informa business

The information contained in this publication is believed to be correct at the time of
manufacture. Whilst care has been taken to ensure that the information is accurate,
the publisher can accept no responsibility for any errors or omissions or for changes
to the details given.

A CIP catalogue record for this book is available from the British Library
A Library of Congress CIP catalogue record has been applied for

ISBN 0 11 702380 9
ISBN 13: 978-0-11-702380-2 (pbk)

CONTENTS

LIST OF TABLES AND FIGURES

CONTRIBUTORS

Dr Anna Giunta (Editor)
Dipartimento di Economia Politica
Universita degli Studi della Calabria
Italy

Dr Arnoud Lagendijk (Editor)
Faculty of Policy Sciences
University of Nijmegen
The Netherlands

Dr Andy Pike (Editor)
Centre for Urban & Regional
Development Studies (CURDS)
University of Newcastle
Newcastle upon Tyne
UK

Mr Peter Ache
Department of Planning
Strathclyde University
Glasgow
UK

Mr James Cornford
Centre for Urban & Regional
Development Studies (CURDS)
University of Newcastle
Newcastle upon Tyne
UK

Dr Stephen Driver
School of Sociology and Social Policy
Roehampton Institute
London
UK

Ms Anna Dudleston
Centre for Residential Development
Department of Building and
Environmental Health
Nottingham Trent University
UK

Professor John Goddard
Centre for Urban and Regional
Development Studies (CURDS)
University of Newcastle
Newcastle upon Tyne
UK

Professor Ann Markusen
Hubert Humphrey Institute of
Public Affairs
University of Minnesota
Minneapolis
USA

Mr Richard Naylor
Centre for Urban and Regional
Development Studies (CURDS)
University of Newcastle
Newcastle upon Tyne
UK

Dr Iva Pires
Centros de Estudos Geográficos
(CEG)
Universidade de Lisboa
Faculdade de Letras
Portugal

Joachim Thiel
Technische Universität Hamburg-
Harburg
Arbeitsbereich Stadt- und
Regionalökonomie
Germany

Dr M. Concepción Torres
University of the Basque Country
Facultad de Filología, Geografía e
Historia
Departamento de Geografía,
Prehistoria y Arqueología
Spain

Dr Mário Vale
Centros de Estudos Geográficos
(CEG)
Faculdade de Letras
Universidade de Lisboa
Portugal

Dr Michelle Wood
Researcher
Durham University Business School
Durham
UK

PREFACE

The link between innovation and territory stands high on the European agenda. Since the 1980s, the European Community and subsequent European Union has devoted more attention and resources to the theme of innovation, not only by supporting business collaborations through its Framework Programmes but also through shifting priorities in the Structural Funds.

The link to territory, in this context, has a double connotation. On the one hand, innovation is geared to improving Europe's industrial performance against that of competitor territories – North America and South-East Asia. This ambition has been a response to the perception that Europe's industries, from traditional (e.g. textiles) to modern (e.g. aerospace), were losing out as a consequence of internal and often national market fragmentation as well as a lack of international orientation. Also, Europe is seen as lagging behind in the development of new industries, in the areas of information and communication technologies and new media.

On the other hand, innovation is closely associated with regional development. In a stream of work underscoring its revival as a strategic site of economic development and policy-making, the region has been identified as an appropriate territorial level for policy interventions aiming to strengthen Europe's innovative performance and to contribute to social cohesion within the Union. Born out of this sometimes uneasy alliance between the harder objectives of 'competitiveness' and innovation, and the softer objectives of a more balanced and equitable geographical development, the region has become a central object around which a whole range of EU policies and policy instruments have evolved and become intertwined.

Such policy perspectives are mirrored in the academic domain. In many disciplines, from geography and economics to sociology, politics and cultural studies, the region has become not only a significant object of study but also a focal point for developing multi- and inter-disciplinary research.

In several ways, the central themes of this book connect with these inter-related concerns of innovation and territory and the revival of practical and academic interest in the region. More specifically, the volume focuses on processes of industrial restructuring from the perspective of the link between territorial development and changes within the organisation of industries, or – to quote the term used here – 'filières'. This perspective stems from the ambition not only to consider the regional level in isolation, but also to develop a multi-level or scalar analysis of interdependent socioeconomic and political processes. The emphasis on restructuring results from an explicit interest in the experience of less-favoured regions in the European Union. The book does not seek to reveal good practice and produce templates for restructuring and improved 'competitiveness' solely by drawing upon developments in Europe's more prosperous heartlands. The problems and prospects of such an approach have been discussed at length elsewhere. Instead, the intention here is to contribute to the understanding of the complex processes that shape uneven and unequal territorial development and both enable and constrain processes of restructuring. From this closer and deeper interpretation, it is intended that policy may learn to become more effective.

At a more practical level, the present volume was born out of collaborative research work supported by the European Commission through its former HCM (Human Capital and Mobility) Programme. With this support, which financed the exchange of doctoral and post-doctoral researchers and the organisation of international meetings and seminars, six European centres established a research network under the name of EUNIT (European Network on Industry, Innovation and Territory). The participating centres comprised:

- Centre for Urban and Regional Development Studies (CURDS), University of Newcastle, Newcastle upon Tyne, United Kingdom (project co-ordinator).

- Centro de Estudos Geográficos (CEG), University of Lisbon.

- Dipartimento di Teoria e Storia dell'Economia Pubblica (DSTEP), University of Naples.

- The Chair of Spatial Planning (ERP), University of Dortmund, Germany.

- Centre for Infrastructure (INRO-TNO), Transport and Regional Development the Netherlands, Delft, the Netherlands.

- Laboratoire Techniques, Territoires et Sociétés (LATTS), École Nationale de Ponts et Chaussées in Paris, France.

Running from November 1994 to October 1998, EUNIT financed the exchange of researchers between the centres and the organisation of three international seminars, one larger international conference in Lisbon and three Summer Schools.

As reflected in the structure of this book, EUNIT research was organised around filière and territorial studies. The filière studies looked at processes of industrial development and restructuring in six sectors: textiles and clothing, automobiles, aerospace, cultural industries, logistics and advanced producer services. The territorial studies were concerned with regional development within the home areas of the participating research centres. While the results have been disseminated widely elsewhere, this book presents a selection of the papers that connect most closely with the theme of restructuring and the interaction between filières and territorial development. The experience of Europe's regions fills out this canvas of theoretical debate.

EUNIT supported not only joint research activity but also a vibrant professional and social network, much of which remains in place today. Like many of its sister networks, EUNIT contributed to the shaping of social relations, including friendships, across Europe. In so doing, EUNIT has enabled the building of common understanding and visions, as well as the human and social capital which underpins Europe's 'competitiveness' and, more importantly, cohesion. The authors of this book intend that their work will contribute to the debates around these issues.

Professor John Goddard
Pro-Vice-Chancellor, University of Newcastle
Scientist in Charge, EUNIT Network (1994–98)

ACKNOWLEDGEMENTS

A collective endeavour of this nature invariably runs up debts of gratitude. The international nature of this project has ensured that these debts have been both large and capable of crossing national borders. Together, the editors would like to thank the following: the Commission for the European Communities (CEC) for funding the European Network on Innovation and Territory (EUNIT) as part of their Human Capital and Mobility programme; the Regional Studies Association and Ron Martin for including this book as part of their Regions, Cities and Public Policy Series; the contributors to the volume for providing their copy and responding to editorial comment; Sue Robson for putting together the manuscript; the Centre for Urban and Regional Development Studies (CURDS) for supporting the preparation of the manuscript; and the relevant staff at The Stationery Office. Individually, Anna Giunta would like to thank Annalena De Rosa and Guiseppe Giunta for their lovely support. Arnoud Lagendijk would like to thank Christien and especially Anna, for letting Daddy to do some work between the playing. Andy Pike would like to thank Michelle and Ella.

Anna Giunta, Rome; Arnoud Lagendijk, Nijmegen;
and Andy Pike, Newcastle upon Tyne

PART I:

INTRODUCTION

1 Introduction: Scalar Interdependencies between Industry and Territory

INTRODUCTION

In the context of an increasingly liberalised and allegedly 'globalising' economy, the territorial development dilemma has become increasingly problematic. Within the European Union, traditional concerns with the impact of economic and political integration upon the distribution of economic activity and employment at the regional level remain fundamental to the European project (CEC 1996). A change in emphasis has been evident in recent years, however, with a discernible move towards stressing the institutional agency of territories in enhancing their own regional economic development prospects and promoting cohesion. (See, for example, CEC 1997a; Amin and Thrift 1995; Cooke and Morgan 1998.) Integral to this shifting emphasis has been a fundamental reconsideration of the changing relations between the restructuring of industries and territorial development. A deepened understanding of the reshaping of this interface forms the central focus of this volume.

The aim of the collection is to explore the emergent interconnectedness and interdependency of industrial and territorial development in the European context. The tension between two strands of work forms the dynamic for the book. First, in contrast to recent literature proclaiming the emergence of a 'placeless' and 'globalised' economy and society (Reich 1993; Sachs and Warner 1995; Strange 1988), more critical work on the structuring and/or restructuring of economic activities has highlighted an increased sensitivity to the particularities and specificities of both industries and places (Held *et al.* 1999; Kozul-Wright 1995). Here, the character and attributes of localities are seen to make an increasing difference to what types of activities are undertaken where, as well as their implications for local economies. Second, the recent emphasis on the interplay of 'localisation' and 'globalisation' processes in influencing the nature and form of economic development has focused on the role and abilities of territories to build the capacity to facilitate growth and prosperity from combinations of endogenous as well as exogenous sources (Storper and Scott 1995). The institutional agency of places and innovative policy development are interpreted here as integral to shaping economic development trajectories.

The inherent tensions between 'globalisation' and 'localisation' processes imply that the fortunes of restructuring industries and territories are increasingly bound together in concrete as well as subtle and complex ways at the centre of the regional economic development dilemma. Indeed, some commentators suggest that current changes are made or remade across a range of interpenetrating and socially constructed scales (Swyngedouw 1997). The core themes of this book flow from a central concern with this closer co-evolution of the changing relationships between industry and territory.

The main approach taken in the book reflects the emphasis in recent regional economic development writing (Cooke 1995; Grabher 1993; Martin 1994; Martin and Sunley 1996; Sunley 1996) on insights from the recent economic sociology and socioeconomics literature (Hodgson 1999; Hollingsworth *et al.* 1994; Matzner and Streeck 1991). These approaches situate economic action within its social structure and have reawakened interest in 'old' institutionalist economic approaches that emphasise the historical and evolving role of institutions in shaping economic, social, cultural and political life. Such approaches have, to an extent, revived regional political economy by opening it up to human and institutional agency in both individual and collective forms. In addition, the evolutionary concerns of path dependency, as well as complexity and heterogeneity, are within this frame of reference. Questions concerning the roles of culture and governance have also moved centre stage in academic debates (Cooke and Morgan 1998; Keating 1997; Saxenian 1994) and in policy and institutional responses at the EU, national, regional and local scales (Lagendijk 1999a; Keating 1999). This collection endeavours to take a critical line on the convergence of these ideas by examining the industrial and territorial dimensions of restructuring processes in Europe's regions.

This introductory chapter introduces the main themes of the collection in three sections. The next section sets out our position in the 'globalisation–localisation' debate and prepares the ground for the following discussion of the interface between territorial and industrial development. The next section focuses on the institutional approach and how this contributes toward an understanding of industry–territory interrelations in conceptual and theoretical terms. This section emphasises the institutional and cultural underpinning of innovation, which pervades much of the present debates concerning regional economic development. The final section provides an overview of the structure of the book.

BEYOND 'LOCALISATION VERSUS GLOBALISATION'

Since the ideas on flexible specialisation emerged nearly two decades ago (Piore and Sabel 1984) the twin themes of 'globalisation' and 'localisation' have occupied centre stage in debates concerning territorial development (Amin and Malmberg 1992; Savy and Veltz 1995; Storper 1997). As part of this evolving agenda, the focus of research has appeared to shift from the spatial organisation of enterprises and the analysis of larger industrial systems to the region as the central unit of economic activity (Storper 1995; Cooke and Morgan 1998). The region has become important for at least two key reasons. First, in economic terms, the performance and 'competitiveness' of firms is regarded as having become more dependent upon external resources, in particular on their close interaction with other companies in functions including innovation and marketing (Malmberg *et al.* 1996; Maskell and Malmberg 1999). Such interaction, which may be of both a collaborative and competitive nature, is facilitated, so the argument goes, by proximity – or, to use the precise terms deployed by schools of thought seeking to explain such developments, by being 'embedded' in a regional 'innovative milieu' (Camagni 1995), 'industrial district' (Brusco 1992) or 'learning-oriented localised agglomeration' (Malmberg *et al.* 1996). The second reason behind the growing importance of the region is political (Keating 1999). In recent decades, it is argued that regions have been endowed with agency – albeit to differing degrees in different places – through decentralisation and the alleged 'hollowing out' of the nation state (Jessop 1994) and the concomitant devolution and strengthening of regional governance structures (Tomaney 1996). This relative rise in political power is underpinned by the alleged shift from a central 'managerial' state to a more devolved 'entrepreneurial' or 'network state' (Martin and Sunley 1997) and the emergence of a 'response mode' style of regional policy-making. The latter implies that regional policy and initiatives stem from local initiatives responding to calls and opportunities offered by national bodies, and increasingly international bodies such as the EU, instead of just consisting of the local implementation of centrally designed spatial policy. The 'response mode' has become especially pervasive in the area of business support and innovation policy (Lagendijk 1999b).

Inspired by the recent economic sociology and institutional literature, recent debates have sought to bring together these economic and political dimensions of regional development. The result has been more attention to the 'softer' side of economic development, with an emphasis upon the cultural and social elements that are claimed to underpin collective behaviour at the regional level. This collective behaviour, which is elucidated in terms of the localised creation of trust, social capital, and 'institution-building' (Brusco 1995; Malmberg *et al.* 1996) is said to improve the 'competitiveness' of firms in increasingly international markets, to bring about a strategic direction and coherence for the regional economy and to help create locally rooted regional strategic assets. By the collective mediation of processes of innovation and specialisation, regions are said to acquire 'competitiveness' in the global economy. Indeed, such processes of 'localisation' at the regional level – in which the economic and political level are closely intertwined – can be understood as the acute awareness and responses of regional agents to what is going on in the world economy in terms of intensified competition in the context of massive and rapid flows of goods, services, technology, capital and, to a far lesser degree, labour. What is more, localisation, far from being a curious aberration in a globalising world, is presented by some commentators as a prerequisite for 'competitiveness' (Maskell 1999; Kristensen 1994; Oinas 1998). The recent emphasis on the 'learning region' is a clear manifestation of the notion of building 'competitiveness' by a strategy of localised learning-based responses to perceived global 'opportunities' and 'threats'. Some authors have even spoken of the return to a somehow 'natural geography of proximity' (Savy and Veltz 1995).

In its purest form, accordingly, the localisation thesis amounts to an image of a harmonious region (Sabel 1992) that derives its 'competitiveness' from the way localised flexible economic networks are institutionally embedded through the role of cultural, social and political factors. Regional 'competitiveness' is thus defined in the context of 'globalisation' that is presented as a set of relentless pressures continuously challenging the position and role of the region in the spatial division of labour. This is supplemented with the notion of cognate agents recognising certain 'opportunities' to enter new markets, upgrade technologies and so on. To sustain 'competitiveness', regions need to fend off these forces and build upon growth potential by improving learning capabilities and anchoring these in the regional institutional structure, and gearing learning capabilities toward shaping advantages that cannot easily be copied. As Storper argues: 'Economies must therefore be equipped to keep outrunning the powerful forces of standardisation and imitation in the world economy' (Storper 1997: 265). In the academic discourse, localised learning thus becomes framed as a strategic ambition to withstand forces of 'ubiquification' (Maskell and Malmberg 1999). Social, economic and political conflicts are reduced to the narrow, potentially divisive and perhaps introspective formula of the 'region-against-the-external-world'.

The image of a harsh, competitive external world outside against which the region needs to brace itself is upheld, often in even more dramatic terms, in policy discourses at the regional level. Nowadays, regional strategies – economic as well as social – and major resource allocations are almost always justified on the grounds of their alleged contribution to regional 'competitiveness' under the condition of the inevitably rising pressures induced by 'globalisation' – that is, by what is happening 'out there' (Fagan 1996). At the regional level, an important factor in sustaining the perception of 'regions against regions' and the associated 'competitiveness' discourse is the involvement of business in regional strategies that is often induced by the dependency of firms on local resources (Cox and Mair 1991; Oinas 1998). Few commentators have paused long enough to reflect upon whose 'competitiveness' is in question – individual firms, regions or nations? (O'Donnell 1996). Inter-regional tensions are thus triggered by political attitudes and the behaviour of regional agents rather than any inevitable outcome of globalisation pressures.

Similar views of 'globalisation' are invoked to account for major crises or perceived policy failures. In response to a recent series of closures of externally owned plants in the North-East region of England (Pike 1999) – some of which

had been praised before for their spin-off potential in the regional economy–
politicians at the regional and national level were quick to blame 'globalisation'.
This triggered the following response in a regional newspaper commentary:

> Politicians over recent days have referred to the 'global economy' as if it is some
> elusive, mythical monster over which governments have no control. A better
> analogy would be a Frankenstein's monster. The 'global economy' did not emerge
> from the ether, it was created by the actions of politicians and financiers. In the name
> of greater efficiency, the new global economy allows the greatest movement of
> capital, subject to the minimum of regulation. (Tomaney 1998)

Echoing these sentiments in relation to the national level, Zysman (1996) defines
'globalisation' as a kind of code word that does not reflect the inevitably declining
power of the state but rather a change in the point of leverage for political action.
In Zysman's view, historical processes at the national level induce specific political
and economic dynamics that create their own policy and market logic. The
essence of globalisation is that territories, by invoking these logics, compete
against each other. Hence it is national concerns in the form of strategic responses
to national 'competitiveness' discourses that give shape to globalisation processes.
The process of globalisation thus contributes to increased political rivalry
between territories. Hay and Watson (1998), too, stress the need to demystify the
excesses of what they see as the 'overblown' globalisation thesis. Like Zysman and
Fagan, they contend that the 'globalisation pressures' rhetoric should be
understood as part of policy discourse and that politics play a substantive rather
than reactive role in shaping the notion of globalisation and the actions that
sustain it.

Such critical perspectives refer to the view that nation states still have a critical
role to play in mediating and shaping forms of internationalisation since they are
the architects rather than the victims of the 'globalisation' of capital (Hirst and
Thompson 1996) – for instance, through regulating capital flows and formulating developmental industrial and regional policies. The internationalisation of
capital is seen as dependent upon the actions of nation states and can both expand
and restrict policy choices (Boyer and Drache 1996; Weiss 1998). In addition, the
promotion of 'competitiveness' discourses at the regional level can also be
interpreted as part of national strategies to devolve austerity and decentralise
responsibilities for the impact of neo-liberal national policies to the regional level
(Fagan 1996).

The discursive juxtaposition of the 'region' as a strategic site of economic
development and policy, and the 'global' as the level at which the forces of
competition operate can be unpacked with the help of the notion of *scale* (Fagan
1996; Swyngedouw 1997). In Swyngedouw's view the 'local–global' debate has
arisen from an a priori association of particular phenomena with specific spatial
scales, and from this, by developing the 'local' and 'global' as sites for employing
distinct methods of analysis. In the juxtaposition of the 'region' versus the 'global',
this scaling is manifested as follows:

- Various core socioeconomic processes have been scaled down to the regional level. This includes the intertwining of the social and the economic, the emergence of associative tendencies to promote economic development, the encouragement and promotion of innovation and, more fundamentally, the role of socioeconomic institutions, regulation and governance.

- The operation of market forces is *scaled up* to the supranational and global level. This includes the role of 'footloose' capital and of demand, as well as the carriers (transnational corporations, Internet) and regulatory mechanisms that sustain the free floating of capital, finance, technology, goods, services and people (IMF, GATT, EU, NAFTA, etc.).

- The link between the 'local' and the 'global' is thus presented in a binary way. In the regional 'competitiveness' discourse, this comes down to the juxtaposition of a rich image of the 'regional world' (Storper 1997) with an interpretation of the global level essentially as a 'set of forces', a 'black box' of inevitable, unavoidable pressures. While the regional level is endowed with agency, the global is thus largely bereft of agency and of territorial and historical specificity (Held *et al.* 1999). Within this context, the regional position is often gauged in very general terms, that is, in crude categorisations of successful/competitive and unsuccessful/non-competitive regions (Hudson 1999).

As Swyngedouw (1997) acknowledges, the last decade has witnessed some imaginative attempts to articulate the global–local nexus, in part by attempting to unpack the 'global' and to conceptualise, in more concrete ways, the linkages and relations between the region and the external world (Amin and Thrift 1993; Markusen 1996a). Building on earlier criticisms of the localisation thesis (Amin and Robins 1990), Amin and Thrift (1993) argue that the fortunes of localities should be seen, to a large extent, as being tightly locked into the evolving networks of international corporate activity, for which they invoke the concept of the 'filière'. New trends in industrial organisation did 'not imply any simple erosion of oligopolistic or centralising tendencies in the production filière' (Amin and Malmberg 1992: 409), and the re-emergence of spatial agglomerations of economic activities should therefore not be interpreted as a revival of old Marshallian districts (see also Harrison 1992). Rather, 'these centres of agglomeration are, thus, centres of representation, interaction and innovation within global production filières' (Amin and Thrift 1993: 416).

While these critical accounts carefully avoid the relatively crude counter-position of the 'local' and the 'global' approaches, they still exemplify the problem of scaling. In the words of Swyngedouw (1997: 143), these accounts manage to 'meander skilfully around the issue of scale and maintain the position of a binary (local–global) spatial perspective to account for the socio-spatial restructuring processes'. Indeed the major difference between these critical approaches and the localisation approaches seems to reside not so much in the juxtaposition of the 'global' and the 'local' but in the way the 'global' is locally manifested. In the 'localisation' approaches the 'global' is perceived in terms of rather abstract pressures coming from 'out there' against which the region needs to protect itself by concerted actions to sustain a flexible and innovative network economy. In the more critical approaches, the 'global' is embodied in corporate networks, evident within regions in the form of externally owned plants and as major gatekeepers of local supply chains and technological resources. In their view, to counter the forces stemming from these corporate networks, regional governance should be geared to managing dependencies and regulating corporate power. Shaping associational governance should thus present 'simply an attempt to set up networks of small firms and intermediate institutions that can act as a counter to … the power of networks of large corporations and dominant institutions' and an attempt 'to "embed" large corporate networks so that they become more committed to particular regions'(Amin and Thrift 1995: 51). Rather than being somewhere 'out there', then, the mythical monster of globalisation is identified inside local and regional economies, tying them into supranational changes. The policy agenda appears to suggest that regional action should be geared to taming and bribing the monster, by attuning its action more closely to regional interests. So, while a more radical line of reasoning is followed, the role of regional governance is interpreted in roughly the same way: as a collective agency that, by embarking on an associational, learning-based trajectory, creates an appropriate, perhaps even progressive response to the challenges of globalisation (Hirst and Thompson 1996).

In recent years, several commentators have attempted to move the literature beyond the 'local–global' nexus by pointing at the territoriality of allegedly 'global' processes (see *inter alia* Giddens 1984; Harvey 1996). Storper, for example, contends that processes of globalisation tend to *modify* rather than annihilate territorial relationships at different spatial scales. This has important consequences for the perception of the role of the region. Globalisation, rather than inducing solely processes of 'de-territorialisation' and increased 'footlooseness' is interpreted as producing a recasting of the role of territories in intra-organisationally and inter-organisationally linked global business flows. Owing to the territorial dimension of these flows, regions may continue to play an important role: 'Regions are not the Davids facing the Goliaths of global firms' (Storper 1997: 176). While acknowledging this, however, Storper does not manage to escape from the 'global–local' binary perspective challenged above.

In this volume, by acknowledging the importance of scale and the territoriality of 'global' processes, an attempt is made to take up Swyngedouw's challenge to see the role and importance of spatial scale as *resulting from* the dynamics of socio-spatial processes rather than as a predefined and ordered hierarchy stretching from the local to the global. Swyngedouw's suggestion is to reinterpret scale in the context of the regulation approach that sees scale as embodying a temporal compromise through which fundamental tensions in the capitalist system are settled – for example competition, the social relation of monetary exchange and state mediation. Essentially, these fundamental tensions give rise to particular scale politics. Here, however, this volume follows a more modest track in that it focuses upon the way chains of production, markets and processes of innovation are institutionalised and connected at different spatial levels. In so doing, we see 'localisation' and 'globalisation' as socially constructed and material processes that embody an array of often contradictory and contingent tendencies – fragmentation and integration, territorialisation and de-territorialisation – that shape socioeconomic and territorial development. In particular places, the argument in this book seeks to contribute to:

- Interpreting the 'global' and 'globalisation' as a bundle of processes which, although occurring at supra-regional level, are not devoid of territoriality and historical specificity, and which need to be analysed in articulation with other spatial scales. This might be termed 'unpacking the concept and practice of globalisation'.

- Seeing the region as less structurally coherent in both an economic and a political sense, interpreting regional agency as part of complex layers of government and multi-level governance intertwined and co-ordinated at different spatial levels. This can be interpreted as problematising the region.

- Showing that particular phenomena of institutionalisation are related to the (re)construction of production chains, markets and processes of 'scaling down' and 'scaling up'. Swyngedouw labels these multi-level spatial ramifications as 'glocalisation'. What is critical about this 'glocalisation' is that it simultaneously involves the dimension of production–innovation and that of governance (see also Hollingsworth *et al.* 1994). To elaborate this point, the volume draws upon the concept of filières.

TERRITORIES VERSUS FILIÈRES

One way of unpacking the concept and practice of globalisation is to consider the 'world of global business flows' to be just as much a world of individual action and social interaction as is the 'regional world' (Storper 1997). Essentially, this means that any form of proximity imperative or a priori claim that local contexts are somehow more important than non-local contexts should be rejected. This does not mean that, when they are empirically observed or are considered as policy models, the notion of regional contexts should be underplayed. Rather, what it means is that in our approach the study of the development of production chains and innovation and the role of territories therein should not be based on any form of spatial reification. Instead, it should be accepted that technological, organisational, and – last but not least – cultural developments have led to substantive changes in the geography of the world economy, including a continuous and ongoing rearrangement of the role of spatial scales. Individuals can be socially active in global professional networks on a daily basis while being largely disconnected from what is going in the local environment – as, in effect, the activities of many academics testify. Spatial scales are, as Swyngedouw (1997: 142) claims, 'not operating hierarchically but simultaneously, and the relationship between different scales is "nested".' A similar image may arise when activities and processes in production chains or filières are scrutinised.

A filière is characterised by a distinct technical organisation of the production process with a corresponding organisational division of labour at different levels: inside the firm, between firms, inside a sector, and so on (Truel 1983). Within the firm an internal or technical division of labour is created; between firms, an external or social division of labour takes shape (Sayer and Walker 1992). By adopting a filière approach, not only the notion of a production chain is embraced, so too is the embedding of such production chains in socio-political settings. It is this dual focus that makes the filière a relevant concept for studying changes in industrial organisation from a political-economic perspective (Groenewegen 1989). Filières, accordingly, like other meso-level entities in the economy, can be seen as critical sites of political economy (Hollingsworth *et al.* 1994).

Filières may span the globe, but this does not mean they are de-territorialised. On the contrary, what is interesting is how specific organisational forms interact with specific spatial configurations to give shape to the territoriality of filières. A problem is that there is no simple one-to-one relationship between industrial organisation and territorial forms. One cannot be 'read off' from the other. There are myriad ways of co-ordinating and integrating the expanding division of labour to organise production (Sayer and Walker 1992) – similar production activities can be effectively carried out in different organisational forms (Langlois and Robertson 1995). Such organisational forms and institutional arrangements can have different territorial shapes, arrangements and even porosity to local and/or regional influence (Pike 1998a). Co-location may be convenient for the organisation of just-in-time supply, for service provision and consumption or for the co-ordination of innovation and learning between a final producer and its suppliers, for instance, but there are many examples of similar processes being organised at other scales. Spatial organisation, in this context, depends largely on the 'scale capabilities' and 'scale politics' of the firms and related actors involved (Swyngedouw 1997). Hence, while the territorial shape of a filière is certainly not completely arbitrary, it can only be traced through theoretically informed concrete empirical analysis. Its manifestations in particular and specific circumstances are only contingently realised.

So, what then drives the development of a filière? How is its territoriality determined? An analysis of filières should not just be one of mapping organisational and territorial forms. The understanding of how filières evolve, both organisationally and territorially, requires insight into the social networks and institutions that underpin interaction between firms and other institutions. Filières, like the markets through and in which they operate, can be seen as institutional constructs (Zysman 1994). They are shaped through history, and locked in specific forms of behaviour and in particular organisational configurations (integrated or disintegrated) that generally do not change easily without radical ruptures and abrupt changes in trajectory. Their development is, in other words, path-dependent – technologically, organisationally and territorially. They are unavoidably shaped by their own historical evolution (Hodgson 1999). They exhibit different scales of competition: between rival firms within a single production chain, between different production chains or systems (for example Toyota versus Nissan in the automotive filière; the PC versus the Mac in the IT filière), and between different territories in which they are embedded (for example the European versus the American agro-food sectors). What is more, many processes of market competition that drive filière development cannot be couched in universal terms (e.g. 'efficiency', 'innovation'), and cannot be easily matched with a simple array of models of spatial organisation (e.g. 'industrial districts', 'core–periphery'). Instead, what is revealed through more detailed analysis is that competitive processes are historically and territorially specific, driven by a number of issues and trends that, at particular times and places, can dominate social interaction between economic agents. Concepts like 'efficiency' and 'competition' are social constructs that are part of the institutionalisation of markets. The importance of specific processes of institutionalisation is demonstrated, for instance, in the study of the new media sector by Cornford, Naylor and Driver. After revealing that no universal model of spatial-industrial development fits the industry, the authors conclude that:

> Instead the current commercial, industrial and geographical organisation of computer and video games production in the UK primarily reflects *specific* processes of market competition based on the need for portfolio strategies, strong financial backing, information exchange at global nodes (trade fairs), risk assessment and the (contested) dominant position of 'gatekeeper' firms executing strong vertical control. (This volume, Chapter 5, page 107, emphasis added.)

A deeper interest in the specific and particular territoriality of filières, perceived in such a historical–institutional perspective, may help us to acquire a better understanding of spatial–industrial dynamics. This conclusion lends its support to a plea for a revived and expanded 'geography of the enterprise' that moves beyond a narrow concern with the activities of 'prime mover' firms. Additionally, a territorial outlook on filières also points to another missing link in recent geographical analysis in the non-local exchange of information, goods and services. As suggested above, since geographers have tended to apply new insights derived from socioeconomics primarily to what is happening *within* the region, relatively little work has been undertaken regarding the complementary 'non-local' dimensions (although see Markusen 1996a). Regional analysis, accordingly, should be complemented with 'geographies of non-local exchange'. Research should focus more on the geography of global nodes such as trade fairs, of collaborative learning and innovation at a distance, and of filières which are non-local in their nature and structure.

This call for more emphasis on 'non-local' exchange should not be read as a rejection of regional analysis. On the contrary, it is intended as a way to improve the understanding of the regional position by unpacking the concept and practice of globalisation and the interrelated and nested scales through which these social processes work. So what, in this perspective, is the position of the region?

In our view, the region does not present an a priori 'essential' unit of socio-economic development. There are, admittedly, regions which have become or at least are seen as important units because they have acquired a dominant position in a certain filière. Such regions host clusters of agents with the 'scale capabilities' and 'scale politics' to be at the centre of filière development, in terms of representation, organisation and innovation. Another example is the type of region that contains the greater part of a filière within its boundaries, where the organisational division of labour corresponding to one production process is largely located in the region. Such regions, generally labelled as industrial districts, represent situations where the social world of the region overlaps with the social world of the filière (Lagendijk 2000). Hence, for industrial districts, to understand the success of the filière requires an understanding of the 'regional world' (Storper 1997). However, even for the extreme case of a regionally bound filière non-local exchanges are important, as demonstrated by recent studies on Italian industrial districts (Harrison 1994).

Originally, this literature interpreted the phenomenon of the Italian industrial district as a set of closely self-contained processes of industrial dynamics at the territorial level in which the birth, development and death of a firm was restricted to a single district. However, more recent interpretation underlines a change in relations between firms and districts. In particular this involves a modification of the 'frontier between interior and exterior, which had always shown a notable degree of impenetrability' (Rullani 1997: 64). The district boundary is permeated by the entry of externally owned firms into the district, especially of larger firms that come to play dominant roles and condition local development. No less significant is the exit from the district of firms embarking on collaboration and joint ventures, takeovers and investment in other geographical areas (Varaldo and Ferrucci 1997). The movement of firms entering and quitting the districts breaks through the territorial containment of the filière, and fosters a process of disintegration of the territorial economy. The 'non-local' thus becomes a key element of analysis.

More generally, the idea is that the development of a regional filière depends on the way it taps into markets and is tuned to technological developments elsewhere. In some cases, the region may play a fundamental role in actually constructing or reconstructing the market, by setting standards and dominating the 'rules of the game'. See, for example, the history of Silicon Valley in the microcomputer industry (Saxenian 1994). In other cases, such as the 'Third Italy', regions may excel in having institutions that monitor market developments worldwide (Brusco 1992). The role of the region thus depends on its position in the various processes of scaling or rescaling that affect industrial organisation and governance structures. More precisely, what counts is the way various processes that have been 'scaled down', notably in the area of supply-side support policies but also in issues such as the shaping of associative powers and local identities, affect the regional position in areas that have been 'scaled up' (e.g. capital flows, market integration).

A major contribution to analysing and assessing the position of the region is provided by the account of the territoriality of filières. Obviously, there are various aspects of this territoriality that may contribute to regional development. For instance, the co-ordination of complex and novel processes will generally benefit from proximity between economic actors, inducing co-location of related economic activities. Firms dependent on specialised inputs, notably labour, will tend to agglomerate in areas with the appropriate resource base (Langlois and Robertson 1995; Maskell and Malmberg 1999). Whether regions are really able to grasp such potential growth 'opportunities', however, will depend on how the local socioeconomic base chimes or fits with the *specific* conditions that dominate the development of a certain filière (Swann *et al.* 1998). Various chapters in this book are testimony to this notion of historical matching that is temporary, evolving and changing over time. In some cases, regional development is promoted by offering a suitable milieu of inter-firm networking and co-ordinated innovation (Chapter 7 on local innovation policy by Ache and Wood); in other cases, by shaping the capacity to respond to skill shortages (Chapter 4 on the local embedding of the automotive sector by Pike, Lagendijk and Vale). In another case, the capacity to modernise the local SME basis to shift from a low-cost position to a quality one in a global market (Chapter 6 on the globalisation of the textiles filière by Thiel, Pires and Dudleston).

The emphasis on a kind of 'matching' of local socioeconomic conditions, or more specifically the capacity to modify network positions in filières, forms the context for understanding the role of the region. The 'region', in this sense, is not an atomistic unit that is forced by globalisation pressures to compete with other territories. The regional position and its possible future development depend on the overall scale articulations and spatial network configurations conditioning its role in the spatial division of labour. Nor is the region automatically endowed with the agency to modify network positions and play the games of 'scale politics'. As argued by Cox and Mair (1991) and Lovering (1999), this requires a local collective recognition and political articulation of identities and common interests, in this case bearing on the regional position in filières. It also requires a strategic capacity which helps to develop and use place-bound or territorially rooted competencies to be in touch with, and have influence over, various spatial scales. As Chapter 8 by Torres and Lagendijk shows, the presence of a strong regional government and structures for collaboration with business and support organisations may be necessary but not sufficient. Policies at national and local levels may also play an essential role. For instance, Chapter 3 by Giunta on the aerospace sector reveals how a national policy of strong incentives has increased the commitment of a strategic firm to the region, and how, together with additional local policy developments, this has paved the way for the creation of a tissue of local subcontracting firms, and the embedding of an internationalised supply chain. Hence, appropriate strategy-making and action demand not only a regional associational structure but also engagement with what is happening within filières and governance processes across the range of nested scales.

TOWARDS AN INSTITUTIONAL PERSPECTIVE ON REGIONAL DEVELOPMENT AND LEARNING

This introduction started with observing a major imbalance in the socioeconomic study of regional development. While the internal – especially indigenous and endogenous – dimensions of the region has received much attention, resulting in a rich conceptual and theoretical body of work, the closely interrelated external – or exogenous – domain relating to the interpenetration of local and non-local scales of activity has tended to be relatively neglected. To address this imbalance, a conceptualisation of the position of regions – a place concept – in the concept of filières – a scalar concept – has been suggested. The concept presents a way to unpack the concept and practice of globalisation by transforming what is often represented as a set of pressures ('globalisation', increased competition, rapid technological and market change, 'footloosenes') into specific contexts, charac- terised by institutions, influential agents, and historical and territorial specificity. The notion of regional positioning stresses the articulated and differentiated ways the place and role of regions in the spatial division of labour changes as a result of its close interrelation with the ongoing restructuring of filières.

This view, it is acknowledged, is neither novel nor will it fully solve the observed imbalance. The filière approach and the notion of differentiated positioning are merely means to put the emphasis on 'competitiveness' and learning in perspective, and to encourage greater critical scrutiny than is currently often evident in the literature. In this sense, we hope to contribute to some of the basic questions that have been posed in the context of the 'learning region' debate. While learning is undoubtedly important, the question is *what* exactly should be learned at the regional level, and for what broader objectives (Hudson 1999). This raises the issue of the scalar dimensions of learning. The emphasis on learning stems from the recognition that learning is an essential factor in creating and sustaining a 'competitive' economy. However, we do not endorse the view that, under the condition of globalisation and the demands for innovation and flexibility, learning has intrinsically become a largely localised process (cf. Maskell and Malmberg 1999). Rather, we concur with Oinas and Virkkala (1997) that there may be only *some* forms of learning that take place in a local context. Hence there are no 'learning regions' in any comprehensive sense. There is only regional learning, defined by Oinas and Virkkala (1997: 270) as 'inter-organisational learning that is tied to the location where it takes place because it would be difficult or impossible to create the same circumstance for learning elsewhere'. Since such processes of learning tend to be organisationally embedded, not only within single business organisations but also as parts of alliances between firms and with other organisations, it is especially the filière level that may offer insights into the organisational and spatial dimensions of learning. Where such filières are spatially concentrated, this is often associated with high levels of localised learning, as demonstrated in the oft-cited examples of Silicon Valley and the industrial districts in Central Italy.

In our perspective of regional learning, however, we are even inclined to take another step back from the prevailing association between learning and proximity (or milieu). The main incentive to regional learning is not that such learning cannot be organised effectively in a different spatial form, for instance in non-local networks (Oinas and Virkkala 1997). Except for the rare cases where economic activities depend largely on intense face-to-face contacts (e.g. in new emerging high-tech applications, or sophisticated financial services (Clark 1997)), the notion of a territorial imperative should be rejected and replaced by a notion of territorially rooted potential. The interest in regional learning stems from the intention of regional agents to develop such possibilities to create and attempt to at least partly control a more locally integrated production system. In this a learning strategy becomes part of regional 'scale politics', of regional attempts to anchor clusters of related firms and organisations with the aim of the development of their regional interests. Interestingly, many examples of 'high-tech' clusters indeed show that policy incentives have been essential for shaping relations and so-called 'club goods' to trigger and sustain localised and collective industrial growth and learning (Swann et al. 1998)

Particularly in more peripheral regions, regional agents attempt to use innovation and learning approaches as a way to impose strategies of modernisation and internationalisation upon the local firm base (Lagendijk 1999c). The creation of a local institutional base – whether understood as associational governance (Amin and Thrift 1995), 'institutional thickness' (Amin and Thrift 1993), or social capital (Brusco 1995) – reflects a strategy to anchor firms in the region, and to align, as far as possible, their actions to the regional interests of employment and income generation. Simultaneously, such 'embedding' strategies are often pervaded and dominated by the local affiliates of global capital, in an attempt to attune local strategies to their own needs, such as labour supply, infrastructure and the development of supply chains. Obviously, this strategy can work because firms are at least partly dependent upon regional resources, a dependency that can perhaps be increased by local learning strategies. However, the main reason regional learning is so important for regional development may be because it is *regions* that depend on locally established *firms* for local wealth creation. One of the consequences of such an approach is that any applied concept developed under the heading of regional learning, such as 'local innovation system', could be perceived from a social constructivist point of view. It is local actors that really make and substantiate such concepts, instead of an abstract and somehow removed logic of localisation.

When addressing the regional position from a strategic perspective of regional learning, two further themes are noteworthy: culture and governance. Institutional perspectives have placed much emphasis on the relationship between learning and culture. The question of culture, as Markusen's chapter will discuss, is far from an easy one. This is already the case in the prevailing firm-centred models in which cultural factors are seen as crucial for unlocking the potentials for interorganisational learning at the regional level (Cooke and Morgan 1998). A scalar filière approach suggests that such a perspective cannot be restricted to the regional level only. It is through examining the position and role of local groups of the institutions of capital, labour and both the state and quasi-state agents in a larger filière that we may understand how the attributes of any culture – local interpretations, traditions and values – fit in the institutional structure of this filière. The latter will generally be characterised by cultural traits – means and habits of communication, valuation, trading and so on – that transcend the regional level. Hence, it is again the intersection of different cultures at different scales, rather than just the study of regional cultures, that can help us to understand why regional development paths differ so significantly.

In our approach, regional learning is also associated with the notion of *political cultures*. In line with the social constructivist approach, the question is in what way different regional agents (state firms, workers, interest groups) interpret 'competitiveness' and learning discourses, and how, on a collective basis, these interpretations are translated into regional learning strategies. Such translations are not just locally adapted applications of general ideas on regional development; they are socially and politically constructed and articulated models and strategies that will reflect the local political culture, in terms of the way actors articulate their interests and of how balances of power affect the mediation of these interests. The contributions by Torres and Lagendijk on the Spanish Basque Country (Chapter 8) and by Pike, Lagendijk and Vale on embedding in the North-East of England (Chapter 4) pay attention to the way that regional interests of locally established agents are translated in particular forms of 'scale politics'. The Basque chapter in particular shows how fashionable concepts of regional learning (such as 'clusters' and 'regional innovation systems') have been adopted, adapted and promoted in the local political system.

The issue of political culture bears directly on the role of regional governance in the context of emergent multi-level frameworks (Tomaney 1996). While obviously shaped by regional and national political cultures, regional *governance* structures create institutions that frame actors, power relations and ideas, which in turn facilitate, through the articulation and mediation of interest, the process of collective strategy-making. Governance structures, as illustrated by the Basque and North-East cases, provide mechanisms to include the interests of some, while keeping others out. As Ache and Wood claim in their chapter on local innovation policy (Chapter 7), different governance structures underpin different forms of regulation and strategy-making. In particular, the extent to which regions can adopt learning strategies from elsewhere, as the evidence from UK and German regions shows, depends on the way local governance structures allow for, and are able to reflect upon, variation in both the content and organisation of new policies. The issue of regional governance also relates to the deeper question of the changing role of the state and the role of regulation. The obsession with 'competitiveness' has been a central dimension in the alleged transition from the managing–controlling state to an 'enabling' or 'entrepreneurial' state (Jessop 1994; Martin and Sunley 1997). This shift has facilitated the joining of regional authorities, firms and other regional organisations in promoting a kind of mercantilist, network-based strategy of region against region, facilitated by the 'scaling down' of supply-side oriented policy instruments. Interestingly, there is a tension between such local trends and the regulatory processes that have been 'scaled up' to the international level (Heinze and Schmid 1994). The latter are dominated by a neo-liberal 'level playing field' approach, which seeks to restrict the role of the state to safeguarding, rather than intervening in the working of the market. It is only by taking account of such scaling processes that we can understand how such policies can co-exist.

In conclusion, an institutional perspective to regional development requires that the global–local duality is replaced by a perspective that links processes of industrial restructuring, learning, and governance at various spatial scales, and that excludes spatial reification and the representation of scales as part of a pre-determined and ordered hierarchy. By adopting a filière approach, we hope to contribute to a more balanced assessment. In addition, an institutional approach, by the way it focuses on the role of actors and their embedding at different spatial levels, can focus attention to the way perceived cases of successful learning-based regional strategies contribute to regional development. Entrepreneurial approaches often seem to suggest that both are the same – that is, they equate phenomena of regional economic success with cases of regional development. However, as Hudson (1999) warns us: 'Knowledge and learning may be necessary for economic success but they are by no means sufficient to ensure equality, cohesion and social justice.' A study of the role of institutions at different spatial levels may give more insight into the question of how regional economic growth can be translated into socially equitable economic development, by engaging with less advantaged segments of the firm sector, workforce and local populace, by its ability to distribute wealth and create demand, and by contributing to social and environmental goals. These topics go beyond the remit of this book but they are integral to the emergent research agenda in regional development.

STRUCTURE OF THE BOOK

The main focus and core themes of the book are addressed in a four-part structure. After the introductory chapters, this comprises three parts: 'Restructuring Industries and Territorial Development', 'Industrial and Regional Institutions and Policy', and 'Conclusions'. The aim of the present chapter has been to focus on the intersection between the filière concept and processes of regionalisation and globalisation, as part of the development of an institutional approach to regional development. The next chapter, by Ann Markusen, explores the structural and cultural features that hobble or invite transformations and concerted policies for the development of regional economies, and reflects on the role of regional culture. The aim of the chapter is to underline the main economic, institutional and cultural forces which promote the transformation of a region. The chapter relies for illustration on four case studies and it builds four typologies of transformation, presenting the following paths: a hub-and-spoke district proliferating new hubs (the case of Seattle); a government-centred district which attracts new hubs (Colorado Spring); a hub-and-state-centred district evolving to the creation of Marshallian-type districts; and satellite platforms evolving into hub-and-spoke districts (South Korean cases). The chapter underlines the role played by economic forces and institutional actors in shaping the development trajectory, concluding that an exhaustive comprehension of the transformation needs to take into account the role played by regional cultures.

The second part is the core of the book and explores the experience of linked industrial and territorial development. This starts with an examination of the interplay between the development of filières, the localities in which they are embedded and the innovative strategies attempting to connect industrial and territorial concerns in several regions. Evidence is provided of the experience of the complex ways in which pressures for restructuring, including internationalisation or even 'globalisation', intensified and changing competition, technological change and so on, have been mediated by formerly nationally 'rooted' industries in Europe becoming increasingly integrated owing to ongoing processes of technological and organisational innovation, and political regulation.

The stories of change are discussed in the following industries and regions: aerospace in Campania in southern Italy; the automotive sector in the North-East region of England; new media in the UK regions; and textiles and clothing in Portugal. Mature industries such as the aerospace and automotive sectors show most clearly how change at the filière level impacts upon local economic structure, but also how the latter not only adapts but also contributes in its own way to filière development. Anna Giunta's chapter looks at organisational change in the aerospace industry, and examines the industrial and spatial effects on the supply chains to Alenia plants in southern Italy. Interestingly, because of the specific local circumstances southern firms seem to score better on technology indicators than northern firms. Recent organisational change however has led to rationalisation in the local supply base, in which primarily externally owned firms have survived and prompted particular public policy responses. While, in a situation comparable to the automotive case, the hub firm Alenia has encouraged some diversification among local suppliers, the future of the local system remains highly dependent on the specific filière position of the hub firm. The question is what this will mean in the future for the firm's commitment to Italy's South.

Since Granovetter's (1985) seminal paper, the analytical category of embeddedness has become increasingly widespread in economic geography and popular in other related disciplines. Yet, despite – or perhaps because of – its popularity, the embeddedness concept seemed to lose its sharpness and explanatory potential once it was used as a 'catch-all' category. The main aim of Chapter 4, by Andy Pike, Arnoud Lagendijk and Mário Vale, is to produce a sympathetic critique of the existing ways in which embeddedness is currently used in the economic geography literature. To accomplish this goal, the authors confront several critical issues. Among these is the distinction between embeddedness and embedding and how to research such concepts. The final empirical section assesses the usefulness of the theoretical and methodological insights developed earlier in the chapter by exploring the evolution of labour market governance and training in the automotive industry in the North-East region of England. Here, the case study revealed the dynamic and evolutionary nature of the embedding process that ebbs and flows for particular participant interests.

In Chapter 5, James Cornford, Richard Naylor and Stephen Driver discuss new media and regional development and challenge the much-vaunted idea of agglomeration among new industries. At the filière level, the specific process of market competition is explained in terms of the needs for portfolio strategies, strong financial backing, information exchange at global nodes (fairs), risk assessment, and the (regained) dominant position of 'gatekeeper' firms executing strong vertical control. This contrasts with the institutionalist approach featuring the link between vertical disintegration and agglomeration, and with a romantic, technologically induced view of the information industry as a placeless 'boutique/cottage industry'. At the local level, the analysis leads to reinterpreting the phenomenon of clustering and a new understanding of local–global inter-action in the context of contested vertical linkages and 'functional footlooseness'.

Joachim Thiel, Iva Pires and Anna Duddleston's contribution on globalisation and the Portuguese textiles and clothing filière in the post-GATT climate (Chapter 6) provides another sound illustration of how global processes affect the position of local production systems, and how local action emerges to respond to threats to the regional economic position in a filière. Changes in the filière amount to an idea of 'global shifts', with interesting tension between pushes from and pulls towards advanced economies. This creates specific opportunities for semi-peripheral countries such as Portugal. Also interesting are the specific changes in the organisation in the filière, such as the position of intermediaries and the new forms of retailer–factory relationships.

The third part of the book focuses on industrial and regional institutions and policy in the context of dilemmas emerging from the interplay of restructuring industries and territorial development. These chapters examine the current wisdom concerning institutional strategy and policy for local economic develop-ment in Europe's regions. Included are studies of innovation and technology policy in Germany and Wales and industrial policy in the Basque Country.

In Chapter 7, Peter Ache and Michelle Wood focus on how institutional configurations (regional government, agencies, consultancies, partnerships and conferences) impact upon the regional economic position especially through innovation and technology development in South-West Wales and the eastern Ruhrgebiet. The configurations are explained in terms of regulatory regimes. A link is made between the regulation perspective and the filière approach through the concept of clustering and through considering to what extent governance modes may be transferred between regions. While the analysis thus endorses the need for strategic approaches at the regional level, through its institutional analysis it highlights the obstacles to innovative forms of local action as well as the obstacles to inter-regional exchange.

Chapter 8 by Concepción Torres and Arnoud Lagendijk relates in some interesting ways to the previous policy-oriented accounts. Like other regional governments, the Basque government has attempted to integrate structural and technology policies as part of its ambition to promote regional economic development. Even more than in the case of North Rhine Westfalia (NRW) and Wales, this policy has been grafted in the last decade onto the cluster concept. The analysis of how the cluster approach and other ideas have been adopted in new policy approaches underpins the importance of institutional and cultural specificity. On the one hand, the Basque government manifests a potent strategic capacity that builds on a strong regional identity. This underpins a strong culture of planning and support, and a certain level of preparedness to learn from previous experiences. On the other hand, the political culture in the region seems to work against active engagement and consultation in the phases of detailed policy design and implementation. The result is that, despite the rhetoric on collaboration and engagement, policy initiatives do not seem to have the broad regional benefit claimed for them.

Chapter 9, forming the concluding section of the book, distils the lessons from the preceding contributions' discussions of the interdependencies between industrial and territorial development, and explores what they mean for Europe in terms of future routes to prosperity and regional economic development.

2 Transforming Regional Economies: The Roles of Economic Structure, Developmental Activism and Regional Cultures

INTRODUCTION

Regional economies are seldom static. Few regions, whether fast-growing, stable or in decline, maintain a single structural form indefinitely. A decade of research on industrial districts has focused on structural features facilitating or impeding innovation, but rarely on the conditions under which one structural type of region can transform itself into a more diverse or robust form. In this chapter, I summarise the results of exploratory research on a number of successful transformations. Although generalising from these cases is problematic, I believe each case helps to reveal structural and cultural features that hobble or invite transformation as well as concerted policies which have been successful.

I present four paths to transformation, based on my earlier work on distinctive industrial district types (Markusen 1996a):

- a hub-and-spoke region proliferating new hubs (the case of Seattle);

- a government-centred district parlaying these assets into the construction of a satellite platform and then into the recruitment of new hubs (the case of Colorado Springs);

- a hub-and-state centred district amplifying itself through the creation of a Marshallian industrial district (the case of Silicon Valley);

- satellite platforms evolving into hub-and-spoke districts (the South Korean cases).

In each, the behaviour of economic agents and the strategies undertaken on behalf of the region have been significant in shaping the fate of the region. Although most other chapters in this book are based on European cases, my empirical examples are drawn chiefly from South Korea and the US. While there may be important insights and lessons to be learned, it remains to be seen whether these types fit the European experience.

The research results presented here demonstrate that economic assets, economic structures and economic motivations alone are insufficient to explain how a region might move from a simple form to a more complex one. In a later portion of this chapter, I reflect on the difficult question of regional cultures. Work by Saxenian on Silicon Valley poses emphatically the issue of regional cultures and the roles they may play in facilitating or inhibiting diversification and resilience. Although cultures are of course shaped by economic and political history, I conclude that there are nevertheless habits governing regional outlook and behaviour that cannot be associated monotonically with industrial structure. In the final section of this chapter, I reflect on why it has been difficult for regional economists, regional scientists and economic geographers to integrate the analysis of regional cultures into our work, and I present a number of speculations on features of regional cultures that might facilitate more progressive forms of regional development.

ROUTES TO TRANSFORMATION

Under what conditions can an industrial district with an inherited structure attempt to diversify away from that form? Which agents in the region are instrumental in such efforts, and which are obstacles? What kinds of strategies have proven successful and can they be mimicked in other regions? Preliminary answers to these questions are suggested by the following cases.

DIVERSIFICATION OF HUB-AND-SPOKE REGIONS

Hub-and-spoke regions possess economic structures dominated by a few large, export-oriented firms in one or more industries, around which other firms cluster as suppliers or customers. Districts of this sort face the problem of the domination of regional resources, politics and culture by large, oligopolistic, outward-facing firms. For instance, the American cities of Pittsburgh and Detroit suffered in the post-war period when the large steel and auto companies crowded out other sectors and suppressed entrepreneurship (Chinitz 1961; Checkland 1975; Markusen 1985).

But such an outcome is not determinant. Seattle is an American region with a similar hub-and-spoke structure, dominated in the post-war period by the world's most successful aerospace firm, Boeing. Seattle suggests that certain mechanisms and strategies are available to a region to avoid stultification and to transform a potential liability into an asset. Seattle's success lies in its ability to sprout additional hub-and-spoke configurations in other sectors, a product both of the harnessing of Boeing- and university-related talent and of the reinvestment locally of earnings from oligopolistic firms. The case of Seattle is explored at further length elsewhere (Gray et al. 1996), but I briefly recapitulate this experience here.

A prominent aspect of Seattle's evolution is the activity of local highly successful entrepreneurs in new sectors. In the resource-dedicated, turn-of-the-century city, William Boeing began to build wooden seaplanes, starting a firm which now employs more than 100,000 in the region. Despite Boeing's success and acknowledged dominance of the regional labour market, the firm did not suppress a new round of accumulation in computer software, with the emergence of Microsoft. Indeed, Boeing's high-tech culture and considerable software operations contributed to the region's nurturing of a software industry.

In addition, Boeing heavily supported the improvement of the University of Washington, whose training in engineering, software and biotechnology has played a significant role in engendering both of the newer sectors. While Boeing never significantly invested in other sectors in the region, apart from the educational infrastructure, key founders of Microsoft have remained in the region and invested considerable sums in the emerging biotechnology and communications industries. The emergence of a strong local venture capital industry is one of the few institutional innovations that help distinguish Seattle's success. Thus while Boeing suppressed the development of the regional aircraft supply industry, it played a passive but facilitative role in the emergence of other sectors.

The Seattle example suggests that the way a region organises and finances its educational institutions may help to transcend hub-and-spoke problems. In contrast, Detroit relied chiefly on low-skilled immigrant labour, a deliberate strategy on the part of Henry Ford, and the auto companies made no similar investments in city educational systems. Chinitz (1961) suggests that the auto companies' domination of the region's finance, labour force and civic life thwarted entrepreneurship in other sectors, and starved the region of capital by reinvesting in their own international operations. The Seattle example also suggests that the recycling of sector-specific oligopolistic profits within a region, a relative rarity in the post-war period, can enable a region to diversify beyond a single hub-and-spoke structure.

An unsettling aspect of the Seattle experience is that other than the organisations noted – Boeing, Microsoft and the University of Washington – regional institutions, public and private, have had very little to do with charting and shaping the region's economic trajectory. Without strong economic development institutions and with surprisingly little networking, Seattle evolved a regional culture conducive to entrepreneurship and innovation. Seattle's diversification suggests that an active boosterist faction is not necessary for transformation to take place. Nor do dominant oligopolistic firms necessarily act in the fashion posited by Chinitz. Operating in a capital goods industry highly vulnerable to economic and political cycles, the dominant firms wanted to avoid being blamed for periodic downturns and thus did not oppose new sectors emerging.

While it may challenge received notions of regional ossification under the hegemony of an ageing, oligopolistic industrial structure, the Seattle case is not atypical. Other American cities and regions have been able to transcend hub-and-spoke structures – Denver in mining, Los Angeles in aerospace and entertainment, Boston in textiles and machining. The extent to which similar trajectories have been experienced in Europe remains an empirical question. Our relatively poor understanding of the causal forces distinguishing the Seattle-type transformations from the relative failure of Detroit-type stasis suggests that much good research remains to be done.

FROM A STATE-CENTRED REGION TO SATELLITES AND HUBS

A state-centred industrial district is one in which one or more government facilities – national or state capital, public university, military base or private sector enterprise chiefly dependent on state clientele – predominate in the local economic structure. State-centred districts possess an amalgam of assets and liabilities, often distinctive, which may be the grist for transformation. A state-centred region may share features with hub-and-spoke districts or satellite platforms, but since its livelihood is expressly bound up with the political arena, an analysis of its dynamics requires the incorporation of institutions of the state.

A satellite platform, the third distinctive type, consists of a region which hosts one or more branch facilities of external organisations, where the units involved are embedded non-locally in corporate or hierarchical relationships and are engaged in little or no local networking, of either a horizontal or a vertical nature. Such satellite districts, including those centred on government facilities, may succeed in transforming themselves beyond the strictures of their structures by employing 'recruit and parlay' strategies. In this process, one round of accumulation implants locally a set of assets – an infrastructure, labour force, technical expertise, amenities – which may be parlayed into lures and incentives for another round of investments recruited externally (Gray and Markusen 1999). Generally, this process requires active intervention and marketing on the part of some regional group, public or private, and it occurs most often in localities with satellite platform or state-centred structures.

Colorado Springs is an outstanding example of how this process has worked over more than five decades. In the depression, waning mining and tourism activities threatened this small city on the eastern flanks of the Rockies. Local capitalists with large fortunes from earlier periods of mining and commercial activity pooled resources and energies to compete for army and air bases then being sited as part of the World War II build-up. They successfully attracted one. In addition, during the war, they used a magnificent mountainside hotel, the Broadmoor, as a rest and recreation spot for top military officers, including General Eisenhower. The exposure and goodwill they earned from this effort was then parlayed, in the post-war decade, into the diversification of military-related facilities: a large army base, the North American Air Defence operations of the air force, and the plum, the new Air Force Academy (Markusen *et al.* 1991).

This set of state-centred institutions, with the exception of the Air Force Academy and perhaps later the Space Command functions, were continually subjected to the threat of closure. But they brought to the community a large, skilled, blue-collar workforce and enabled it to meet a minimum threshold size. In the 1960s, a group of local businessmen with a memory of the active effort to recruit the Air Force Academy, aggressively recruited electronics branch plants from Silicon Valley and abroad, emphasising the good work ethic and blue-collar skills, cheap land with a view, and the high-tech veneer accorded the community by the academy and the air force electronics complex. They succeeded in recruiting more than half a dozen sizeable plants, which brought manufacturing expertise and once again ratcheted the city up in size, despite the fact that they remained captive to their parent companies and vulnerable to closure in the longer run.

When the shutdowns came, however, the city had already moved on to parlay its improved infrastructure, skilled labour force and reputation for relatively conservative politics and culture into bids for headquarters operations of competitive sports and religious organisations. The city enticed the US Olympic Committee to relocate there and subsequently the large conservative Christian organisation, Focus on the Family. Each in turn attracted smaller organisations with related interests to the city. Via these waves of recruitment, the 'recruit and parlay' strategy worked, overcoming the disarticulation of 'satellite' facilities to attract successive rounds of new satellites.

Has Colorado Springs been able to move beyond its state and satellite dependency? The sports and Christian sectors each show some signs of evolving. The presence of the Olympic Committee has drawn headquarters and operations of other national sporting groups to the region, but my findings suggest this is chiefly an agglomeration phenomenon, without the interrelationships characterizing a Marshallian industrial district. However, the fundamentalist Christian groups have created a dense networking of interacting, self-sustaining organisations and firms that benefit from the proximity which may indeed be considered an incipient industrial district. The region remains very dependent on a substantial flow of resources and incomes from Washington, for the huge army base, the Air Force Academy and Space Command. But this case demonstrates that local private sector boosters have been able partially to diversify the region by parlaying various assets into attractors for other sectors.

A HUB-AND-SPOKE AND STATE-CENTRED REGION HOSTS A MARSHALLIAN DISTRICT

Silicon Valley is one of the most highly profiled fastest-growing American regions (see, for instance, Saxenian 1994). However, the region remains oddly understudied as a complex whole. Recent interest in the electronics complex and its relatively unique culture tends to obscure the continued presence of hub-and-spoke structures, state-centred activity and satellite operations within the valley. Elsewhere, my colleagues and I have attempted to remedy this lopsided emphasis by presenting a more comprehensive interpretation of the current structure of the regional economy and its evolution over time (Golob *et al.* 1999). Although the valley has been portrayed as hosting an industrial district in electronics, we show that it was originally a hub-and-spoke district, organised around the massive and significant presence of Stanford University and the Lockheed Space and Missiles complex, the latter almost completely (and to this day) federal government-dependent.

Continual large infusions of R&D money from the Department of Defence and National Space and Aeronautics Administration and government-subsidised recruitment of highly skilled scientists and engineers from other regions enabled Silicon Valley to evolve into a more complex, diversified structure. Through spin-offs and customer–supplier relationships, Stanford and to a lesser extent Lockheed produced a growing number of smaller electronics firms, also benefiting from government research and procurement contracts for Cold War missile and space operations. Some grew into larger firms – Intel, Hewlett-Packard – and were joined by large branch plants of firms headquartered elsewhere – IBM, Sylvania.

Over time, as commercial applications emerged, the combined inducement of large civilian and government sales and continued military research funding helped to create the relatively unique sector of smaller firms so much admired in the literature, as well as new large firms like Apple and Sun Microsystems (Saxenian 1994). An additional contingent of branch operations has been added over the past decade as foreign firms, especially Asian companies, have set up offices in the valley to monitor American technological advances and transfer these back to home offices. Thus Silicon Valley today is really an amalgam of structural types.

Although the success of Silicon Valley has created problems of 'liveability' and a dualised income distribution (Saxenian 1983; Siegel 1998), the diversification of its structure has unquestionably strengthened it as a regional economy. When the semiconductor industry experienced distress in the 1980s, the regional effect was mitigated by the extraordinary upswing in military spending, which was particularly generous to Silicon Valley, with about $4 billion a year in defence prime contracts.

Like Seattle and unlike Colorado Springs, the transformation of Silicon Valley took place largely without any local boosterism or organisational steering. During much of its recent history, local groups have been most concerned with trying to limit the negative externalities of growth, while efforts to form co-operative business associations with an agenda of regional governance à la Third Italy have foundered because trade associations are more nationally oriented and many entrepreneurs consider themselves simply too busy (Saxenian 1991).

SATELLITE PLATFORMS INTO HUB-AND-SPOKE STRUCTURES

The majority of innovative regions in the developing world are of the satellite platform type (Park and Markusen 1995). In South Korea, for example, virtually all the fast-growing regions outside the three major cities may be regarded as either satellite platforms or hub-and-spoke districts. Pohang and Ulsan have assumed hub-and-spoke forms – the Posco Steel company serves as the hub in Pohang, while initially petrochemical plants and now automobile plants are the hubs in

Ulsan. Even here, however, the companies are headquartered in Seoul and many suppliers remain there. Kumi, Changwon, Ansan and Masan, four of the fastest growing cities in South Korea, are satellite platforms, each with a distinctive mission (Park and Markusen 1995; Markusen and Park 1993). Even Taeduck Science Town can be regarded as a satellite platform because R&D centres in the science park have few inter-establishment linkages and are predominantly embedded in external linkages (Jeong and Park 1999).

South Korea's satellite platforms originally owed their competitive advantages to national government incentives such as tax exemptions, provision of infra-structure, cheap supply of industrial land, and financial supports, as well as to cheap regional labour. But in the late 1980s, as a result of democratisation, successful union organising, rapid wage increases and labour shortages, satellite platforms have undergone significant industrial restructuring. With government support, firms have chosen to increase subcontracting activities, invest their earnings disproportionally abroad in China and South-East Asia, and pursue technological change (Park 1995).

As a result, growth in the satellite platforms has slowed dramatically – employment in a city like Masan has actually fallen. Some larger firms have closed operations and moved elsewhere in East Asia. Others have subcontracted out large volumes of particularly routine work, often to smaller firms in the vicinity, some of whom have been set up by former employees. This creates, then, a degree of local linkage and co-operation between large and small firms within the regions that did not exist before. For the most part, however, the larger firms remain dominant and the smaller firms stay dedicated to a single customer, resembling hub-and-spoke rather than Marshallian structures. The higher tech spin-offs in Taeduck may be an exception. Since 1990, more than 20 spin-offs have emerged from institutions in Taeduck Science Park, although they remain small (Jeong 1995). A modest number of spin-offs are also beginning to emerge from Research Triangle Park in North Carolina in the US, another higher-tech satellite platform (Luger and Goldstein 1990).

The South Korean national government continues to be active in shaping industrial relationships, in the form of supports for collaboration between large firms and small-to-medium firms. Many of the governance functions that reside locally in the Third Italy are exercised here by the national government. Large chaebol parent firms have been encouraged to build co-operative links with suppliers to stabilise customer markets, to promote technology development and the specialisation of the small firms, and to provide technical and managerial assistance for small- and medium-sized supply firms. Small- and medium-sized firms joining such organisations of co-operative supply firms to a specific large parent firm are given priority in government subsidies for plant automation and loan guarantees (Jeong 1995). For the hub firm, the national government provides incentives for labour training, technical guidance and co-operative R&D with suppliers.

These linkages among large parent firms and burgeoning numbers of small- and medium-sized supply firms have contributed significantly to the appearance of local networks in the new industrial districts. They owe their existence, however, chiefly to the drive to control labour and keep costs low. In this regard, they are unlike Marshallian industrial districts, with no dominant firms or locally based regional governance structures that are responsive to small-firm members and attempt to co-ordinate responses to disruptive markets in ways that preserve firms and capabilities. They are, however, remaking the face of industrial districts.

For the most part, however, the features hypothesised to block the diversification of satellite platforms are quite robust. The Kyushu regions of Oita and Kumamoto in Japan have not been able to diversify, and Manaus in Brazil is finding it quite difficult to outgrow its satellite platform status (Diniz and Borges 1999). In all countries, the external embeddedness of private sector firms and the absence of locally articulated linkages make it very difficult for regional agents to organise around a strategy for regional transformation.

REGIONAL CULTURE: AN ASSET FOR INNOVATION?

The work of my international colleagues and US team suggests that economic assets, economic structures and economic motivations alone are not sufficient to explain how and why a region might move from a simple form to a more complex one. The role of the state and politics is an essential ingredient, albeit complex and theoretically challenging (Markusen and Park 1993; Jessop 1994). But beyond the political and the economic lurks the underexplored role of culture in regional development, and not just in the guise of institutions of civil society, but deeper, in the less well-organized and even unintentional habits, practices and outlooks of regional societies. In this final section of the chapter, I explore these 'meta-cultures', distinguishing them from the more concrete (and therefore more easily researched) regional social and cultural institutions pioneered by the social capital school (Jacobs 1961; Granovetter 1985; Coleman 1988; Bolton 1992, 1998; Putnam 1995) and the filière approach explored in this book.

The question of meta-culture is not a simple one for regional scholars. Why is it so difficult for us as economists, geographers and regional scientists to acknowledge the distinctive roles of regional culture in assessing comparative regional development and change? We work in an intellectual tradition that privileges economic analysis and incorporates only a crude comprehension of the role of politics and political institutions in regional development. Yet cultural practices – habits of thought, behaviour, kinship and community life – are strong forces in distinguishing among regions' ability to thrive and change. Interest in regional cultures has been stimulated by pioneering work on places like the Third Italy (Goodman and Bamford 1989; Piore and Sabel 1984; DiGiovanna 1996) and Silicon Valley (Saxenian 1994), but characterizations of cultural traits remain underdeveloped, and issues regarding their researchability and integration into regional economic geography are only just beginning to be debated (see, for instance, Lee and Wills 1997).

It is easier to explain why the role of culture is understudied than to remedy the situation. The exercise poses both conceptual and operational problems. First, the rise of post-modern thinking has made it nearly impossible to pass judgement on the superiority or inferiority of individual experience or group culture. Second, a lack of agreement on what constitutes regional 'success' makes it difficult to weigh cultural attributes that contribute differentially to outcomes. This is a predicament intrinsic to capitalist development, which can produce growth with inequality, intolerance or environmental degradation. Third, an effort to appreciate culture as a causal force creates difficulties of conceptualisation – how do we characterise or classify cultural traits? Imagine an SCC – a standard cultural code – to accompany the industrial and occupational codes we now have. A simple reflection on the notion of 'trust' demonstrates this point.

Even if we could agree upon certain cultural traits worthy of investigation – anthropologists and social psychologists certainly have done so – we confront daunting problems in generating evidence. Even where we can generate a clear definition of a particular cultural feature, there may be no existing data on it, and it may be impossible to gather. There is the intractable problem of 'stance', long brooded over by anthropologists. One's view and evaluation of another culture is irreparably tainted by one's own experience and embeddedness.

Finally, we may hesitate to study culture because we might not like the outcome. In the United States, for instance, it would be difficult for me as a woman and white Anglo-Saxon Catholic to have to conclude that the success of the Mormons in Utah may have something to do with their culture, which has traditionally been explicitly sexist and racist.

However, most regions of the world will be developed under capitalist economic and social relations for the foreseeable future. The problem for the policy-oriented researcher, then, is to determine which outcomes are desirable and then study whether particular cultural qualities help to achieve them. Some of these may be compatible with capitalist incentives. Others will require some form of regulation.

To illustrate the power and perils of the cultural category, let us reflect on the case of Silicon Valley, particularly the account recently published by AnnaLee Saxenian (1994). Her work is principally cultural in focus and lauds the relatively freewheeling, co-operative, fast-paced work environment in this new region, comparing it favourably with the more settled, family-oriented and hierarchical culture of the Boston area. While pathbreaking in simply taking on culture, her work is controversial in several ways. Her cultural interpretation is challenged by some, and others reject the strong relationship posited between this culture and regional performance. Her normative judgements on culture are criticised by others, and the replicability of the Silicon Valley experience doubted. Even her method, relying intensively on interviews with selected regional actors, can be questioned (Markusen 1999).

A more robust approach might be systematically to derive from comparative cultural studies those features which can be used to characterise cultures but which do not have labels such as 'Mormon' or 'Irish' or 'Arab' stamped upon them and which are not immediately judged 'good' or 'bad'. In fact, the same qualities that make for economic 'success' and/or a 'good life' are to be found across vastly different cultures and political systems. Here, economists, geographers and regional scientists might do well to incorporate the insights of social psychology and anthropology.

At this juncture, I would like to state five traits that I believe reside in regional (and sometimes national) cultures and which play a significant role in innovation. First, a culture that is optimistic and assumes the best from its residents and others will be more innovative than cultures that are pessimistic, suspicious of new ideas and/or vengeful. In the US, for instance, regions like Seattle, Silicon Valley, Minneapolis and Colorado Springs exhibit cultures of this sort, while older regions such as New Jersey and portions of the black belt South are relatively more pessimistic and ingrown. Sicily might be a good European example of the latter. Persistent net outmigration with little 'new blood' tends to exacerbate pessimism and inflexibility.

Second, cultures that tolerate failure, thus engendering a willingness to learn, will be more innovative than cultures with heavy sanctions for failure and fear of exposure. Silicon Valley is celebrated as a place where no one cares much about failure, since many successful entrepreneurs have failed several times, whereas failure is less acceptable in the North-East of the US (Saxenian 1994). These failure-tolerant cultures will also tend to exhibit a more nurturing attitude toward youth and apprenticeship, acting as magnets for younger people. Despite its extraordinarily high per capita income, New Jersey experiences persistent outmigration of its youth towards regions in the West, like San Francisco and Seattle.

Third, inclusive cultures which operate with a sense of breadth of community will be more innovative than cultures preoccupied with rank, membership, and boundaries, be they class-, caste-, race-, religion-, neighbourhood- or otherwise based. Inclusive cultures are likely to be more tolerant of and attractive to immigrants, and if there are welcoming and helpful structures of incorporation, immigrants can strengthen the innovative potential of the region. Saxenian's (1999) recent monograph on Chinese and Indian entrepreneurial immigrants illustrates this draw in Silicon Valley. Seattle aggressively welcomed Asian business and immigrants over the past two decades, including redoing its street signs in Japanese as well as English. In contrast, many European and Asian regions, as well as smaller cities in the US Midwest and South, lack this diversity and source of innovation. The elimination of millions of entrepreneurial Jews from many European cities during World War II has had a long-term effect in suppressing innovation.

Fourth, a regional culture with a distinctive aesthetic sensibility and associated skill, be it in art, craft, theatre, music or some other sphere, is more likely to be innovative than one without such a sensibility. Often, this aesthetic offers a region a means of anchoring itself in a past to be proud of while permitting an experimentation and openness to change. It also renders the region understandable, attractive and distinctive to outsiders. Many European cities distinguish themselves in this fashion, as do some Canadian and American cities (Montreal, Toronto, Vancouver, New York, San Francisco, Los Angeles, New Orleans and Santa Fe). In the developing world, many second-tier cities live in the shadow of cultural concentration in and domination of the largest cities, and yet cities like Rio de Janeiro and Kyoto manage to parlay their particular aesthetic traditions into continued success. Aesthetic qualities often operate indirectly, through their role in attracting and retaining creative individuals who are willing to experiment and innovate in order to live in the region despite inadequate infrastructure, absence of networks or agglomerative advantages (Markusen 1996b).

Finally, a region with an appreciation for its natural environment and with a commitment to building, using and living within that environment in a way that preserves its originality and productivity will in the longer run be more innovative than a region that builds, exploits and operates without regard to its setting. In the US, cities like San Francisco, Boulder, and Minneapolis were precocious in their concern for establishing and preserving public parklands and open space, reminiscent of greenbelt initiatives in Britain but tailored to the distinctive topography and climate in each case. Recent outmigration from California towards western cities like Seattle, Boulder and Albuquerque is attributed to eroding environmental quality in California. Cities like Seoul and São Paulo face a very difficult future in this regard, having evolved with little preservation of public space or parkland and with growing pollution problems. A combination of aesthetic and environmental values may explain the rootedness of Seattle's software entrepreneurs and their willingness to reinvest their earnings in the region.

These are the propositions, then. Numerous caveats should be attached to them. Many of these features are produced historically by economic and political forces and are not easy to reverse or reproduce. Many are not as achievable in regions with poor economic prospects, suffering from geographical isolation or already environmentally degraded. However, in the century to come, the integration of capitalist market economies will force many regions to face difficult questions of cultural preservation and adaptability. They are every bit as deserving of attention as are the economic and political structures with which regional scholars currently appear to feel more comfortable.

Acknowledgements
The author would like to thank her colleagues Sean DiGiovanna, Klaus Kunzman, Yong Sook Lee, Sam Ock Park, Annalee Saxenian and the editors of this book for their helpful comments.

PART II:
RESTRUCTURING INDUSTRIES
AND TERRITORIAL DEVELOPMENT

3 Large Firms and Subcontracting Relations in the Commercial Aircraft Industry: A Case Study of Campania, Southern Italy

INTRODUCTION

In the 1960s and 1970s, with the relatively generous support of a fiscal and financial incentive scheme, a number of large, state-owned and exogenous private firms played the role of undisputed protagonists in promoting the development of the industrial structure in the least developed area in the South of Italy – the Mezzogiorno. Subsequently, the propulsive force associated with that particular development model became progressively weaker. The 1980s saw a drastic streamlining of large units of production caused to a large extent by restructuring processes, aggravated by crisis and waning interest in intervention policy in state-owned companies. In the meantime, the growing general consensus among Italian researchers and policy-makers – shaped by experience in the 'Third Italy' – was increasingly in favour of a rather different regional growth model based on the development of small and medium (SME) local enterprises specialising in light industries. Since then the role performed by large and small enterprises in the Italian debate has been much like two players in a sort of zero-sum game, where success for the small firms means failure for the large ones and vice versa. As a consequence, the role that large firms have and continue to play in the Mezzogiorno has subsequently been underrated. Very little research has dealt with the subject over the last 15 years, and our knowledge of the situation has become decidedly patchy, while the stereotypical image of the large firm working in the South lingers on. It is still seen as a predator, backward in organisational systems and largely devoid of any productive connections with the small firms in the area. However, two recent studies that have been produced on the issue (Latella 1996; Giunta 1998) reveal a rather different picture.

While large firms are still receiving only scant attention in Italy, a number of economists in other countries point to the current organisation system adopted by large firms as a potential driving force for local economic development (Barquero *et al.* 1997; Gray *et al.* 1996; Harrison 1994). It has been shown that when, for their own advantage, large firms take on responsibility for 'care and cultivation' of the local environment, such behaviour can eventually favour the development of local small firms via subcontracting relations.

Alenia, the Italian state-owned aeronautics company, is a paradigmatic example. In a golden period of growth in the aeronautics industry in the 1980s, it promoted the development of a local tissue of small firms acting as a means of transmission for entrepreneurial, organisational and technological know-how in the Campania region of the Mezzogiorno. The end of the Cold War in 1989 had severe repercussions on Alenia's performance, forcing Italy's leading aeronautic company into a complex process of reorganisation, especially in terms of subcontracting relations. The impact on the local supplier firms has been almost completely neglected.

In this context, this chapter aims to analyse the restructuring processes of the subcontracting system undertaken by Alenia and to investigate its impact on subcontracting firms located in Campania where the production of aerostructures for civil aviation is concentrated. The combined analysis of these two aspects offers a number of pointers for reassessment of the role large firms can play as potential catalysts for the development of less-industrialised areas. Indeed, the case of Alenia reveals that it has adopted efficient systems of organisations involving the collaboration of local firms that raise serious doubts about the stereotype of the large firm as a predator devoid of roots in or connections with local and/or regional productive structures.

The remainder of this chapter sets out this argument in several sections. First, the theoretical studies and empirical research carried out on the forms that procurement can take in the aeronautic industry are renewed, highlighting the scarcity of such material. Nevertheless, what is emerging is a so-called 'lean' procurement model that has many features in common with that in the automobile industry (see for example Womack *et al.* 1990). Second, a profile of Alenia and the role it played in Campania during the 1970s and 1980s is outlined. Third, an assessment of the procurement model now utilised at Alenia is made relative to the aeronautical industry model of lean procurement. Fourth, focus is given to the impact of the changing procurement model on SMEs at work in the Mezzogiorno. Fifth, an analysis is presented of the problems regarding the future positioning of Alenia in the international alliance system and the role industrial policy may play in fostering the commitment of large firms such as Alenia to less-developed regions like Campania. The final section sets out conclusions.

The methodology and analysis are based on information from various interviews with Alenia's procurement division managers and a survey of 20 subcontracting firms, located in Campania, which survived the selection process at the heart of the new lean procurement model.

CURRENT PROCUREMENT MODE IN THE COMMERCIAL AIRCRAFT INDUSTRY

The commercial aircraft industry has a marked division of labour between firms operating at the international scale. With the high costs and risks involved in R&D and engineering, the complexity of the product cycle and the application of extremely diverse technologies (for example aerodynamics, materials and structures, equipment and propulsors) requires the involvement of a number of specialised enterprises to play their various parts.

Notwithstanding this complex division of labour, the organisation structures and subcontracting relationships among aircraft firms is a relatively under-researched area. Indeed, in this increasingly strategic part of an aeronautic firm's competitiveness, disclosure of such sensitive information is often problematic.

Yet, on the evidence of the few available studies, there seems to be a growing awareness that the large aeronautic firms are moving toward a 'lean' organisational model.[1] This model was adopted by Japanese firms in the automobile industry but is now becoming widespread among manufacturing firms worldwide as part of a more efficient or even 'world class' economic strategy. The lean production model incorporates some key features of the Japanese procurement system including long-term commitments with fewer and more carefully selected suppliers, price premiums, small lots, absence of inspections, risk-sharing mechanisms, single sourcing and system supply strategy (Aoki 1984 and 1990; Asanuma 1992; Sako 1992; Okamuro 1995).

The aim of this section is to provide a review of the relatively few recent studies and to assess the prevalence of this lean organisational model in the commercial aircraft industry (Bozdogan 1998; Lefebvre and Lefebvre 1998; Boyer 1997; Giunta 1997; Beckouche 1996; Gray *et al.* 1996; Kechidi 1996; Paliwoda and Bonaccorsi 1994; Todd and Simpson 1986). On the basis of the empirical evidence gathered in such studies we cannot go as far as saying that the unified system of Japanese-style lean procurement model has been adopted in its entirety. However, these researchers suggest that quite a few features of the system are becoming popular within the commercial aircraft industry as a result of an intensive restructuring process undertaken by major aircraft firms at the beginning of the 1990s. What follows is a concise description of the stylised facts of this new procurement mode in the commercial aircraft industry.

Vertical Integration

Even though existing empirical studies do not rely upon commonly used indicators, such as added value on turnover (Adelman 1955), it seems that, as in the automobile industry, the production process in the aircraft industry is now characterised by a declining degree of vertical integration. Three major forces appear to be at work in this process: first, the increasingly sophisticated technologies, such as materials, electronics and avionics, embodied in the aircraft construction require an extensive participation by several specialised firms; second, increased outsourcing has aimed to lower costs and realign in-house production around 'core' business (Bozdogan 1998); and, last, offset agreements have been sought by foreign governments as part of their industrial policy – in the developing countries in particular – that requires the participation of their aircraft industry as a prerequisite for aeroplane orders by their national carrier.[2]

Supply base

In the aircraft industry the adoption of the industry 'good practice' of lean procurement has led to the rationalisation of the supply base and the reduction in the number of suppliers. The subcontracting chain is organised according to a pyramid structure, the top of which is occupied by the lead firm. In the commercial aircraft industry there are Boeing and the Airbus Consortium.[3] The second level is occupied by the preferred suppliers that maintain privileged relationships with the lead firms and share a proportion of the industrial and financial risk of the project. In the third tier and lower are those suppliers that do not have direct links with the lead firm, and work mainly as local subcontractors for the second-level firms (Kechidi 1996).[4]

The Nature of the Relationship and Selection Criteria

The rationalisation of the supply base requires a changed relationship and selection of the most proficient suppliers. Long-term business agreements and subjective selection criteria prevail in the aircraft industry.[5] According to Paliwoda and Bonaccorsi (1994), the formal vendor rating scheme has been replaced by the subjective judgements of people in the customer company. Such subjective judgements are rooted in long-term relationships, as suggested by Gray et al. (1996) drawing on evidence from Boeing in Seattle and by Kechidi (1996) with reference to Aerospatiale in France.

Supply Policy

The establishment of a pyramid structure of preferred suppliers is also dictated by current organisational needs, which require the adoption of the 'system supply strategy' as opposed to the traditional policy of supplying individual commodities (Basile and Giunta 1993; Paliwoda and Bonaccorsi 1994). In fact, aircraft companies are increasingly delegating part of the integration task to component suppliers, through their preference for purchasing complete systems. In comparison with the traditional supplier policy, system supply guarantees product reliability and reduces the costs of identifying the responsible party should the system prove defective after final assembly of the single components. This centralisation of liability in the hands of the preferred supplier, now providing a fully assembled system, is today one of the key ways of reducing costs.

Sourcing Supply Policy

Multiple or overlapping sourcing is a specific supply policy that is adopted when buyer firms make two or more subcontractors compete in order to obtain equilibrium prices near minimum long-term average production costs. Such a policy maintains a market mechanism within the supply chain and has been a complementary feature of the American automobile procurement system. By contrast, single sourcing characterises the Japanese system. Such a policy is shown to be more efficient in an 'environment where a quality premium addresses the moral hazard problem' (Taylor and Wiggins 1997: 612). As quality assurance is essential in the aircraft industry, it is plausible to infer the superiority of the single sourcing policy and the empirical evidence of its utilisation (Paliwoda and Bonaccorsi 1994).[6] Even though investments are specific, in the aircraft industry mutual trust appears to overcome the bilateral monopoly problems which were envisaged in the transaction cost literature (Williamson 1985).

Just-in-Time Delivery

The system supply strategy goes along with the adoption of the just-in-time delivery system, previously introduced in the automobile industry and now becoming common practice in the aeronautical industry because airframe manufacturers are unwilling to carry all the necessary stock in-house.[7]

Geographical Proximity

Very few studies raise the issue of geographical contiguity in relation to the new procurement models. According to Beckouche (1996), the French aircraft industry is characterised by the geographical proximity of supplier firms. The highly specified nature of subcontracting firms coupled with production complexity require frequent exchange between the prime contractor – Aerospatiale – and its supplier firms. Others (Bozdogan 1998; Lefebvre and Lefebvre 1998; Gray et al. 1996) argue that offset agreements might pit the viability of a local aircraft supplier base against the need of prime contractors to exploit both foreign markets, especially in the Asian countries, and international industry capabilities. This array of developments in the evolving procurement model in the commercial aircraft industry has led to a wave of reorganisation and restructuring. The experience of Alenia and its subcontractors in Campania is instructive and is the core which will be considered in the following sections.

ALENIA: A FIRM PROFILE

The commercial aircraft industry has recently became a two-player game, in which the US firm Boeing-McDonnell Douglas (McDonnell Douglas having been recently acquired by Boeing) maintains a 60 per cent market share and the

European Airbus Consortium the remaining 40 per cent. As already mentioned, Boeing and Airbus develop the aircraft programme and organise the collaboration network at a global level with second-level firms. The latter, lead firms in their own countries, are involved in the production of the aircraft through a range of different collaborative methods that, indeed, go from international subcontracting to partnership. In their turn, these second-level firms organise the lower tiers of an often localised supply chain, mainly within their own country. It therefore follows that the position reached in the international division of labour by a second-level firm, like the core of Italian Alenia, has a considerable bearing on local development through the involvement of local subcontracting firms in its supply chain.

Alenia is the leading state-owned company in the Italian aerospace industry.[8] It was formed in December 1990 from the fusion of the aircraft manufacturer Aeritalia with the high technology electronics specialist Selenia.[9] Alenia has now been reorganised into four divisions: aeronautics, space and communications, aeroengines and naval systems.

The aeronautics operations of Alenia competes in the aerostructure segment where, following upon the entry of a number of South-East Asian countries and the reconversion of some military firms into commercial industry, the number of participants has become considerable.[10]

In the 1970s, by establishing subcontracting relationships with both McDonnell Douglas and Boeing, Alenia laid the foundations for its position as a second-tier supplier in the international division of labour in the aircraft industry. A significant upgrading of its role was reached in 1980 with the co-operation agreement with the French group Aerospatiale for the joint production of the ATR42 commuter transport aircraft. This was the first time Alenia had entered into an international agreement as partner.

Since 1980, Alenia's role has evolved into an array of relationships with prime manufacturers (Table 3.1). In spite of the long-standing relationship with Boeing, Alenia still holds only a 'risk and revenue' partnership, even though it has been granted the privileged status of 'sole source' for some specific items.

Alenia also operates as a mere subcontractor for aircraft produced by the Airbus Consortium, while continuing its participation in a joint venture with the French group Aerospatiale in the ATR programme of commuter aircraft production.

Alenia's Role in Southern Italy

As in other countries, aeronautical production is highly regionally concentrated (see for example, Bekouche 1996; Gray et al. 1996). In Italy, there are two regional poles: in Turin, in Piedmont, in the North; and in Pomigliano d'Arco, in Campania, in the South. The spatial division of labour between the plants has led to the establishment of aircraft integration and test functions in the North and the construction of structures for transport aircraft in the South (see Figure 3.1).

The current geographical production structure is the outcome of a 20-year intervention policy by the Italian state where the country's need for a competitive

TABLE 3.1: ALENIA'S COMMERCIAL AIRCRAFT PRODUCTS, COLLABORATION AGREEMENTS AND WORKSHARE, 1997

Company	Products	Collaboration agreements	Workshare
Boeing-McDonnell Douglas	767 wide-body jet	Risk sharing and single source supplier	Flaps, slats, aerilons, spoilers, elevators, rudder, vertical fin, wing tips, radome
	777 wide-body jet	Single source supplier	Outboard flap, radome
	717/200 (exMD95) 120 seats	Risk sharing and single source supplier	Forward, centre and after fuselage barrel
	MD80/90	Single source supplier	Fuselage panels, aerilon, rudder
	MD11	Single source supplier and risk sharing for the new parts	All fuselage panels, vertical stabiliser, rudder, winglets, nose, after fuselage section
Airbus Industrie	A300/310 wide body	Subcontractor	Tail cone
	A321	Subcontractor	Fuselage section
Aerospatiale	ATR42 ATR72	Partner (50%)	Fully equipped fuselage, vertical fin, rudder, horizontal empennages and related systems

Source: Based on data from Alenia, 1998

aeronautical industry has been married with the objective of promoting the regional industrial development of the South. A regional policy of financial and fiscal incentives was utilised to encourage the location of plants in the South.[11] In the early years an expansion of the productive base in the South was attained. A growth trend in profits characterised the whole of the 1980s, which could be defined as the decade of consolidation for Alenia. The rise in commercial sales contributed to positively increasing its share of total turnover from 12 to 42 per cent between 1971 and 1988. Similarly, an absolute and relative increase in the size of the workforce was evident in the area of commercial aeronautics, especially in the southern plants.[12]

The growth in activity yielded immediate spin-off benefit for local development. The whole experience stands as one of the successes of the growth poles development policy adopted by the Italian government between the early 1960s and the mid-1970s. The development of the local productive network was the result of the 'non-isolationist' and inclusive behaviour of former Aeritalia, which acted as a transfer centre for entrepreneurial, technological and organisational skills. Indeed, by the 1980s the use of local firms to carry through stages of the manufacturing process become systematic, thus favouring spin-off processes and enlarging the productive base through the creation of a network of local firms.

FIGURE 3.1: LOCATION OF PLANTS

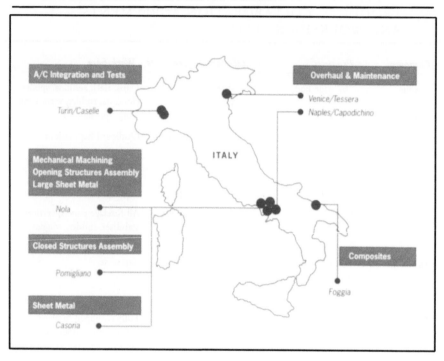

Small and medium-sized subcontracting firms did not enjoy an autonomous position in the international market. Rather, they acted as indirect exporters, since they supplied forward users who in turn served the international market.

Moreover, in contrast with the more commonly diversified practice in more evolved industrial contexts, these SME suppliers operated in a monopsonistic system. Their productive capacity was saturated with the orders of the lead firm – the former Aeritalia.

Some details of the structural characteristics of the SME subcontractors in Campania can help to fill out the cognitive picture. The data are drawn from field research carried out in 1993 in the middle of the crisis period of dramatic restructuring on a representative sample of 26 small and medium-sized subcontracting firms located in Campania (Basile and Giunta 1993).[13]

This empirical study confirms the positive correlation between the position held by Alenia in the international division of labour and the thickening of the local supply network. In fact, less than half of the firms were created between the latter 1960s and the first half of the 1970s, the remainder starting up in the boom period of demand for commercial aircraft that coincided with a substantial upgrading in Alenia's position in the international division of labour.

Indeed there is evidence of a considerable spread of entrepreneurial spill-over processes that confirms the role of the large firm as a mechanism for transferring know-how. Over half the entrepreneurs had worked for Alenia before starting up their new firm. Almost all entrepreneurs were local; only 12 per cent came from the Centre–North of Italy. These were subcontractors for Alenia in Piedmont who were induced to transfer their production units to Campania. This indicates a pulling effect of suppliers, which, as I show below, was to have important repercussions in the 1990s. A final point of interest here is the limited technical dimensions of the local firms: most were small and showed a very poor division of functions, confined solely to manufacturing. The prevalent productive specialisation was machining.

The particularly positive results both in corporate terms and in terms of local multiplier effects met with a serious and prolonged standstill as a result of the 'outbreak of peace' in 1989, aggravated by the downturn in the global economy marking the early 1990s. It was in these years that a dramatic process of restructuring in the aeronautical industry was set in train. Firms sought to cope with the effects of a crisis in which changes of a structural nature – the process of political détente between East and West – combined with the slump in demand for air transport.

THE RESTRUCTURING PROCESS: A NEW SUBCONTRACTING SYSTEM FOR ALENIA

In the early 1990s the need to face up to the crisis drove Alenia to work out a complex restructuring plan, currently near to completion.[14] The plan involved changes in the internal organisational structure, rationalisation of operations, reduction in the workforce and, finally, the adoption of a new subcontracting system called 'strategic sourcing'. As other researchers have pointed out (Paliwoda and Bonaccorsi 1994), this is one of the areas in which it is extremely difficult to obtain significant information. Our data originate both from a survey carried out by Alenia in 1995 among 20 subcontractor firms and from several interviews with managers of the procurement department carried out between 1995 and 1998.

This section considers the main features of the emergent lean procurement system discussed above in order to assess – on the evidence of the data we have access to – how closely Alenia is working to the prevailing procurement model. As ascertained by other scholars (Paliwoda and Bonaccorsi 1994; Kechidi 1996), our information demonstrates that procurement reorganisation proceeded slowly and with difficulty. Since 1992 it has been centralised in a single purchasing unit which supplies both Alenia's southern and northern plants.

Vertical Integration

Data regarding the degree of vertical integration of Alenia's plants in selected years was unavailable. However, our interviewees observed that vertical integration has fallen in recent years. The main reasons for this externalisation were given as:

- economic – some activities could be carried out externally at lower costs because they did not include overhead costs;

- financial considerations–some manufacturing costs 'weigh down' invested capital;

- operating flexibility – flexibility was needed in order to offload the risks and costs of cyclical fluctuation in demand;

- the contractual requirements of work-sharing offset agreements with international suppliers.

Supply Base

An acquired datum is the screening of the subcontractor list and the outlining of a pyramid-style organisational structure, according to the Japanese-style lean procurement model. Supply base reduction went ahead in a piecemeal fashion, to be fully accomplished only in 1998. A major step was taken in 1994: 20 subcontractor firms survived the selection process, accounting for a total of 1420 employees. Subcontracting firms were subdivided into two groups: major and minor. There were four major firms, all with owners from the Centre–North, with plants in both Piedmont (North) and in Campania (South). The 16 minor firms include 11 southern firms and five firms located in the Centre–North of Italy.[15] The selection thus rewarded firms with owners from outside Campania, promoting them to the status of major.

Nature of the Relationship and Selection Criteria

As regards the nature of the relationship between preferred suppliers and Alenia, very little information was available and the supplier survey revealed very little. Both major and minor firms have a guaranteed 20-year-long relationship with Alenia. Technical assistance is provided by the leading firms, with frequent visits to the plants of preferred suppliers.

As regards the type of contract, during the 1980s Alenia operated in a monopsonistic environment, and the competition for subcontracting contracts was regulated thus: Alenia established a price ceiling – a price that could not be exceeded – and on this basis launched a competition for subcontractors to reach the lowest price. The fixed-price contract, where all the risk of cost fluctuation was taken by subcontractors, was then hegemonic, as one would have expected given the conditions of monopsony. Unfortunately, information was unavailable concerning the current contracts. We might reasonably assume that the change in the environment – the shift from monopsony to bilateral monopoly-coupled with long-term relationships and the establishment of preferred suppliers would call for a cost-plus contract – i.e. the risk being partly absorbed by Alenia. In this light, subcontracting relations would act as an insurance mechanism (Aoki 1984; Okamuro 1995).

Little information was also available regarding the selection criteria, although some of them can be inferred from the structural variables characterising preferred subcontracting firms.

First, the subdivision between major and minor firms clearly signals that a hierarchy system is at work, in accordance with the empirical findings of other researchers (Beckouche 1996). Second, there is more than one layer in such a pyramidal structure, as can be seen by considering the incidence of purchases over turnover for each type of the selected firm. The percentage averages around 39 per cent for major firms, 32 per cent in Centre–North minor firms and 31 per cent for southern minor firms. What these data show is that the preferred suppliers – both major and minor – are in turn externalising phases of production to other firms, which do not have direct relationships with the firm at the top of the pyramid, namely Alenia. In this way there exists a fragmentation of the production process with centralisation and liability for the final product, ordered by the top firm. The incidence of purchases over turnover can also be interpreted – see below – as a very crude proxy for managerial capacity, meaning the ability of the preferred supplier to organise the work of lower-tier suppliers. Third, geographical proximity is relevant, since 75 per cent of the preferred suppliers are located in the South. Finally, the major firms evidently have a wider command of technology (such as sheet metals, machining, assembly, bonding, tools and composites), while the minor firms are predominantly mono-technological, as they are specialised in machining, although minor southern firms show a greater propensity toward multi-technology (Figure 3.2).[16]

Supply Policy

Since technological capacity played a crucial role in the supplier selection process, it can be inferred that Alenia is attempting to move toward a system supply policy. As described above, aircraft companies are delegating part of the assembly task to suppliers through the purchase of complete systems. The ability to adhere to the supply system, or in other words to carry into effect the assembly of different components inside the firm's own plant, is to a greater extent a function of technological capacity.

Sourcing Supply Policy

At the time of the supplier survey in 1995, multiple sourcing was still prevalent. Rather than the outcome of a deliberate policy favouring a competitive bidding system, it seemed to be a legacy from the past growth period and, as interviewees pointed out, doomed to be replaced in the near future. It has been declared that multiple sourcing is retained only when an offset agreement is stipulated: in this case the other supplier is obviously located abroad.

FIGURE 3.2: PHASES OF PRODUCTION ACCORDING TO THE TYPE OF SUPPLIER FIRMS, 1994

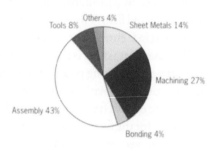

Phases of production in major firms

Others 4%
Tools 8%   Sheet Metals 14%
Machining 27%
Assembly 43%
Bonding 4%

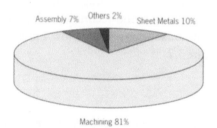

Phases of production in minor centre – north firms

Assembly 7%   Others 2%   Sheet Metals 10%
Machining 81%

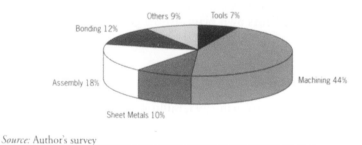

Phases of production in minor southern firms

Others 9%   Tools 7%
Bonding 12%
Machining 44%
Assembly 18%
Sheet Metals 10%

Source: Author's survey

Just-in-Time Delivery

No information was forthcoming on the just-in-time system. While it does not seem to be a major concern for Alenia's procurement managers, the preference for geographical contiguity of subcontracting firms suggests that there is potential for just-in-time to be easily adopted in the near future.

Customer Portfolio

As we saw earlier, a diversified customer portfolio does not appear as a characteristic feature of the new supplier system in the aircraft industry. Yet the interviews and surveys reveal that it does constitute a specific requirement that Alenia stipulates to preferred suppliers in order to reduce their dependence.

All the subcontracting firms surveyed maintain four customers, each accounting for substantial levels of sales (Table 3.2). The capacity to diversify the customer portfolio and thus to reduce the risk connected with variation in demand appears high among 20 firms, and greater than expected, since the technical possibilities of production diversification in the aeronautics sector are somewhat limited.[17] Thus, the recession acted as a disciplining mechanism for those who survived. Subcontracting firms were forced to look for alternative markets releasing them from the monopsonistic system in which they operated throughout the 1980s.

TABLE 3.2: PERCENTAGE OF TURNOVER IN 1994 ACCORDING TO TYPE OF SUPPLIER FIRM AND CUSTOMER IMPORTANCE

	Major firms	*Minor southern*	*Centre–North minor*
First customer	45.3	44.5	46.4
Second customer	21.5	20.3	18.0
Third customer	14.5	14.0	11.9
Other customers	18.7	21.2	23.7
Total	100.0	100.0	100.0

Source: Based on data from Alenia, 1995

A comparison now can be made between the models of procurement adopted by the major firms operating in the sector of civil aviation described above and the degree to which Alenia conforms to this model (Table 3.3). The first column in the table shows the individual features of procurement, the second shows the specific organisational modes adopted by the major firms operating in the aeronautical sector and the third the extent to which Alenia conforms to this model. On the basis of this comparative analysis we may conclude that the majority of the features of the new style of procurement evident in the sector were adopted by Alenia as a result of an intensive process of organisational restructuring.

TABLE 3.3: PROCUREMENT FEATURES BOTH IN THE AIRCRAFT INDUSTRY AND IN ALENIA

Procurement features	Aircraft industry	Alenia
Vertical integration	Decreasing	Decreasing
Supply base	Reduced	Reduced
Nature of the relationship and selection criteria	Long-term relationship and subjective criteria	Long-term relationship Technology is relevant, as well as managerial ability
Supply policy	System supply policy	System supply policy
Single sourcing	In use	About to be implemented
JIT	In use	No evidence
Geographical proximity	Contrasting evidence	Relevant
Customers' portfolio	No evidence	Relevant

Source: Author's interviews and supplier survey

THE NEW SUBCONTRACTING SYSTEM: THE IMPACT ON LOCAL SUPPLIERS

This section considers the impacts of this lean model of procurement organisation on the local subcontracting firms in Campania. A number of points are worth underlining here, beginning with the resulting rationalisation of several firms. The fundamental change in the supplier base has led to the closure of many southern subcontracting firms that were established during the 1980s during the marked increase in demand for commercial aircraft. This increase meant that Alenia systematically turned to the market with consequent spill-over effects. However, as the crisis broke out, most of these firms were subsequently found to be marginal, unable to adapt to the stringent conditions imposed by the new procurement trend, incapable of finding alternative markets outlets and therefore forced out of the market. Few firms managed to survive this process. Eleven subcontracting firms in the South actually did so, although they were positioned at a lower level of the subcontracting chain. In comparison with the minor northern firms, the minor southern firms appear to have on average an equal capacity for customer portfolio diversification (Table 3.2), greater technological versatility (Figure 3.2) and, as I show below, higher managerial expertise. In fact, in running a regression using the data from the Alenia 1995 survey of 20 supplier firms to investigate the explanatory weight of the variables of managerial expertise and the degree of comparative advantage shown by minor southern firms, the following regression equation was estimated:

$$PGS = a_0 + a_1 LOC + a_2 S94 + a_3 WCE + a_4 FI$$

Here, the dependent variable PGS is the purchase of goods and services by subcontracting firms in 1994. As mentioned above this is used as a very crude indicator of managerial ability. LOC is a dummy variable for location, taking 1 if the subcontracting firm is located in the Centre–North and 0 otherwise. S94 is turnover in 1994. WCE is the proportion of white-collar employees of the total workforce, indicating the presence in the firms of functions other than just manufacturing. Finally, FI is the proportion of total sales accounted for by the first customer, i.e. Alenia.

Table 3.4 reveals the estimation results of the regression equations. In our preferred equation (number 2), the explanatory variables show the expected signs and are statistically significant at a 5 per cent level. The southern firms evidently have a comparative advantage over their Centre–North counterparts, the sign of the location variable being in fact negative. This result gives further support to the conclusion of our descriptive analysis. As expected, all the other variables are positively correlated with the managerial capacity of subcontracting firms. More specifically, the positive and significant coefficient of sales in 1994 (S94) signals that a sustained level of sales improves managerial ability. Moreover, the sign of WCE indicates that the higher the number of white-collar employees, the higher also is the managerial ability. It might also suggest that an externalisation process is under way, and that higher value-added functions are held inside the firms. Finally, the sign and the coefficient of FI (percentage of sales to Alenia) suggest that the larger the subcontracting firm's proportion of sales to Alenia, the greater is their managerial ability.

The third point worth making here concerns the hierarchy, which seems to work as a system for the transmission of know-how. As we have seen, the current

TABLE 3.4: ESTIMATION RESULTS OF PURCHASE OF GOODS AND SERVICES OF ALENIA'S SUPPLIER FIRMS IN 1994

				Independent variables				
Dependent variable	C	LOC	S94	WCE	FI	BE	BHE	R^2
1. PGS	−0.028 (−0.027)	−0.08602 (−1.434)	0.0000082 (2.375)		0.46317 (2.107)	0.77934 (2.034)		0.25
2. PGS	0.00347 (−0.03)	−0.1144 (−2.177)	0.0000085 (2.813)	1.0472 (1.933)	0.50272 (2.446)			0.26
3. PGS	0.0519 (0.379)	−0.08944 (−1.260)	0.0000078 (2.200)		0.3989 (1.793)		0.15778 (0.703)	0.17

Note: *t*-statistics in parentheses

Key: PGS = purchase of goods and services by subcontracting firms in 1994
C = constant
LOC = dummy variable for location (1 = Centre – North; 0 = South)
S94 = turnover in 1994
WCE = white-collar employees/total employees
FI = proportion of sales to the first customer
BE = employees with a bachelor degree/total employees
BHE = employees with a bachelor degree or a high school diploma/total employees

procurement trend has led to a more markedly tiered supply structure. The selection process has rewarded firms with owners from outside the region of Campania, promoting them to major status. This pulling effect of suppliers should not be underestimated. Apart from the obvious multiplier effect of increasing local employment, one other aspect needs to be stressed. Moving to the South, these entrepreneurs act as a co-ordination structure for firms placed at a lower level in the supply chain, favouring top-down transmission of entrepreneurial know-how. This is an asset in chronic short supply in southern Italy, as well as in other less-favoured regions in the EU.

Furthermore, the established hierarchy among supplier firms is not a static equilibrium, since it offers each firm chances to move up to the higher levels of the supply chain. A process of upgrading can be set in motion, the outcome of which will depend on the ability of local firms to adopt the more highly developed organisational and productive models that are currently shaping local markets as well.

Finally, there are some observations to be made about medium-term success. Here we need to go back to the demand side, because both the economic future of the Campania region and the further development of the Italian aeronautical industry are highly dependent on the role of Alenia in the international division of labour.

THE ITALIAN AIRCRAFT INDUSTRY AND LOCAL DEVELOPMENT IN THE NEAR FUTURE: SOME ISSUES

As we showed above, there is an obvious positive correlation between the workshare Alenia gains on the international market and local multiplier effects. In fact, spin-off processes came into effect in Campania during the 1980s, resulting from full partnership with the French group Aerospatiale to build regional aircraft together with an increased demand for commercial aircraft at the international level. In the 1990s the scenario appears to have changed drastically on account of various factors: these included declining military demand, increasing concentration of European firms, privatisation processes among a number of European firms and the slow recovery of international demand owing to the Asian crisis. The close connection between local multiplier effects and Alenia's positioning in the international division of labour raises serious questions about Alenia's future role in the international system of alliances. Favourable and developmental positioning in the commercial aircraft industry is reached through a step-by-step process, which usually begins with international subcontracting, then passes through a risk- and revenue-sharing partnership to full partnership. The question that arises is therefore: now that the commercial aircraft industry has become a two-player game, what role can Alenia play in co-operating with Boeing and/or the Airbus Consortium? There seem to be two main issues, which are closely interlinked.

First, nearly 30 years on from its establishment, it would be a decidedly positive development if the Italian firm moved in the direction of partnership-based solutions. This would involve an upgrading of Alenia's relative position, shifting to relations characterised by high co-ordination and low dominance.

Second, with which of the two main firms is Alenia likely to be linked? On the one hand, the natural outcome of a long-standing relationship with Boeing would be the attainment of partnership, even with a minority share at the outset. Such a partnership would guarantee a fixed participating share for Alenia in Boeing's programmes, thus protecting it from future competition from Asian firms, and particularly from Japan; however, a contractual agreement of this kind that was tried in 1995 with the former McDonnell Douglas had no success. In fact, the failure has crystallised Alenia's position inside a risk and revenue partnership, even if, as we saw in Table 3.1, it has been granted a considerable workshare and the privileged status of sole source for specific items.

On the other hand, recent talk of a unified European aerospace and defence group seems to be pointing forcefully toward a European solution to the matter. In fact, the so-called 'E Company' – the European Aerospace Defence Company – is said to be open to having other European companies, including Alenia, join in the restructuring. However, since the establishment of the Airbus Consortium, the role of Alenia has been marginal and confined to relatively minor subcontracting production. Moreover, the formation of the 'E Company', being a gradual process based on separate link-ups between operating companies, and raising the issue of converting Airbus into a proper company, seems to have a long way to go before it becomes reality.[18] Last, but not least, the Italian company has played no significant role in recent international consolidation manoeuvring: British Aerospace is merging with Marconi, Spain's Casa is being bought by the German company Dasa, and, more importantly, there is to be a merger between Dasa and Aerospatiale Matra. Furthermore, the ownership structure of Alenia is becoming more anachronistic because state ownership itself is gradually disappearing in the European aircraft industry.[19]

Analysis of the present situation shows Italy's lead firm indisputably lagging behind. It is therefore a matter of some urgency to launch an investment process to enhance the position of Alenia and make it a valuable potential partner in future alliances. At the same time, and in close connection with this, it appears equally urgent to speed up the process of privatisation of the company, as this is seen by European partners as a necessary condition for Alenia's participation in future European programmes. This may well lead to further restructuring and job loss. However, while privatisation of the firm is included in the aims which the new Italian government has set itself to be achieved by June 2000, as far as new investments are concerned, the tool for industrial policy described as 'planning agreements' (*contratti di programma*) between government and the large state-owned firms appears to seek both the relaunch of the firm and the development of the local supply chain. Together with the 'territorial agreements' (*patti territoriali*) and 'area contracts' (*contratti d'area*), these planning contracts form part of the package of measures (Law 662/1996) introduced to favour local development in southern Italy. Unlike the territorial agreements and area contracts designed to promote local entrepreneurship, however, the planning contracts are intended to encourage the inflow of external resources into the area, thus reviving some features of the old (and, by some, heavily criticised) strategy of 'growth poles of development'. Financial incentives are accorded by the government to large firms and/or consortiums of SMEs provided that they carry out industrial investment, research and staff training projects in the Mezzogiorno regions, and moreover commit themselves to favouring the development of local firms through subcontracting relations (Florio and Giunta 1998). Appreciated as favouring a broader base for southern Italy's slender productive structure, this tool of industrial policy eases the way to technological re-equilibrium and the division of labour among firms, and is particularly opportune at the present moment with streamlined procedures applying to the transference of resources to firms. Drawing up a planning contract between Alenia and the government would therefore be a desirable move to relaunch Alenia's investment activities and, by so doing, reinforce the firm's commitment to the objectives of regional industrial development in Campania.

CONCLUSIONS

The main aim of this chapter was twofold: to investigate the extent to which the organisational procurement model prevailing in the aircraft the industry has been adopted by the leading Italian firm, Alenia, and to analyse the likely impact of this new procurement model on the local supply chain.

With regard to the first point, I began by arguing that there is a serious deficit of research. In the last 15 years, very few articles in Italy have been written and even less empirical research has been undertaken. With its virtual disappearance from the research agenda, the outcome of restructuring processes and the current organisational models of large firms located in southern Italy are largely unknown.

Nevertheless, existing studies prove that the large southern firms, although drastically reduced in number, have embarked on radical restructuring processes involving profound transformation of their supplier relations in common with large firms in other industrialised countries. Alenia, a leading Italian firm in the aeronautical industry, is a case in point. This chapter underlines a major change in Alenia's subcontracting model.

To pursue its lean procurement strategy, Alenia followed the trend of increased outsourcing, reduction of the vendor list, implementation of system supply policy and single sourcing. It also built up a hierarchical structure in the supply chain, driving supplier firms to find alternative markets. The final configuration shows some resemblance to the core–ring system where supplier firms are organised by the 'visible hand' of the prime manufacturer, Alenia.

As regards the other main point of this chapter, namely the likely impact on local supplier firms, it can be concluded that the outcome has been severe and profitable at the same time. Reduction in the workforce and the exit of several marginal firms have represented a loss in an area where the industrial structure is weak and the unemployment rate significantly above the national average. However, such negative trends are common nowadays owing to a structural crisis combined with the effects of the Asian recession.

The survival of eleven southern firms is a sign of their technical and managerial ability, which now qualifies them to participate in the global supply chain and benefit from the transmission of entrepreneurial know-how flowing from the top of the hierarchy. In connection with this, the active role played by Alenia as a governance structure fostering and supporting the selected suppliers has worked as a significant upgrading mechanism.

I have stressed the relevance of the present and future role of Alenia in the international division of labour in the aerospace industry since it has important repercussions on local development. While a joint-venture partnership is highly preferable to a risk-and-revenue partnership, in order to become a truly valuable partner Alenia needs to strengthen and upgrade its core competencies. The industrial policy tools available open the way for relaunch of the Italian firm's investment activities. It is suggested in this chapter that a viable solution may lie in drawing up a planning agreement between the government and Alenia, thus speeding up the upgrading process of the firm and indirectly fostering and ensuring Alenia's commitment to regional development in the South of Italy.

NOTES

1. In the defence aerospace industry, the lean procurement model has taken hold in the form of the Lean Aerospace Initiative (LAI). LAI was launched in 1993 when leaders from the US Air Force, the Massachusetts Institute of Technology, labour unions and defence aerospace businesses began a partnership to revolutionise the industry, reinvigorate the workplace, and reinvest in America. See <http://web.mit. edu/lean/index.html>.

2. Offset agreements are defined as mandates for technology transfer or incorporation of local production, or a variety of other performance requirements typically requested by the purchasing government (National Research Council 1997: 5). On the role of offset agreements as a common path for the development of a national aircraft industry, see Scott and Creighton (1994) who shed some light on the Asian aircraft industry. Gray et al. (1996: 657) underline that only 15 per cent of total Boeing's suppliers are local, owing to the weight of offset agreements acting as a bias against awarding contracts to local suppliers.

3. Airbus is a consortium of four European aircraft firms. It is one of the main examples of international collaboration in civil aeronautics. The principal partners are Dasa (Germany) 37.9 per cent, Aerospatiale (France) 37.9 per cent, British Aerospace (Britain) 20 per cent and Casa (Spain) 4.2 per cent. Because of the very recent merger of Dasa and Casa, the combined company will be in the near future the single largest member within Airbus consortium, once the deal is approved by the European Commission competition authorities. Unlike the Europeans, Boeing has not yet entered into any true joint ventures with an equal sharing of responsibility. Instead, the US airframe manufacturer has pursued a risk-sharing subcontract collaborative agreement, in which the junior partner companies share launch costs, accept some of the commercial risk and provide market access in return for production work, potential profits and the development of national capacity (*Aerospace* 1994: 17).

4. This highly structured hierarchy was created by Aerospatiale at the very beginning of the 1990s. It was inspired by the Japanese keiretsu, as reported by Kechidi, 1996.

5. 'Only 20% of the total of an airframe manufacturer is purchased through competitive procedure' (Paliwoda and Bonaccorsi 1994: 237). Contrasting findings are in Bozdogan (1998) although referring to the defence aircraft industry. He underlines that most firms in the industry have adopted formal supplier rating, certification, and selection systems.

6. Single sourcing also prevails in the defence procurement system (De Fraja and Hartley 1996).

7. Airframe manufacturing is less rigid than car manufacturing on the assembly line, but it is much more expensive in terms of working capital committed to production (inventory of raw material, subassemblies, components); see Paliwoda and Bonaccorsi 1994: 238.

8. The entire Italian aerospace industry is grouped under Finmeccanica, the high-technology branch of IRI, a vast state-owned conglomerate.

9. The merger was dictated mainly by the necessity to reach a competitive critical mass, which allowed Alenia to stand comparison with the most important European firms, as well as the need for managerial and commercial rationalisation.

10. This is the case of the recent risk and revenue partnership stipulated by Boeing with Japan for the 777 aircraft (a wide-body jet), in which Japan was accredited a work share equivalent to 20 per cent of the total cost of the aircraft. The Japanese government financed this venture with the objective of developing the local industry. A similar experience occurred in Italy in the 1970s: the Italian firm gained a 15 per cent share in the development of the 767 aircraft (another wide-body jet).

11. In France as well as in Spain the aeronautics industry has been created to promote the development of the South (Beckouche 1996). In Italy, when it was established in 1969, the name of the company was Aeritalia. It was created with the joint participation of FIAT (a private group) and Finmeccanica (state-owned IRI group). In 1976 the IRI group bought Fiat's share, thus becoming the sole shareholder. On the Italian case and the attempt made by the Government to link the aerospace sector into its strategy for southern regional development, see also Todd and Simpson, 1986.

12. The number of people employed in southern plants increased from 12,286 in 1983 to 13,662 in 1987.

13. The universe consisted of 50 supplier firms.

14. The reduction in activity level caused a drastic reduction in employment level of the southern plants, which shrank from over 10,500 in 1991 to 7,585 units in 1995 (−27.7 per cent). The restructuring process also implies a reorganisation of the mission of each plant. A plant in the North (in Turin) has been closed. Operating since 1996, two new plants with a high level of automation have been created in the South (called NOLA1 and NOLA2). Apart from company resources, the establishments of these two plants was brought into effects due to the financing from Law 181 of 1989. The automation strategy pursued clearly aims at reducing labour costs in the attempt to compete with South-East Asian countries. For fuller details on the various aspects of Alenia's restructuring process, see Giunta (1997).

15. Out of 1,420 employees, 61.2 per cent are in major firms, 28 per cent in southern minor firms and 10.8 per cent in Centre–North minor firms. The average size of the major firms is 271 employees, the minor southern firms averaging 36 and the minor Centre–North firms 30.

16. Bonding is the preparation of parts in composites such as fibre glass and carbon fibre. Tools are needed to build single pieces and assemble them. An example of a tool is the jig, namely the slip for mounting panels. The importance of technological capacity is addressed and tested for 384 small and medium-sized subcontractors, operating in the USA, the UK and Canada, by Lefebvre and Lefebvre (1998).

17. In fact, the customers other than Alenia are all operating in the same industry and all belong to Finmeccanica conglomerate.

18. As a French *groupement d'interet économique*, Airbus consortium now enjoys a tax-free status. There are two more difficulties in converting Airbus into a proper company. One is agreeing the values of the assets to be pooled. A second is agreeing on the management structure and governance of the company (*The Economist* 1999: 81).

19. The privatisation of French aerospace has now taken a step forward. Lagardère Group will pay as much as $343 million for a 33 per cent stake in the merger between its Matra defence arm and Aerospatiale. The French government will remain the largest shareholder with 47 per cent, while 20 per cent will be floated later this year, market conditions permitting.

Acknowledgements
Special thanks are due to Alenia's representatives who granted me interviews and information. However, this chapter reflects my opinions and Alenia holds no responsibility for the same. I would also thank Alfredo Del Monte, Arnoud Lagendijk and Andy Pike for valuable comments on an earlier draft and Ann Markusen for support throughout the final writing stage at PRIE (Project on Regional and Industrial Economics, Rutgers University). I also acknowledge financial support from the Italian National Research Council (short-term mobility fellowship) and the Human Capital and Mobility Programme of the European Union.

4 Critical Reflections on 'Embeddedness' in Economic Geography: The Case of Labour Market Governance and Training in the Automotive Industry in the North-East Region of England

INTRODUCTION

'Embeddedness' has increasingly become common currency in economic geography to describe and explain the relations between economic agents and their context across a range of geographical scales. The idea that economic action is 'embedded' in ongoing spatial systems of social relations has often been used as a touchstone – usually dealt with by reference to Granovetter (1985) – for the recognition of the various 'turns' – social, cultural and institutional – currently pervading the sub-discipline (Amin 1998; Lee and Wills 1997).

However, as currently employed, 'embeddedness' appears to be a somewhat vague and ambiguous article of faith. It tends to be over-used in careless ways that often empty the term of much of its meaning. While the concept directs attention to integral issues in economic geography, there is growing recognition in some quarters of dissatisfaction with the conceptual and theoretical specificity and weak understandings of embeddedness. Oinas (1997: 24), for example, claims that:

> however popular, [embeddedness] remains a vague concept – not the least as it is employed in the economic geography literature, it needs to be complemented by more penetrating concepts, theorisations and empirical analysis.

This chapter does not attempt to re-engage with the historical evolution of the idea of embeddedness through the work of Polanyi and Granovetter in order to try and provide some sort of definitive account. Such worthy analyses have been tackled elsewhere (Oinas 1997; Granovetter and Swedberg 1992; Zukin and DiMaggio 1990). Instead, the intention here is to produce a sympathetic critique of the existing ways in which 'embeddedness' has been employed in the recent economic geography literature. A distinction is drawn between embeddedness and embedding prior to revealing some of the problems evident in recent economic geographies. A more clearly specified conceptual and theoretical framework and methodological approach is suggested. If one significant future research agenda entails 'constructing a contextual economics and economic geography, in which socio-spatial embeddedness is moved centre-stage, since economic events are necessarily contextual, that is embedded in spatial structures of social relations' (Martin 1994: 43) then a better understanding of embeddedness is required. Such a revised approach is then utilised to examine preliminary empirical material concerning the 'embedding' of the automotive industry in the North-East region of England.

EMBEDDEDNESS AND EMBEDDING

Our critique stems partly from the notion that work on embeddedness has changed its emphasis over the last decade but that the nature and implications of this shift have not been fully understood. This change has involved, in particular, a shift in attention from 'embeddedness' to 'embedding'. Embeddedness, essentially, refers to the claim, as set out by Granovetter (1985; see also Granovetter and Swedberg 1992), that all economic action contains significant social elements. Embeddedness, in this sense, presents an article of faith, asserting the blurring of the distinction between the economic and the social, and rejecting the tendency towards atomisation of human action in mainstream economics and sociology. Granovetter thus advocated a perspective in which 'attempts at purposive action are embedded in concrete, ongoing systems of social relations' (Granovetter 1985: 487). These relations are held, primarily, with known actors (Oinas 1998). In addition, placed in a broader context, this view of embeddedness can be linked to an institutional perspective, which sees social relations shaped and constrained by informal (e.g. traditions, customs) and formal institutions (e.g. organisations, administrative systems). As McDowell (1997: 120) claims:

> Economic decisions, like other forms of interaction and behaviour, are socially constructed, made and carried out in a set of social circumstances and institutions which have a history and a present, and are based on sets of vested interests and alternative power bases.

What is relevant for economic geography is that these social relations have a necessarily spatial structure, because they are evident between and through inter-related scales (Massey 1995). Their territorial expression is both a cause and a consequence of the embedding process rather than simply a manifestation. Each thread of socio-spatial relations comprises an array of different but closely inter-related economic and social dimensions, as well as political, cultural and cognitive ones. According to Oinas (1998), perhaps a better metaphor for this interpretation of embeddedness is 'rootedness'.

'Embedding', on the other hand, draws attention to a process in which (socio)economic actions of certain *subjects* are seen to become intertwined with *objects* that do not necessarily form part of the actor's original network of social relations (G Grabher 1993). The process of embedding economic action can be seen to ebb and flow – hence the possibility of *dis*embedding – across a series of intertwined – rather than discrete and separate – threads that are structured by social relations – between capitals, capital and labour, the state and quasi-state institutions, as well as gendered and ethnic groups. In the territorial context, the object of embedding is generally a demarcated area, a region or country, while the subject may be a firm or industry located in this area. Embedding can then refer to a process of anchoring or tying the subject to the object.

PROBLEMS WITH 'EMBEDDEDNESS' AND 'EMBEDDING' IN ECONOMIC GEOGRAPHY

Both 'embeddedness' and 'embedding' seem to have become prerequisites in writing economic geography in recent years. There may be many reasons for this. Perhaps the terms provide conveniently broad, catch-all categories for the analysis and explanation of the influence of social, political and cultural concerns that can simply be added onto the more traditional and purely economic interests of the sub-discipline. Difficult issues regarding the influence of political culture upon economic action, for example, may be explained away by appealing to a vague notion of their embeddedness within the historically constructed and often localised social structure. 'Embedding' too has become associated with the notion of anchoring firms and industrial assets to regional contexts as part of public policy and regional competitiveness debates. If we are to be clearer about both embeddedness and embedding then we need to address several themes of criticism of the current utilisation of the ideas in economic geography.

WHAT IS EMBEDDING OR BEING EMBEDDED IN WHAT?

The pervasive use of the notions of embeddedness and embedding in economic geography is such that the focus of research and analysis has become somewhat clouded. It is simply not clear in some accounts just what is being embedded or is being involved in embedding. Superficial readings of the notion tend to focus upon a loosely conceived idea of economic action as the key. Dominant research in this tradition therefore often focuses upon capital – in a private, firm-centric manner – as both the research object and subject of the embeddedness (e.g. Oinas 1997; Sally 1994). Although significantly, more recent attention has been given to different institutional, social and cultural forms of capital (Dicken and Thrift 1992; Harrison 1994; Schoenberger 1996). Unlike economic sociology where a diverse range of studies are evident – concerning migration and discrimination for example (see Smelser and Swedberg 1994) – in economic geography other areas of ostensibly economic action – including the public and voluntary sectors, organised labour and community groups for example – have received relatively less attention, although recent work has been undertaken on local exchange trading systems (Thorne 1996) and local government (Halford and Savage 1997). Until what is being embedded is clarified and its explanatory evidence broadened, then the concept remains constrained.

The context of embeddedness and embedding has suffered from similarly imprecise treatment. Accounts are often unclear about what is being embedded in what and what embedding is occurring within. Both terms have sometimes been utilised as somewhat crude spatial metaphors to describe and explain physical links in terms of infrastructure and/or organisations. In addition, there has been a tendency in geography to conflate the notion of embedding in the sense of anchoring and embeddedness as a principle of rootedness, at the expense of a proper understanding of the role of concrete, ongoing and dynamic spatial structures of social relations. As a result of this imprecision and lack of conceptual clarity, the use of embeddedness in economic geography has arguably produced the same problem of the atomisation of economic actors and the denial of the ongoing influence of social relations identified in the original analysis of 'under-socialisation' in economics and 'over-socialisation' in sociology (Granovetter 1985; G Grabher 1993). Without proper recognition the impact of class conflict and alliance inherent in the social relations under capitalism upon socio-territorial development is underplayed.

With under-socialisation, 'embeddedness' is subject to economistic reductionism and treated as a question of narrowly conceived 'economic' links and relations. Ongoing social relations are perceived to have a minimal impact. For instance, much work in economic geography has focused on geographies of linkage formation and the purchasing of goods and services (e.g. Markusen 1994; Phelps 1993; Turok 1993). Such issues are tangible and have their own research history and conventions. While critically important, however, their narrow economic analysis often provides only a partial – under-socialised – view of embeddedness. Their accounts are often only part of the story, albeit an important one.

In terms of over-socialisation, some recent treatments of embeddedness have similarly reproduced the atomisation of economic agents and denied the influence of ongoing social relations. In an attempt to emphasise the different social formations of capital – marked by their own particular consensually developed and internalised norms, values and traditions – each is identified and often generalised such that their behavioural patterns of decision and action are assumed to be common and homogeneous. For example, analysis of the specific social forms of capital evident in South-East Asian formations and embodied in Japanese, South Korean and Taiwanese firms are often assumed to operate in particular and identifiable ways that are often assumed to be common to each and are claimed to be 'as much social as economic institutions' (Yeung 1997). This can be problematic, as Sayer (1997: 22) cautions:

> 'Political economy' has become more cultural with the recent emphasis on networks, communication, learning, management 'philosophy' and 'corporate culture'; when researchers explain the changing fortunes of industries without bothering to assess costs or cash, something is seriously wrong.

The influence of ongoing social relations is downplayed in such accounts. The attributes of the particular social forms of capital are given more explanatory emphasis.

Similarly, the importance of the spatial context within which firms are said to be 'embedded' has become a focus for study with the utilisation of concepts including 'untraded interdependencies', 'milieux' and 'atmospheres' (see Lagendijk 1996). Again, these concepts appeal to a set of often geographically rooted behavioural patterns and suggest that they have been internalised by economic agents within such territories. Again, ongoing social relations have often been afforded less causal weight in such accounts.

The examples of significant but often over-socialised work sometimes represents a problematic and often vague appeal to difficult and less tangible phenomena – often swept up into the catch-all 'social' category – in some sense outside economic agents that are critically important but not easily dealt with in more conventional analysis (see Markusen's Chapter 2 in this volume). As a result of such work we move only marginally closer to knowing what is being embedded or is embedding in what.

HOW MUCH EMBEDDEDNESS AND EMBEDDING, AND FOR HOW LONG? ARE THEY 'GOOD', 'BAD' OR INDIFFERENT THINGS?

Closely related to the previous problem are questions regarding the extent and temporal construction of embeddedness and embedding. Recent accounts are ambiguous and unclear concerning the conceptualisation and analysis of the extent and normative implications of embeddedness and embedding. Put simply, such work is vague on understanding what is meant by how much embeddedness and embedding and whether they are 'good', 'bad' or indifferent things. Some studies contain the implicit or explicit assumption that more embeddedness or embedding is somehow better than less and is necessarily more developmental and progressive (e.g. Amin and Thrift 1994; Crewe 1996; Dicken *et al.* 1994). Other accounts place more emphasis upon the ambiguity and acknowledge issues of dependency and underdevelopment related to the extent and implications of embeddedness and embedding (e.g. Oinas 1997; Turok 1993). Questions regarding the absolute and/or relative nature of embeddedness and embedding remain unanswered.

A related problem concerns the temporal nature of embeddedness and embedding. The literature sometimes contains the questionable assumption that the longer the economic action within the social structure persists over time the more embedded it is or becomes (e.g. Dicken *et al.* 1994). In this sense, accounts appear to be utilising an implicit linear and even programmatic model of the evolution of necessarily increasing levels of embeddedness or embedding over time. The temporal dimension of embeddedness or embedding becomes almost deterministic. Once an agent becomes embedded or begins embedding, the logic appears to run, then it will become ever more so. These treatments of the extent and temporal nature and implications of embeddedness and embedding in existing economic geographies are questionable and often vague. Such contributions make analysis and assessment of questions of how much embeddedness or embedding and for how long little easier to resolve.

THE SCALE AND GEOGRAPHIES OF EMBEDDEDNESS AND EMBEDDING

The treatment of scale in the existing accounts tend closely to associate and align embeddedness or embedding with specifically local geographies (e.g. Amin and Thrift 1994). More recent work has taken a more balanced view and has focused upon the specifically 'non-local' embeddedness of economic action (Park and Markusen 1995; Oinas 1997), including work that privileges the national (Kenney and Florida 1993) and international (Sally 1994) scales. Clearly, depending upon the precise specification of embeddedness and embedding the geographical scale is not necessarily limited solely to the local. The local and even regional arenas may be where the facets of embeddedness or embedding are contributing to or denigrating economic development, making them more evident and tangible and perhaps relatively easier to research. Indeed, the fact that local and regional development is a traditional concern within economic geography and the object of territorial development policy may also help to explain this focus.

A further problem exists with the geographies of embedding in the sense of anchoring. Often the direction of causation runs, sometimes 'top-down', from the economic agent (as subject) to the territory (as object). Economic agents are seen to embed themselves within the localised social structure. More recent accounts have examined how territorially based institutions have sought to embed or anchor economic agents within their local and regional economies and, in turn, have been 'captured' by corporate interests (e.g. Phelps *et al.* 1998). In this case, the causation comes from both directions – 'top-down' and 'bottom-up'. These problems of the scale and geography of such embedding receive uneven discussion in recent accounts.

EMBEDDEDNESS AND EMBEDDING FOR WHOM?

The question, 'Embeddedness and embedding for whom?' receives limited attention in recent economic geography. Conceptualisation and analysis of in whose interests embeddedness and embedding are occurring often goes little further than acknowledging that the social relations within which economic action is 'embedded' or embedding are each marked by power asymmetries. For example, dominant studies tend to focus on the influence of large firms upon local economies (e.g. Dicken *et al.* 1994) and the inter-firm dynamics of geographically proximate networks of small and medium enterprises (e.g. Harrison 1994). Insufficient attention has been given to the issues of power, control and public and industrial democracy wrapped up in the question of embeddedness or embedding for whom. Power is not an unproblematic concept, owing to the overlapping modes through which it is exercised – such as authority, coercion, manipulation and seduction (Allen 1997). The utilisation of embedding as a concept or strategy by particular interests – capital, labour, the state and quasi-state organisations – receives relatively little consideration. In addition, questions of divisions and inequalities relating to gender and ethnicity are rarely discussed in economic geographies of embeddedness and embedding (for exceptions, see Halford and Savage 1997; McDowell 1997).

This brief critique suggests that the recent utilisation of embeddedness and embedding in economic geography needs to confront several issues: to clarify what is being embedded or embedding in what; to more clearly specify their extent and temporal nature and normative implications; to address the question of their scale and geography; and, to engage critically with the question of embeddedness and embedding for whom.

BRINGING EMBEDDEDNESS AND EMBEDDING TOGETHER

The sympathetic critique put forward here suggests the need to think about embeddedness and embedding in a more coherent way. A clearer conceptual and theoretical specification of what both terms mean and how they relate is required. The intention therefore is to develop an integrated and holistic approach to understanding the myriad interrelations between economic agents in their context of ongoing spatial systems of social relations with their associated cognitive, cultural, political and social dimensions. The challenge is to conceptualise how the ideas wrapped up in the notions of embeddedness and embedding might be utilised to understand and explain the interaction between concerns – sociological, political and cultural – that lie outside the realm of the traditional or conventional domain of analysis in the economic geography sub-discipline but have become an increasing preoccupation within the 'new' economic geography (Lee and Wills 1997).

In terms of the critique outlined above, the first task is to understand how the embeddedness article of faith should be interpreted. Granovetter's (1985) contribution opens up the issue of the interpretation and understanding of economic action as rooted in concrete and evolving social networks. However, even this well-cited work says little about the substance of embeddedness – that is, about how this rootedness enables and constrains action. It is also vague about its precise meaning and perhaps represents only the first step in an ongoing exploratory process (Friedland and Alford 1991; Oinas 1997). In particular, what constitutes economic action needs to be problematised and expanded upon. One possible way of understanding it is as the decisions and behaviours of agents – both purposeful as well as unintended – with economic outcomes in a direct and/or more indirect sense. Examples might include a direct market exchange of a good or service or an administrative reorganisation either of which seeks an intended and direct economic outcome. Selective recruitment practices might produce rather more unintended or ignored and less direct labour market segmentation. The understanding of economic agents can be individual and collective in the sense that they can involve individuals working in independent or collective ways (Oinas 1997), for example through individual routines, groups or collective organisations. It is not just whole organisations that are 'embedded' but often their key decision-makers and employees who build and maintain the underlying social relations and networks. Such action may cohere over time into institutions that can be informal (e.g. conventions, traditions) and formal (e.g. organisations, legal and administrative systems) (North 1991).

For both *embeddedness* and *embedding*, the emphasis on the relation to the context in concrete, ongoing socio-spatial relations is paramount. In the case of embeddedness, the structure of social relations can also be described as the *environment or context* in which action takes place, while with embedding there is more emphasis on a structure of social relations as *object*. However, it is a clear that in the long term, 'object' may become 'context'. This means that, in the end, subjects such as businesses, other organisations or individual actors influence, shape and affect the very economic action and institutions within and through which they are reproduced and constituted. The problem of clearly distinguishing the subject from the object in any analysis and account is therefore inherent. The rest of systems of concrete, ongoing socio-spatial relations can be understood thus: concrete may be seen as real and meaningful. 'Ongoing' can refer to their change and evolution over time as well as the ways in which their development trajectory is path-dependent – that is, unavoidably shaped by their own history (Hodgson 1999). Spatial refers to the fact that the social relations have a scale or level between and through which they are constituted. Scale itself may be seen as a social construct of class struggle and alliance (Swyngedouw 1997). Territory is both a cause and consequence of such a process rather than simply a manifestation. Systems refer to their interrelation and interdependence. The geographical political economy reading of social relations is the fundamental relationships between capital and labour – which are inherently spatial and cross-cut by the questions of gender and ethnicity – where conflict and co-operation condition economic action, social division and the historical evolution of social forces (Massey 1995). A more institutionalist reading would perhaps emphasise how these relations have cohered over time into informal and formal institutions (Hodgson 1999). For each approach, such relations are regulated and mediated by state and quasi-state forms and relations. These social relations structure the intertwined series of threads across which the embedding process occurs – with each being porous and interdependent – and each comprises various different but interrelated dimensions – political, cultural and cognitive.

The latter approaches hint at a perspective in which embeddedness and embedding may be brought together. Embeddedness underpins the notion that all economic action is socially shaped through its rooting in concrete and evolving social networks. Since these networks are territorially and historically specific, there is a spatial dimension to embeddedness manifested by the work on 'milieus', 'districts' and spatial networks. Embedding refers to the processes through which subjects of economic action, while embedded in their own set of social networks, become integrated in a selected spatial object, such as the region in which the subject is located. Thus we can address at least some parts of the critique and move beyond the simplistic and narrow focus solely on capital through private sector and firm-centric studies, crude physical and spatial metaphors, and the problems of under- and over-socialisation. Several issues will be discussed now in more detail. These comprise the historical and spatial dimensions of embedding, and the role of power.

The notion of the embedding of subjects in ongoing spatial systems of social relations links directly to the idea of their historical evolution over time and through space. This idea can be clarified by taking an explicitly institutionalist line of thinking that interprets the socioeconomic system as a 'cumulatively unfolding process' (Hodgson 1999). Such social systems and processes are not without their ruptures and systemic flaws, although this runs against the relatively simplistic view of the 'firm–environment relation' (Oinas 1997: 23), which reveals an underlying systemic thinking and suggests that each may be seen as somewhat closed containers which have clearly discernible links. The diversity and complexity of the real world suggests that each instance or formation of embedding is moulded unavoidably by its own history and evolution. Such ideas can tackle the issue of the strength or weakness of embedding – that is, the critical question posed of how much embeddedness or embedding and for how long. Over the longer term, therefore, embeddedness can be seen as a historical product of interrelated and ongoing processes of embedding and disembedding. As Sayer (1997: 19–20) notes:

> While all economies are socially and culturally 'embedded', in advanced economies, division of labour, markets, money and capital are also disembedding forces, it is normal for embedding and *disembedding* forces to interact and indeed to be interdependent. [Original author's emphasis.]

Some work in economic geography has touched upon this thinking, for example in the analysis of the importance of the historical evolution of forms of capital: 'business organisations are [...] "produced" through a complex historical process of embedding' (Dicken and Thrift 1992: 287). Harrison (1994) similarly discusses embedding within industrial districts where the actions of economic agents are affected by the trust is created through their ongoing engagement within and through social relations supported by third parties such as the church and political activity. Thorne (1996: 1362) too utilises the notion of 're-embedding': 'to describe purposive action to enhance collective social well-being in exchange relations, a way of talking about resistances to the unevenness and disempowering of an embedding local economy'. Moreover, when projected upon a specific context of regional development, the developmental implications of embedding would not be directly linked to the extent and degree of how much embedding has actually occurred. Indeed, Oinas (1997: 30) suggests that embedding can equip firms with resources *and* incapabilities wherein established custom and practice 'lock in' organisations and inhibit learning. In this context, implications are difficult to establish a priori.

Acknowledgement that embeddedness incorporates spatial systems of social relations requires some conceptualisation of scale and the geography of the embedding process. If embedding is inherently territorial then it needs to be conceptualised how this is so. Cox and Mair's (1991) notion of scale divisions of labour conceives of what roles in the social division of labour exist at different spatial scales. This idea contributes to the accommodation of both embeddedness – interpreted in a network context allowing for different spatial levels – and embedding – projected upon a specific spatial object (locality) at a specific spatial scale (region, city). Since embeddedness is constituted through social relations, scale is better understood in terms of nested and interdependent layers rather than more rigid hierarchical levels. Applying the scale-divisions-of-labour approach in this manner also invokes Cox and Mair's notion of interdependency. In particular, the ways in which the geographical context may be both cause and consequence of embedding – that is, the forms of interdependency between economic actions and territory – need explicit recognition. These points support the view of the extent and temporal construction of embedding having a scale and geography.

The concrete and ongoing social relations within which economic action is (dis)embedding are underpinned by asymmetrical power structures. Yet we need to go further than this commonly made point. Granovetter (1985: 506), for example, noted that status and power are also 'rational' objectives for economic agents. Oinas (1997: 28) notes that:

> Where agents may be embedded in numerous sets of social relations simultaneously
> – multiple embeddings – a hierarchy is likely to exist where some embeddings are
> more consequential for their action than others.

The relations and balance within and between the hierarchical power structures that shape these embeddings evolve over time and through space with the detail of the extent and nature of the embedding process. Their ongoing balance and resolution are to varying degrees subject to public and industrial forms of political debate and conflict resolution within and without organisations. For example, the shifting and unfolding balance of power between capital and labour is manifest in periods of conflict and collaboration, often formalised through industrial relations procedures. The ability of economic agents – through their *embeddedness* in wider social networks – to comprehend and both consciously and knowingly shape their context of social relations in which they are *(dis)embedding* is increasingly central to questions of power and control. This interactive process can be understood in terms of 'reflexive' agency (Giddens 1984; Storper 1997), whereby social action and context are becoming increasingly mutually constitutive and interactive. 'Top-down' manipulation of that context in the particular interests of economic agents is possible, for example in the instrumental actions of firms attracting public subsidy through supporting local economic development institution embedding initiatives based upon supply chains and training.

The notion of attempting to bring more closely together the conceptualisations of embeddedness and embedding outlined here enables some of the lines of criticism of its use in recent economic geographies to be addressed. It is not claimed to be a definitive reworking of the concept. Rather, the intention is to propose some ideas for its clearer and more coherent utilisation.

RESEARCHING EMBEDDING

In common with and related to the vague definitions and conceptualisations addressed above, the analysis and interpretation of embeddedness and embedding are often little clearer. Methodological approaches of how to research embedding are also limited. The nature of the embedding process, wherein the threads and dimensions between and through which it is manifest are necessarily interrelated, makes analysis inherently problematic. The suggested conceptual and theoretical specification of embedding suggested above requires some elaboration and separation of its constituent dimensions for analytical purposes (e.g. McDowell 1997; Zukin and DiMaggio 1990). As Oinas (1997: 28) argues:

> Even though the 'economic' and the 'social' seem intertwined and inseparable from one another empirically, it does not mean that we could not and should not analytically separate 'the economic' from the rest of what is 'social', even though it might be difficult in some instances. Let us maintain a separation between the complex and confusing real world and conceptually clear analysis.

Accepting such a standpoint raises some difficult questions: how can we analyse the extent and temporal nature of embeddedness? How can we discern the direction of the (dis)embedding process and assess its implications? How is (*dis*)embedding along one thread of social relations and its associated dimensions linked to (*dis*)embedding across other threads?

Recent attempts at the analysis of embedding have sought to identify the level, aspect and combinations thereof. In terms of level, debate has focused on the appropriateness and interrelated nature of analysis across and between functionally differentiated levels of embeddedness, ranging from micro, individualised, face-to-face interaction up to macro, large-scale and systemic considerations (Granovetter 1992; Oinas 1997). Aspects have been concerned with *individual embeddedness* that is captured through its coincidence with the notion of embodiment whereby individuals and their actions reflect the organisations within and through which they act. Here, the separation of structure from agents is overcome, for instance in seeing the changing gender composition of the workforce as part and parcel of the restructuring process rather than an outcome (Halford and Savage 1997). *Structural embeddedness* – in Zukin and DiMaggio's (1990) reading – refers to social networks composed of individuals rather than the wider structure of society. *Political embeddedness* refers to economic agents and non-market actors such as the state and social classes involved in power struggles. *Cultural embeddedness* concerns the evolution of shared and mutually interpreted understandings that shape economic behaviour (Oinas 1997; Zukin and DiMaggio 1990). The combinations occur in relation to the question of the scale of embeddedness – addressed above – and regarding cognitive embeddedness which captures the ways in which agent's regularised and structured thought processes constrain and limit rational economic logic and decision-making. Although these insights provide useful contributions, they are necessary rather than sufficient. Even with these concepts it remains difficult to build the analytical tools and methods with which to ascertain the nature, extent and direction of the embedding process. This is especially the case if it is accepted that such processes are contingent, indeterminate and require empirical investigation.

This chapter suggests an analytical approach and method that tries to disentangle the different and necessarily interrelated threads of social relations comprising dimensions through which the (dis)embedding process unfolds. Initially, the object of the (dis)embedding process needs to be established – be it an individual, group, organisation, network, or local or regional economy. Then, its social relations and their scales of operation, their types and their organisational forms need to be mapped out. These social relations comprise links between capitals (e.g. suppliers, competitors, business organisations), capital and labour (e.g. employees, trade unions, households), capital and the state (e.g. central and local government) and quasi-state organisations (e.g. quangos). Significant gender and ethnic questions may also be incorporated into the analysis at this stage. This method builds on Cox and Mair's (1991) discussion of the analysis of localities in terms of what social relations constitute the localised social structure. After this, the analytical focus needs to sharpen, in part to start to understand the complexities of embedding for each social relation and its linkages but also to make the study manageable. The choice made from the series of threads of social relations across and through which the (dis)embedding process occurs – with all its various and inter-related dimensions (political, cultural, etc.) – can then be opened up to scrutiny. Clearly, which thread is chosen depends upon the research questions being asked. An account can then be formed of how the extent and nature of the (dis)embedding of our entity with whose economic action we are concerned have unfolded.

Such an analysis requires both the disentangling of the threads of social relations through which the (dis)embedding process unfolds and their constituent and various dimensions, while simultaneously remaining alive to their necessary interaction. In this way, each segment of the unfolding process of disembedding can be analysed and pieced together to provide a more holistic account.

The following empirical research concerning the embedding of the automotive industry in the North-East of England attempts to utilise and assess the usefulness of such an approach. The empirical material considered here is not an exhaustive study. Rather, the work is intended as preliminary in nature to explore the scope and limitations of the theoretical and conceptual understanding of embedding suggested in the chapter.

EMBEDDING THE AUTOMOTIVE INDUSTRY IN THE NORTH-EAST OF ENGLAND

Historically, there was little coherent automotive industry within the North-East of England, with only a handful of firms acting as suppliers to assembly plants outside the region.[1] The catalyst for the development of the automotive industry in the North-East was the arrival of the Japanese transnational Nissan's assembly plant in the mid-1980s. The region was a greenfield territory ripe for experimentation with the labour process and relations between labour and management and with component suppliers. Nissan's 'transplant' in Washington was among the most significant investments in the UK during the 1980s, being the first new Japanese car assembly plant in Europe, the first new UK car plant since the 1960s and the first car assembly plant in the North-East region (Sadler 1992). The investment was established as a 'bridgehead' into the European market and reflected the parent company Nissan Motor's broader 'globalisation–localisation' strategy, which sought to make the firm 'at home worldwide'. The UK was chosen for Nissan's first European assembly plant because of the competitive labour and exchange rates, grant support framework, high selling price market and lack of a strong domestic manufacturer (Rover was perceived to be weaker than VW in Germany, Fiat in Italy or Renault and PSA in France). The UK was also Nissan's largest European market in which the government had legislated in favour of a milder labour climate, curbing the previously strong influence of trade unions (Garrahan and Stewart 1992). The UK's basic history of automotive know-how, proximity to Europe and the English language were also contributory factors in affording Nissan a relatively low-risk strategy to work with European suppliers (Pike 1994). Washington near Sunderland was chosen out of the 40 local authority bids that were initiated for the plant site. The investment was interpreted as evidence of the emergence of a 'performance plant' with much more progressive implications for local and regional development (Pike 1998a). The press lauded the plant as 'Nissan's ray of hope in a grim landscape' (Garnett 1985) and the 'Jewel of Wearside' (Tighe 1988).

The plant has currently reached the sixth stage of its development, with the addition of a third model and substantial in-house component manufacture. Investment has now exceeded £1.25 billion and employment has grown to over 4,000. Nissan's transplant has provided the focus and catalyst for the growth of an automotive industry in the North-East region. Significant inward investments in the automotive sector have arrived via new greenfield developments, joint ventures and take-overs of indigenous firms to supply Nissan, and many other goods and services suppliers in the region have reoriented at least part of their business toward growth opportunities within the sector (Pike 1994). The Northern Development Company (NDC) – now part of the new Regional Development Agency – hold the names of over 235 companies in the northern region with experience of supplying the automotive sector, employing close to 38,000, in their database for the automotive 'cluster' (Watson 1996), although many of which firms are general service companies and component suppliers to other sectors.

As a consequence of such development, the North-East was the only region that experienced employment growth in the automotive industry in the UK between 1981 and 1993. The number of jobs rose by nearly 4,000 (64 per cent) to over 9,500, compared with a net loss of 190,000 jobs (55 per cent) nationally (Table 4.1). The automotive industry also increased its share of total employment

TABLE 4.1: UK AUTOMOTIVE SECTOR EMPLOYMENT CHANGE BY REGION, 1981–93

Region	Year 1981	Year 1993	Change No.	Change %
South East	36 627	19 827	−16 800	−45.87
East Anglia	37 277	15 226	−22 051	−59.15
London	33 381	9 342	−24 039	−72.01
South West	9 410	5 332	−4 078	−43.34
West Midlands	114 787	46 196	−68 591	−59.76
East Midlands	10 180	4 576	−5 604	−55.05
Yorkshire & Humberside	12 299	9 695	−2 604	−21.17
Mersey	17 847	1 602	−16 245	−91.01
North West	36 684	18 847	−17 837	−48.62
North East	5 863	9 596	3 733	63.67
Wales	19 330	12 108	−7 222	−37.36
Scotland	11 290	2 880	−8 410	−74.49
Total	344 975	155 227	−189 748	−55.00

Source: National On-Line Manpower Information Service, 1997 (an on-line database)

in the region to 1.26 per cent, compared with 0.85 per cent nationally (Pike 1998b). Only the West Midlands and Wales have a higher proportion of their total regional employment accounted for by the automotive industry. The early-1990s slowdown led to the shedding of some jobs that are only now being recovered. Nearly 90 per cent of the North-East's automotive sector employment in 1993 were male full-time jobs and the remainder female. Part-time employment in the North-East automotive sector in the same year was significantly lower than in other UK regions, and was almost wholly female employment (Pike 1998b). Using the broadest definition of the automotive industry developed by the NDC which includes companies supplying goods and services to other sectors within the North-East region at the county level, the majority of the firms are concentrated in County Durham (owing to its dominance of the supplier base) but employment is dominated by Tyne and Wear (owing to the Nissan plant) (Figure 4.1).

NISSAN AND THE AUTOMOTIVE INDUSTRY IN THE NORTH-EAST, FIFTEEN YEARS ON

In future, people will see the arrival of Nissan as a great pivotal step in the transformation of the North-East of England. (Ian Gibson, CBE, Managing Director and Chief Executive, Nissan Motor Manufacturing (UK) Ltd., quoted in Tighe 1996).

FIGURE 4.1: SUB-REGIONAL GEOGRAPHY OF AUTOMOTIVE-RELATED FIRMS AND EMPLOYMENT IN THE NORTH-EAST REGION OF ENGLAND

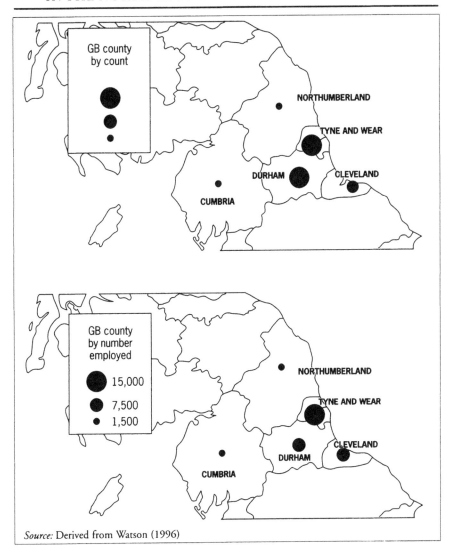

Source: Derived from Watson (1996)

There is no doubt that a substantial automotive industry has built up in the North-East centred upon Nissan's investment. Nissan claim that their 'world class manufacturing operation contributes £400m to the North-East economy' (Port of Tyne Authority 1996). Nissan appears to have made itself as much at home in the UK as US-owned Ford and GM Vauxhall but in a relatively shorter period. Since 1991, Nissan has received the recognition by the Society of Motor Manufacturers and Traders (SMMT) as a 'British Manufacturer', won numerous Queen's Awards for Export Achievement from the Department of Trade and Industry (DTI) and displays the slogan 'British Made World Class' on its trucks.

FIGURE 4.2: NISSAN – COMPANY DEVELOPMENT LIFE
CYCLE

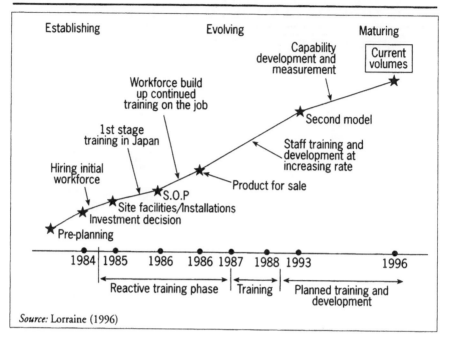

Source: Lorraine (1996)

Nissan has even utilised the language of embedding to conceptualise their own
'company development life-cycle' within the North-East, moving through the
'establishing', 'evolving' and 'maturing' stages (Lorraine 1996) (Figure 4.2).
The emergence of an automotive industry in the North-East of England provides
fertile ground for examining the process of embedding – in the sense of anchoring
the subject (the automotive industry) in the object (the North-East region). An
industry having been developed from scratch, the experience discussed here can
reveal much about the embedding process. Analysis can begin with mapping out
the threads of social relations across and within which the economic action within
the industry in the region is embedding. Table 4.2 summarises the social relations,
scales, types, specific organisations and sectoral/general roles. It attempts to
assign institutions to social relations rather than simply describing them as purely
'state' or 'quasi-state'. It is significant that there is a broad range of economic
actions in the process of embedding within the spatial structures of ongoing social
relations, especially beyond those purely concerned with production itself. In the
longer term, a follow-up question is how this embedding will affect the context for
economic action in a more fundamental way, that is, how the rootedness of such
economic action has changed.

   Attention has been given elsewhere to questions about the embedding process
in relation to the automotive industry in the North-East, especially those
concerning supplier linkages (e.g. Pike 1994; Sadler 1997), infrastructure (Peck
1996), the labour process and labour–management relations (Garrahan and

Social relation	Scale(s)	Type	Organisation	Sectoral role and/or initiatives	General role
Capital–capital	Local, regional, national, international	Assembler	Firm (only Nissan)	Vehicle assembler and core of automotive industry in the region	'Flagship' inward investor Symbol of industrial regeneration
	Local, regional, national, international	Suppliers	Firms (e.g. indigenous: Kigass; foreign-owned:TRW)	Parts and services suppliers	Automotive industry linked with and beyond Nissan
	Regional	Business organisation	Nissan Local Supplier Group	Sharing information and upgrading of Nissan and non-Nissan automotive suppliers	Building self-sustaining supply base for automotive sector in North East and beyond
	Regional	Business organisation	Manufacturing Challenge		Raising manufacturing output and exports from the Northern region
	Regional	Business organisations	North East Chamber of Commerce Northern Business Forum Northern CBI[1] Engineering Employers' Association	Representation and lobbying	Voice of business in the North East region
Capital–labour	Factory level	Trades Union	AEEU[2]	Workforce representation and membership services	General engineering union
	Factory level	Company Council Council	Nissan Company Council	Workforce representation	
Capital–state	Regional	Integrated regional office	Government Office for North East	Sectoral watching brief SMMT/DTI Motor Industry Forum[3]	European and national grant allocation (e.g. ESF and RSA)[4] Inward investment and technology support

continued overleaf

TABLE 4.2: EXAMPLES OF ORGANISATIONAL INTERESTS IN THE AUTOMOTIVE SECTOR IN THE NORTH-EAST OF ENGLAND, *continued*

Social relation	Scale(s)	Type	Organisation	Sectoral role and/or initiatives	General role
Capital–state (continued)	Regional and district	DfEE[5]	Employment service		Labour market vacancy notification and applicant matching
	Local	Local authority	City of Sunderland Council	Automotive team 'The UK's fastest-growing automotive centre' initiative Automotive international annual conference	Economic development Leads on 'Advance manufacturing centre of the North' partnership Public service delivery and management
Capital–quasi-state	Regional	Regional Development Organisations[6]	Northern Development Company	Automotive team and investment manager	Inward investment Strategic supply chain initiative/ DTI regional supply office High volume manufacturing initiative
	Sub-regional	Economic development agency	Tyne and Wear Development Company (TweDCo)	European Research Centre of Automotive Excellence	Business support services
	Sub-regional	Training and Enterprise Councils (TECs)	Sunderland City TEC	Sectoral training initiative partner	National training programme contract
	Regional, national and international	Higher education	Sunderland University	Department of Automotive Engineering and Ergonomics Centre for Achievement in Manufacturing Management (CAMM)	Under- and post-graduate education Management training and research Industry networking and business support

Capital–quasi-state (continued)	Regional, national	Further education	City of Sunderland College	The Industry Centre Sectoral vocational training (e.g. multi-skill technician course)	General vocational training
	Local	Schools	Thornhill, St. Aidan's Secondary	Curriculum support and project work	Secondary education
	Regional	Sectoral development and training organisation	Automotive Sector Strategic Alliance (ASSA)	Automotive sector development Design and delivery of dedicated automotive sector training programmes	Advocacy of automotive sector
	Sub-regional	Urban Development Corporation	Tyne and Wear Development Corporation (TWDC)[7]	Supplier Park Hub initiative	Urban regeneration
	Regional	Technology support	Regional Technology Centre North		Technology, development, training and support
	Local	Economic development agency	Sunderland Business Link	ASSA board member	Business support services

Notes: 1 Confederation of British Industry. 2 Amalgamated Electrial and Engineering Union. 3 Society of Motor Manufacturers and Traders and Department of Trade and Industry. 4 European Social Fund and Regional Selective Assistance. 5 Department for Education and Employment. 6 Regional Development Organisations became Regional Development Agencies in the English regions in April 1999. 7 All the Urban Development Corporations were wound up in 1998.

Source: Authors' research and interviews

Stewart 1992; Pike 1994). Given the flavour of the above critique, this chapter focuses on one relatively neglected thread of social relations and its integral dimensions across and through which the embedding process has developed: labour market governance and training. This issue provides a brief empirical example through which to explore the ideas developed in this chapter.

LABOUR MARKET GOVERNANCE AND TRAINING

The relatively rapid expansion of the automotive industry combined with its lack of history within the North-East region has created tensions. These have been exacerbated by the associated extent and nature of its labour demand. Indeed, the regional concentration of the industry can be seen as part of the root cause of the problems of labour market governance and training. Perceived skills shortages have led to wage inflation for skilled grades (e.g. maintenance technicians, tooling engineers and electrical and mechanical engineers). These shortages have undermined the rationale for in-house training and have left vacancies unfilled. Concern has arisen regarding stagnation within a low-skill equilibrium if the incentive not to train and to buy skills in the labour market becomes too ingrained (Finegold and Soskice 1988; One North East 1999). Staff retention and poaching problems have arisen as a result. It is perceived that Nissan is very adept at training its engineers but less competent in retaining them, particularly in terms of matching salaries available among the automotive suppliers and other manufacturing companies as well as the business support organisations within the region. Experience of working with Nissan's lean production system is much sought after and the organisational interests (Table 4.2) in the region are littered with former Nissan employees.

Mismatches between labour supply and demand are also evident within the region. The North-East has levels of unemployment consistently above the national average at each stage of the business cycle, owing mainly to the long-term shrinkage of its traditional manufacturing base (Pike and Tomaney 1999). However, the nature of labour demand within the relatively more recent 'greenfield' investments in the automotive industry requires relatively higher entry qualifications, the ability to work in teams and the capability and willingness to become 'multi-skilled'. Each of these attributes tends to marginalise and undervalue the skills offered by the workers made redundant from the traditional industries (Tomaney et al. 1999). Hence, vacancies within the sector cannot always be linked seamlessly with the available labour supply in the region.

There are signs that, to combat these problems and their associated costs and burdens upon the 'competitiveness' of the automotive sector in the region, firms within the automotive industry within the North-East have developed a collective view regarding the need to intervene in the governance and regulation of labour market. The consensus appears to be that firms need collectively to 'grow their own' and create a plentiful supply of appropriately skilled staff by reintroducing apprenticeship programmes at entry level and enhancing the skills of their existing staff. Agents within the automotive industry in the North-East have consequently become active in building a dedicated institution to address this labour market governance and training concern. The regional concentration of the industry has sown the seeds of a collective interpretation of the problem and response. This collective action was prompted by Nissan's concerns regarding the availability and turnover of suitably skilled staff both within its factory and in the broader supply chain, particularly in the context of the addition of the third model and the expansion in labour demand by 850. Originally, training was delivered through a direct linkage between Nissan and Sunderland City TEC utilising both national and European funds. It was recognised that to serve the wider supply base and regional industry a more broadly based and quasi-independent alliance was needed to draw down funds. Such a model was adapted from a similar organisation utilised by Fiat in Piedmont, Italy, as a means of matching planned labour demand with supply. The Automotive Sector Strategic Alliance (ASSA) was established in 1997 as a membership organisation whose subscribers include Nissan and over 40 automotive suppliers within the North-East region. The board membership includes representation from Nissan, local authorities, TECs, further and higher rducation, NDC and Sunderland Business Link.

ASSA's concern is human resource development for the automotive industry in the North-East, and it aims 'to support the growth and competitiveness of the sector through the development of a skilled labour force, helping to create job security' (ASSA 1998). Activities include information-gathering and creating a co-ordinated and centralised resource for training needs analysis, development and delivery, especially for traditionally harder-to-reach SMEs in the lower tiers of the automotive supply chain. The intention is to 'cascade' the 'training culture' down from the assembler through the tiers and both persuade and support traditionally reluctant SMEs collectively to invest in training. A series of accredited and nationally recognised vocational training courses have been developed specifically for the range of occupations within the automotive sector. The client groups targeted are at entry level for apprenticeships and at intermediate level among existing staff for team leader, technician, IT and supervisory training. ASSA also makes claims to a broader role in providing a forum and voice for the automotive industry in the North-East region. Indeed, ASSA is being utilised as part of building a coherent image of the North-East as an automotive region in order to attract future inward investment and more design-oriented projects in the industry.

Significantly, ASSA includes the growing segment of the automotive industry within the North-East that supplies both Nissan and other companies. The establishment of ASSA was prompted rather than directed by Nissan, although Nissan's influence and name was used to secure the initial involvement of the suppliers. Some suppliers were critical and initially viewed ASSA as a further means for Nissan to govern their supply chain. However, after establishment, ASSA's medium-term strategy is to create a self-sustaining, sector-led initiative that serves as a common training resource to the industry in the region. From then onwards, ownership of the organisation was with the region and this allowed Nissan to distance itself from the initiative. Clearly, this was functional to Nissan as a means of externalising a significant element of training provision while simultaneously upgrading skill levels within the regional supply base. Critical to the emergence of the new organisation were strong personal networks between individuals working within the human resources section of Nissan and the European programmes team of Sunderland City TEC. The North-East being a greenfield automotive industry centre, it was also easier to propose a fresh initiative free from the influence of established vested interests.

This issue of labour market governance and training provides an example of a passage of heightened activity in the process of the embedding of the automotive industry in the North-East of England. The decisions and behaviours of individuals, in the personal relationships that initially fostered the idea of ASSA, and of collective organisations, in the concerted responses of the assembler and suppliers and local organisations, engaged in purposeful economic action. These actions had intended and directed economic outcome in terms of reducing the costs incurred by the problems of fragmented labour market governance and training. Actors sought to develop a formal institution – in the guise of ASSA – to design, develop and deliver a co-ordinated resource and provide a forum and voice for the industry in the region. In tandem, the building of an informal institution – in the shape of the training culture – was emphasised particularly in relation to creating training habits and norms among the small and medium-sized firms in the supply base. In this sense, the needs of the firms within the industry became closely aligned with institutions – particularly the Training and Enterprise Council – through a shared concern with the potential to damage the 'competitiveness' of the industry in the region.

This example reveals how the embedding process flows across a series of inter-twined and ongoing social relations – in this case between capitals (the assembler and suppliers) and between capital and state and quasi-state organisations (assembler–suppliers and the TEC, local authorities, NDC, ASSA). Such social relations were evident through and within spatial structures comprising the local and the regional – the ASSA membership – and the international – the assembler and some suppliers were part of foreign-owned and often transnational firms. The territorial concentration of the automotive industry in the North-East region was to an extent at the root of the problems of labour market governance and training and, in providing a platform for regional collective action, was part of its potential solution. In this sense, the historical development of the automotive industry in the region shaped how the process unfolded. Analytically, the account here has sought to disentangle the threads of social relations while simultaneously recognising their interdependence. The empirical material has revealed the indeterminate and contingent nature of how the embedding process unfolds in the longer term, although acknowledging the purposeful action and interaction of the various social agents involved in the process.

CONCLUSIONS

While embeddedness has become commonplace in recent economic geographies, its conceptual, theoretical and methodological clarity has been underdeveloped. Given its apparent importance, the present shortfall in the debate has prompted the development of this sympathetic critique of the existing ways in which embeddedness has been utilised in the economic geography literature. In so doing, several issues have been suggested for resolution concerning embeddedness: distinguishing embeddedness (rootedness) and embedding (anchoring), what is being embedded or embedding in what; their extent, temporal nature and normative implications; their scale(s) and geographies; and embeddedness and embedding for whom. As a means of moving the debate forward, a more clearly specified conceptual and theoretical framework and methodological approach have been suggested.

This work has focused on the process of the embedding of economic action within spatial structures of ongoing social relations, with a case of the development of the labour market governance and training in the automotive industry in the North-East of England. Economic action is interpreted as the purposeful as well as unintended decisions and behaviours of agents in individual and collective terms that have direct and/or indirect economic outcomes. Informal and formal institutions may develop from the prolonged and enduring repetition or organisation of such action. The process of embedding this economic action can wax and wane across a series of closely interrelated – even inseparable – threads that are formed by enduring social relations operating through and between scales and territories within spatial structures. Each thread contains a range of different but necessarily interdependent economic, social, political, cultural and cognitive dimensions. It is perhaps these latter dimensions of embedding that recent economic geographies have latched onto and prioritised without sufficiently grounding them in an appropriate theoretical and conceptual context. These studies have also failed to show how active embedding processes impinge upon the embeddedness of economic action in a territorial sense.

In analytical and methodological terms, the approach recognises the need to disentangle these threads at the heart of the embedding process while simultaneously acknowledging their necessary interrelatedness. The embedding process is claimed to be indeterminate and contingent – implying that the particular extent, nature and normative implications of embedding remain an empirical question. The process unfolds in an evolutionary manner, unavoidably shaped by its own history (Hodgson 1999). Further debates on embedding will need to address contingencies at the various levels of analysis involved in the process: the region, the firm, networks (of firms and other organisations), and larger industrial systems (in which firms and other organisations are embedded). In particular, the right balance needs to be found between 'top-down' directions of embedding – such as firms embedding themselves in a region – and 'bottom-up' ones – the drive of territorially based organisations to anchor firms within regional economic networks and business coalitions.

While theoretical, conceptual and methodological in purpose, the case of the embedding of the automotive industry in the North-East of England was utilised as the empirical material through which to explore the scope and limitations of the suggested approach. In particular, the issue of labour market governance and training was examined. This provided an example of the embedding process in full flow, perhaps moving in a relatively progressive and developmental direction at least for some of the participant interests. The analysis of this issue revealed both the potential and the limits of the approach. The thread across which the embedding process unfolded needed linking to other threads simultaneously to provide a more holistic account. The empirical account could just as easily have explored the ebb of the disembedding process by drawing material from a period of retrenchment and employment decline in the automotive industry in the North-East. That it did not reflects only the format and purpose of this particular work rather than its limitations. The purpose of this chapter was never to provide an exhaustive narrative and definitive account of whether and how the automotive industry is embedding in the North-East region. Rather, it has sought to contribute to the theoretical, conceptual and methodological debates concerning embedding. The process described here and exemplified in the empirical material is dynamic and evolutionary – with embedding and disembedding tendencies simultaneously evident. This piece has sought only to provide some frameworks to support a better understanding of what is going on.

NOTE

1. The empirical research discussed here has been drawn from a number of research projects. The studies have involved in-depth interviews with the main agents within the automotive industry in the North-East, including firms, trade unions, state and quasi-state organisations. This primary material was supported by secondary material from both published and unpublished sources.

Acknowledgements
This work draws upon research undertaken both individually and collectively as part of the European Network on Innovation and Territory (EUNIT). Thanks for her comments to Anna Giunta. Thanks also to the economic development institutions, employers, trade unions and workforces who participated in research from which this paper is drawn. The usual disclaimers, as always, apply.

5   New Media and Regional Development: The Case of the UK Computer and Video Games Industry

INTRODUCTION: THE PROMISE OF NEW MEDIA

Since 1990, we have witnessed dramatic developments in new information and communication technologies (ICTs). These have given rise to speculation and anticipation concerning the convergence of traditional computing, IT, telecommunications and media industries, ideas that have become widely accepted as actuality within public policy (e.g. CEC 1997b; DTI 1998a). In events related to these developments, we are also (apparently) witnessing the birth of something called 'new media'. The precise make-up and composition of new media is, however, indeterminate. The definition of new media offered by the Coopers & Lybrand *New York New Media Survey* indicates the elasticity of the term:

> The New Media industry combines elements of computing technology, telecommunications, and content – information, entertainment, personal/group communications and transactions – to create products and services which can be used 'interactively' by consumers and business users. (Coopers and Lybrand 1996: 16)

This Coopers and Lybrand study provides an important reference point as, at the time of its first publication in 1996, it was one of the earliest reports to construct new media as an object of study, and has since become much cited in both policy and academic research. New media, then, is a broad category that includes (at least) online and CD-Rom or DVD delivered products and services such as publishing, design, advertising and training for a corporate clientele, together with games, reference and 'edutainment' or educational products for the consumer market.

As the definition above implies, new media is closely allied to, and some might say commensurate with, the more established heading of 'multimedia', at least in an Anglo-American context. At the same time, new media also covers those products, activities and firms identified by more recent concepts such as 'digital media' (cf. Digital Media Alliance 1998) or 'interactive media' (cf. Coopers and Lybrand 1998). We would argue that, while there seems to be a multiplication in taxonomic categories, the most recent labels – 'digital', 'interactive' and 'new' media – all seek to foreground 'content'. The increasing importance of the creation, manipulation and packaging of digital content has additionally been identified in existing studies of multimedia (Scott 1995: 5; Henning 1997) and more widely in debates related to the 'information economy' (OECD 1998).

The excitement that surrounds new media tends to promise a fundamental transformation of the media and communication industries, in what is anticipated as a new era of abundance and diversity in entertainment and information. Unsurprisingly, then, the new media industries, and digital content creation in particular, have been widely identified as a key area for employment growth over the next decade. For example, in one influential study Chris Freeman and Luc Soete argue that the 'multimedia project co-ordinator' may well be the fastest-growing occupation of the next decade, although it has not yet entered the official classification (Freeman and Soete 1994: 145). However, there is little agreement about the locational dynamics of these industries, about where these much hoped-for new jobs will be created. For some, the novelty of new media includes not just new products and markets but also new industrial dynamics and, importantly, new locations for media production. Such arguments have led regional agencies and local authorities throughout the world to see the development of new media companies as strategically important and as offering a 'window of locational opportunity' for capturing a new growth sector (Fuchs and Wolf 1997).

In this chapter we briefly review these arguments before examining the concrete example of one of the more mature 'new' media sub-sectors – the computer and video games industry in Britain. A final section draws out some of the wider conclusions for economic geography.

RESTRUCTURING THE MEDIA LANDSCAPE?

The traditional, or old, mass media industries – publishing, music, film, radio and television – have developed relatively discretely over the past century, each based on a distinct set of analogue production technologies, business practices and regulatory principles, albeit ones that have evolved over time. These industries were, to varying degrees and with important exceptions, focused principally on domestic markets. The structure of the media industries has typically been one of a public monopoly or private oligopoly (often tightly regulated) with a small number of 'gatekeepers' – major publishers, major record companies, film distributors, broadcasters – dominating the distribution and finance of cultural products (Frith 1987; Picard 1989; Vogel 1990). In many cases, these dominant companies directly organised the majority of production in-house; in other cases, they contracted smaller companies to produce material for their distribution networks' products (Gordon 1973; Staiger 1983, Bagdakian 1983). Production activity has tended, to a greater or lesser extent, to gravitate around these key gatekeepers.

The picture presented above is, of course, a rather ideal-typical description of the structure of the media industries. We should emphasise that real world media structures are far from static, but rather in a constant state of flux. What is more, there are long-running trends within the media industries – globalisation, liberalisation and an increasing interpenetration of various media businesses – that must be acknowledged (Barnouw 1997). Nevertheless, provision by a handful of companies is still the typical mode of organisation for most media products and services today.

Traditionally, the geography of the media industries in the advanced economies has followed, and exaggerated, that of the urban hierarchy as whole with, as Allen Scott (1997) details, major cities dominating cultural production. In strongly centralised national systems, such as Britain and France, the cities of London (see e.g., Pratt 1997) and Paris possess a hugely disproportionate volume of media activity. In more balanced urban systems, such as Germany or the United States, the distribution of media activity is concentrated in a small number of major cities (in Germany, principally, Berlin, Hamburg, Cologne and Munich; in the US, Los Angeles and New York).

Different cities may dominant in different media. For instance, Sträter (1997) notes that regional specialisation within the German media is highly evident, with broadcasting primarily concentrated in Cologne, newspapers centred on Berlin, magazine publishing most evident in Hamburg and Munich strongest in the film industry. Different cities may also dominate within different media segments. So, 'news' in the US media (whether this is the major television networks or print journalism) is disproportionately concentrated in New York and Washington, given the propinquity of the financial and political centres, whereas entertainment media are concentrated in and around Los Angeles (Hollywood).

THE 'NEWNESS' OF NEW MEDIA

The transformation of the media space economy that is most commonly asserted with the introduction of new information and communications technologies (ICTs) is a technologically induced vision of decentralisation, the collapse of media empires, a new level playing field, and a perfect marketplace of ideas. From this perspective the new media technologies are seen as having such radical potential – in terms of their costs, availability, accessibility, and ease of operation – that traditional media systems will be washed away in a flood of decentralised, grass-roots activity. Many of these contributions stem from the rather disparate collection of (mainly North American), industry gurus and futurologists built up around such institutions as the MIT Media Lab, Microsoft and the magazine *Wired*. The novelty of new media lies, these writers argue, in the increasing ease with which text, pictures, video and sounds can now be digitally combined, manipulated and distributed using new ICTs.

Two major claims are deduced from this premise. First, the locational needs of industry are transformed because firms will no longer need to concentrate within territorially based clusters to benefit from agglomeration economies, since physical access to these economies based on proximity can be supplanted by the ability to communicate and transfer products 'over the wire'. Consequently, this ability of ICTs to overcome the 'friction of distance' allows for a far greater geographical spread of activity and employment in the new media sector than has been the case with previous knowledge- or information-intensive growth industries (*The Economist* 1995).

Second, it is argued that new ICT-based networks, particularly the Internet, will undermine existing distribution networks and, with them, those actors effectively operating as gatekeepers between producers and consumers. The mass media, it is predicted, will be at the sharp end of this process of 'disintermediation': the traditional role of the distributors (broadcasters, publishers, etc.) as gatekeepers will be weakened as the Internet and other new distribution channels allow producers and consumers to bypass them and transact directly, in a model of what Bill Gates (1995) has termed 'friction free capitalism'. Entry barriers will, it is argued, also be reduced through the rapidly falling capital costs involved in new media production, underpinning the emergence of a mass of new cultural producers.

Nicholas Negroponte, co-founder of the MIT Media Lab, is perhaps the best-known exponent of this view. For him, the advent of digital media – what he refers to as moving 'bits' of information instead of 'atoms' of paper – will have dramatic consequences for media structures. 'If', he asks, 'moving these bits around is so effortless, what advantage would the large media companies have over you and me? Wholly new content will emerge from being digital, as will new players, new economic models and a likely cottage industry of information and entertainment providers' (Negroponte 1995: 18–19). Here, the future is presented as one in which the 'mass' media that we have known are replaced by a myriad of small specialist information and entertainment providers: 'the information industry will become more of a boutique business. Its marketplace is the global information highway' (ibid.: 85).

VERTICAL DISINTEGRATION AND AGGLOMERATION ECONOMIES

If the techno-futurists privilege the underlying technology of new media, then there is a second and increasingly influential school of thought that has diametrically opposite implications for the geographical distribution of new media activity. This perspective, associated most clearly with Allen Scott, and more widely with the 'California School' in regional development studies, is based upon the work of new institutional economists such as Williamson (1975). Scott draws on previous work on 'old' media, such as the Hollywood film industry (Christopherson and Storper 1986; Storper 1989), and highlights parallels with studies of other new technology-based sectors. For Scott, the multimedia industry represents 'a critical point of intersection between high-technology sectors on the one hand and cultural products on the other' (1995: 1).

Scott argues that the constant need for innovation, coupled with the high risks involved with unstable markets and highly differentiated products, results in a process of vertical disintegration and an organisation of media production focused upon industrial districts consisting predominantly of small firms. The agglomeration economies derived from such territorially based clusters ensure that all producers benefit from localised externalities (Scott 1998, 1996). As such, the new media industries assume significance not for their technological singularity but, rather, as a leading edge exemplar of a much wider transition away from mass production and mass consumption towards new forms of flexible, small-scale batch production. Thus Scott characterises the California multimedia industry as 'dense transaction intensive complexes, made up of many small-and medium-sized producers working together in tightly knit social divisions of labour and drawing on regional external economies' (Scott 1995: 27). While Scott does acknowledge the worldwide 'commercial reach of the industry' which is mediated by 'large and specialised distribution companies' (ibid.), these actors form only a background element in his account of the dynamics of the industry. Centre stage is given to the relationships between small production companies and their suppliers.

POLITICAL ECONOMY OF THE CULTURAL INDUSTRIES

The California School plays down the role of large companies in the distribution and finance of media activity. However, a third perspective that can be brought to bear on the development of new media activities places these large firms at the centre of the story. Building on a number of early studies (e.g. Hirsch 1972; Peterson and Berger 1975), there is a well-established body of literature on what can be described as the political economy of cultural industries (Garnham 1990). This research tradition argues that it is misleading to focus on production *per se* when analysing media industries. Rather, it argues that in order to understand how an industry manages the kind of pressures which Scott identifies as inherent in cultural production – constant innovation, highly differentiated products and high levels of risk – the analysis needs to focus upon the relationship between production and finance/distribution (Miege 1987; Driver and Gillespie 1993a, b). For this approach, the central dynamic in media industries is concerned with the contested relationship between large (finance and distribution) and small (production) firms.

The cultural industries perspective has a strong empirical background, developed over a number of years through cumulative and longitudinal studies of media markets. Analyses repeatedly highlight the central and recurring importance of particular firm strategies, such as the struggle to secure what Hirsch (1972) calls the 'gatekeeper' function within the industry system. Peterson and Berger's classic (1975) account of the recorded music industry, for example, points to the waxing and waning of the dominant position of the majors in the US record industry. The majors' fortunes varied as they struggled to come to terms with changes in technology and popular culture (specifically, the rise of rock'n'roll and the introduction of the 45 and 33 rpm record formats), first losing market share to new smaller producers but subsequently clawing their way back as they restructured and regained control of the market.

The organisational capacity of large, often vertically integrated enterprises helps to guarantee a ready market for media products, generates economies of scale in, for instance, marketing and sales, and allows companies to offset the many 'titles' or products (i.e., television programmes, records, books, web sites, computer games, etc.) that fail against the much smaller number of titles that succeed. Only by having a large portfolio of product can the profits from the small number of hits cover the losses from the majority of misses.

It is this structure of costs that gives rise to the typical oligopolistic structure of cultural industries: a small number of companies with global reach enjoying a pivotal position in terms of the financing and distribution of cultural products – e.g., the Hollywood studios, the five 'major' record companies, and so on. These majors either source their production from in-house production units, or outsource it to smaller independent production units, financing individual productions through advances, in return for intellectual property rights (IPRs) and distribution rights. When production is not vertically integrated with distribution, small and/or independent producers typically find that they must still enter into 'loose-tight' contractual relationships with large-scale distributors – often involving a surrender of their IPRs – in order to survive (see Robins and Cornford 1992 on the TV industry; Hesmondhalgh 1996 and 1998 on the record industry). Political economy, then, introduces a concern with power and control into accounts of the dynamics of media industries (Garnham 1990; Aksoy and Robins 1992).

Both Negroponte and Scott, it should be noted, share a common assumption that the emergence of new (or multi-) media industries is associated with a shift in the balance of power in favour of smaller firms. However, the hypotheses offered by these perspectives concerning the locational distribution of new media firms are diametrically opposed. For Scott, the forces of geographical agglomeration are enhanced, as factors such as tacit knowledge and localised learning 'spillovers' become ever more crucial to maintaining competitive advantage. For Negroponte, by contrast, the emphasis placed on the substitution of physical proximity by *network* proximity suggests a 'post' geography position, where, as Negroponte (1995: 6) proclaims, 'the digital planet will look and feel like the head of a pin'. For the cultural industries approach, with its central dynamic of the shifting balance of power between major publishers and/or distributors and the producers of content, the geographical outcomes are much more contingent.

THE UK COMPUTER AND VIDEO GAMES INDUSTRY

In examining the relative merits of these three positions, we will use the empirical example of the UK computer and video games industry.[1] In many respects, computer and video games are the most mature and developed of the new media industries. The trade journal *Screen Digest* estimates that the global interactive leisure software market – predominantly computer and video games – is now worth more than US$14 billion while in Western Europe leisure software now surpasses the cinema box office as a revenue earner (*Screen Digest* 1998). According to research commissioned by the European Leisure Software Publishers Association (ELSPA – the trade body for computer and video games publishers), the UK dominates the industry in Europe with 71 per cent of total development investment in 1998. The UK computer and video games industry also exported £417 million of software, generating a trade surplus of £225 million in 1997 (ELSPA 1998). ELSPA's most recent and detailed yearly update (*Screen Digest* 1999) reported that annual sales of leisure software in the UK totalled £991 million in 1998, with the sales of games console hardware and dedicated peripherals and accessories amounting to £262 million and £194 million respectively. The same report estimates that full-time employment in the production, publishing and distribution of leisure software stood at 13,053 for the same period, with a further 8,346 full-time jobs in dedicated retail.

ROOTS OF AN INDUSTRY

As Leslie Haddon (1993) describes, computer and video games have a history dating back to the 1960s when programmers developed games to play on large, mainframe computers. The first commercially available video game appeared in the US in 1972. The most prominent of these was a very basic tennis simulation called Pong, designed by Nolan Bushnall and produced by the California-based company he helped to found, Atari. The first iteration of Pong was a 'coin-op' game, that is, the game was played on a coin-operated machine housed in a purpose-built cabinet. Games produced for this platform have subsequently been referred to as 'arcade' games because of the popularity of coin-ops in amusement arcades.

In the same year as Pong, TV distributor Magnavox (now Philips USA) produced the first domestic video game machine that played through a standard television set, based on technology developed by the then US defence-oriented company, Sanders Electronics. But the real landmark in video games technology arrived three years later, when Atari successfully converted Pong from its coin-op original into a domestic machine, utilising semiconductors. The introduction of integrated circuit technology sparked a rapid expansion in the home video game market:

> The particular appeal to the semiconductor companies, such as Fairchild and National Semiconductor, was that video games machines arrived when they were diversifying from capital goods and in the process of building up a consumer products division. (Haddon 1993: 128)

The Pong game platform was followed later in the decade by the first wave of genuine games 'consoles'. Atari, now with financial backing from Warner Communications, produced the market-leading VCS 2600, fighting off competition from old rival Magnavox and new competitors Mattel and Coleco, both of which diversified into video games from the toy industry. Unlike Pong, machines such as Mattel's Intellivision and the VCS 2600 were the first dedicated video game computers capable of playing any number of compatible games. The hardware was 'uncoupled' from the software as games were delivered via a plug-in cartridge, and this enabled a distinct games software industry to emerge. Also, the ability to play a number of games on one machine dramatically extended the appeal and longevity of the game system, and the market expanded accordingly as consumers built up their own games 'libraries' or rented titles from video shops and other retail outlets.

While US companies, and California-based companies in particular (e.g. Atari and Activision), were the first movers in the video games industry, many of the companies that have since risen to prominence in the market are Japanese. These include the three major producers of proprietary games consoles – Nintendo, Sega and latterly Sony – but also software and/or coin-op specialists such as Square, Capcom and Namco.

Sega, formally established in Tokyo in 1960, moved into the production of coin-op arcade games in the 1970s as it fed directly into their core business, which at this time was the production and management of amusement facilities. Nintendo, founded in Kyoto in 1889 and previously a company that specialised in the production of Japanese playing cards, shifted emphasis into the production of basic electronic games and toys from 1969 onwards. Nintendo's decisive move into the video games industry in the 1970s, an industry that it would go on to dominate through the next decade until the early 1990s, was built upon their previous experience of developing games that exploited light-sensitive solar cell technology. What convinced Nintendo of the lucrative future for video games was the falling costs of silicon chips (which made their utilisation in entertainment products possible for the first time) and also the pioneering efforts of Atari and Magnavox. Indeed, Nintendo's first foray into video games was a licensing agreement in 1975 with Magnavox for Japanese manufacture and distribution of their games system (Sheff 1993).

In the UK, games consoles were not initially as successful as in Japan or the US, but electronic games took on a renewed lease of life in the early 1980s. The unexpected boom in relatively cheap home computers, led by the Sinclair ZX Spectrum, the Acorn and the Commodore Vic 20 – later to be followed by the Atari ST and the Amiga – established a sizeable domestic market for computer games that has endured and blossomed into the Apple and IBM PC era. During the mid-1980s, the console market slumped, precipitating the market exit of non-games specialists such as Mattel and Coleco. By the end of the decade, however, the cyclical console market was revived with the introduction of new machines from Japan's two main gaming giants. Nintendo produced the Nintendo Entertainment System and its more successful 16-bit follow-up, the Super Nintendo Entertainment System (SNES), while Sega countered with the comparable Master System and Megadrive consoles. Together with the increasing stability and power of the PC as a games platform, Nintendo and Sega's consoles underpinned the increasing popularity of computer and video games.

By the mid 1990s, the early 16-bit consoles were losing out to increasingly powerful and cheap PC hardware and the PC emerged as the most popular games platform in Western Europe. A new generation of more powerful 32- and 64-bit consoles – Sony's newcomer the PlayStation (PSX), the Nintendo64 (N64) and the Sega Saturn – together with increasing domestic penetration of PCs have underpinned a further expansion of the market in the second half of the 1990s. The next generation of consoles – the Sega Dream Cast and the Play Station II – are expected to maintain the market momentum and, possibly (in Sony's case), to establish games consoles as the *de facto* set-top box for the delivery of a variety of interactive products and services.

FROM BEDROOM TO BOARDROOM, OR THE 'INDUSTRIALISATION' OF COMPUTER AND VIDEO GAMES

As the account above indicates, throughout the 1970s the originators of both video game hardware and software were almost exclusively North American or Japanese companies. The establishment of a *UK-based* computer and video games industry – what became known as 'BritSoft' – originated later from the success of home computers in the early 1980s. Many of the founders of today's successful UK computer and video games companies (e.g. Psygnosis, Rare) started to develop games on these relatively low-cost home computers. As the machines were relatively unsophisticated, individuals or very small teams of two or three could write the games. Today, the hobbyist lone 'programmer in the bedroom' is a stock character in the early period of company histories.

However, the business of developing computer and video games in Britain has grown as successive technological innovations have both expanded the market for games and raised the level of production resources required to produce titles. In particular, the size of the development teams has increased – spectacularly so with the shift to three-dimensional (3D) games. The production of contemporary computer or video games is undertaken by mixed teams, principally made up of programmers and graphic artists. The size of a team can vary dramatically, but the usual parameters would be around six people for a small team and around thirty for a large one.[2] What remains constant, however, is the large number of total development hours that are required to produce a contemporary computer or video game.

So, while a small team may take two years or more to complete a title, larger teams, through a greater technical division of labour, can produce the same game far quicker. Developers themselves prefer smaller teams and there is a general recognition within the industry as a whole that the most creative games tend to be produced by smaller teams. However, the expansion in average team size has been driven by the increasing time pressures faced by publishers (as outlined below) – rather than developer preference – and these pressures show no signs of abating.

Development companies may have one, two or more teams and therefore generally have around 15 to 40 employees, although a handful of very large UK companies have 150–300 typically spread across several sites. Other specialist roles – which may be undertaken by external labour – can include localisation, porting games from one platform to another (e.g., from PC to the Sony PlayStation or vice versa), adding music and voice acting, and the production of short 'full motion video' (FMV) sequences. It should be noted that the bulk of external contracting occurs, then, in essentially 'non-core' areas. The specialist activities outlined above typically amount to little more than 'packaging' activities for different territories and/or different platforms, and these take place when the game itself – and the generation of the key IPRs – is substantially complete. The sector also supports a significant number of recruitment agencies specialising in the placement of experienced staff.

Cost Structures

The need for larger teams – and the capital equipment to support them – has inevitably pushed up the development costs of computer and video games. Most 3D computer and video games currently have an entry-level production budget of £300,000 rising to about £1.5 million, with the occasional game well in excess of even these figures.[3] Marketing games now often costs at least as much again, with costs for expensive productions – so-called 'triple-A titles' – typically way in excess of those for development. Even in the last years of 2D games in 1993–94, marketing budgets for some triple-A games, such as Acclaim's Mortal Kombat II and Nintendo's Donkey Kong Country, were equal to or exceeded US$10 million for the US alone (Schuyler 1995: 47). While the first games to be given these movie-like launches (TV and radio advertising, billboard campaigns etc.) were all console products, the PC market rapidly followed suit. In contrast to marketing costs, the actual manufacturing costs per shrink-wrapped CD-Rom disk (including label, box and manual) remain relatively low, being estimated at between $3 and $4 for a PC or PSX game in 1995 (Schuyler 1995: 45). As with other cultural industries, then, computer and video games share a familiar cost structure of high costs of production, but low costs of reproduction.

Demographic Shift

It is this particular cost structure that produces the pressure for titles to sell in ever greater quantities in order to compensate for their increasing development costs. Integral to this process has been a necessary move away from the audience that first supported games – children, and more specifically, the market segment referred to as the 'hardcore gamer', a term still virtually synonymous with 'adolescent males'. The use of mass marketing techniques and (costly) distribution strategies focused predominantly upon retail multiples has been the means by which the games industry has attained a certain degree of success in moving beyond its original demographic.

Sony's PlayStation in particular, fêted within the games industry for having 'the hardest working marketing department in showbiz', is credited with much of the sales success of their console (for shifting 50 million units between 1994 and 1999), and for broadening the appeal of computer and video games more generally. The average age of a UK PlayStation owner is currently 24 and rising, and the console has even made significant inroads into the notoriously resistant – by industry standards – female market (for a multi-perspective discussion of gender and computer and video games, see Cassell and Jenkins 1998). The shift away from games' original audience is a continued source of consternation in much of the specialist games press, but a clear indication of the realpolitik of games can be summed up by the comments of Bruno Bonnell, chairman of major French publishers Infogames, when asked if his company was now targeting 'the lowest common denominator':

> Why not? Infogames is not a technology company. Infogames is an entertainment company, a mass market entertainment company. Our model is very much like a music business model, a mix of international hits that can be sold everywhere, and very big local business.[4]

Hit-driven, or 'Nobody Knows Anything'

The probability of any *individual* game recovering its development costs are, as in other cultural industries, slim. Once again, at the heart of the games industry is the cultural industries conundrum identified by William Goldman that, at the end of the day, 'nobody knows anything'. That is, there is absolutely no guarantee that any particular title will be successful: in fact, most titles will fail in the market with the losses on them offset by the gains from a much smaller number of hits. Computer and video games are no different in this respect. In 1996, a 'top-forty' PC game in the US sold, on average, some 252,000 units, while non 'top-forty' games sold only 9,375 on average (equivalent UK figures were 52,089 and 1,662 respectively) (*Screen Digest* 1997: 135).

Again, as with other cultural industries, publishers have developed a multitude of strategies and metrics to attempt to reduce the level of risk that they are exposed to. Some of the distribution and marketing strategies in the games industry have been alluded to above. More visibly, however, publishers adopt content or 'editorial' strategies designed to satisfy the same goal.

Despite the myriad technological possibilities, game content is very conventional, confined in the main to a very narrow set of tried-and-tested genres. One games production manager expressed the paradoxical challenge facing publishers: 'coming up with an original idea is the classic thing: we want it to be an original and yet it's got to be like something else' (Richard Leinfellner, Executive in Charge of Production, Bullfrog Productions – authors' interview 1998). Within these game genres, sequels and series proliferate, essentially functioning as brand names. Licensing tie-ins – typically sports or film-based – are also common. Developing game franchises and attaching licences to titles are all strategies that 'massively' increase the odds of making the game a hit in what is now a saturated marketplace: 'People go for brands; they do in every other industry ... you've won half the battle to start with because they already like it' (Joss Ellis, Vice President of Production, Virgin Interactive Entertainment, authors' interview 1999).

A return to the developer of between $5 to $15 can be expected after the retailing, marketing and distribution costs have been accounted for, and after royalty to the publisher – and payment to the hardware licensee such as Sony or Nintendo if the game is a console product, or to another development company should any elements of software (e.g. the game 'engine') have been licensed in the production of the title – have been deducted.[5] With these margins, a game which cost $500,000 to develop has to reach sales of between 33,334 and 100,000 simply to cover its development costs, sales figures that the majority of games will never achieve. Only for the larger publishers, then, can this risk be offset by having a large catalogue of games, within which the profits from the few hit titles can cover the losses from the majority of misses.

Global Restructuring: Vertical and Horizontal Integration

As the scale of finance required to develop, distribute and market computer and video games has increased, so the structure of the industry has changed. In the 1980s, it was common for individuals, 'two-man bands' or very small teams to produce a finished game and then to seek a publisher. A second, popular option was for small companies to develop *and* publish their own titles, generally distributing them through dedicated distributors, via mail order, or through 'cover mount' deals with the burgeoning games press that regularly sought to woo customers by 'bundling' free games with magazines.[6]

Thus, the British games industry in the early 1980s has rightly been described as a 'cottage industry' (Haddon 1993: 135), an observation that bears more than a trace of irony when one considers Negroponte's assertions for the future of today's new media. Games were basic, inexpensive and quick to produce. Distribution and marketing costs were relatively low given that the consumers were a small, relatively homogenous and tightly defined market niche that could easily be reached through the specialist games press and certain computer and toy shops. At this time, then, the games industry in the UK was a relatively competitive market, with low barriers to entry that supported a raft of small-scale, endogenous publisher-developers, together with a number of third-party developers, producing predominantly for a domestic market.

Such a scenario stands in stark contrast to the UK computer and video games industry of the late 1990s. As the technological sophistication of computer games has increased, raising production values, budgets, and the time-to-market, developers have increasingly been forced to turn to large publisher-developers for finance, seeking advances against royalties to enable a game to be produced.

Alternative sources of finance, such as venture capital, are hard to come by but not impossible. Small developers, though, often feel that venture capitalists want a disproportionate equity stake in the company – 50 per cent is quite common – in return for their financial backing. So, stuck between a rock and a hard place, most developers have fallen back on the publisher for finance.[7]

Similarly, with escalating distribution and marketing costs – associated with traditional retail channels, mass market advertising, and export territories – there are fewer and fewer small companies who are publishing their own material. In 1997, *Screen Digest* estimated that 'just eight publishers accounted for around 50 per cent of the PC CD-Rom games market in the US last year [1996], over 60 per cent of the same UK market and 80 per cent of the comparable market in Germany' (*Screen Digest* 1997: 136). While many smaller publishers have gone bankrupt, many more have remodelled themselves or been remodelled purely as developers, either voluntarily or as a result of acquisition. As one small publisher-developer put it when describing the rationale behind curtailing new publishing activity in favour of development:

> . . . developing at the moment the initial reward is there *instantly*. When you produce your own product and sell it and ship it . . . we're still trying to get paid for product we shipped for last Christmas [eleven months ago]! The rewards are greater but there's a lot more risk. (Colin Courtenay, Managing Director of Microvalue-Flair – authors' interview 1998)

Similarly, veteran British developer Bullfrog's high-profile move from publishing their own titles purely to developing them (as a direct consequence of a buyout by the US games giant Electronic Arts, EA), affords Bullfrog a number of major benefits:

> The game I've just launched (*Populus* II) shipped simultaneously in eight languages and we had Chinese and Japanese three weeks after. They organise the detail, we organise actual game stuff. One of the biggest things about EA is it's got huge support functions. (Richard Leinfellner, Executive in Charge of Production, Bullfrog Productions – authors' interview 1998)

Although the beginnings of a steady trend towards oligopoly in games publishing is identifiable in the UK from around 1983–4 (Haddon 1993: 135–6), what has been distinctive during the 1990s, as the latter quote implies, is the global scale upon which this restructuring now operates and the high degree of external ownership that this process has brought into being in the UK.

Latterly, as Table 5.1 indicates, the bigger publishers (including the console manufactures) have sought to buy, or part-buy, development companies and their own smaller rivals (publisher-developers). While horizontal integration is largely concerned with generating economies of scale and building up bigger and more diverse game portfolios, vertical integration is motivated by the desire to control costs and assure a steady flow of product through gaining control over the development process. Control in this instance does not simply equate with cost reduction. Perhaps more importantly, it is also concerned with the imposition of greater time discipline upon games developers.

TABLE 5.1: SELECTED MERGERS AND ACQUISITIONS
WITHIN THE UK COMPUTER AND VIDEO GAMES
INDUSTRY, 1993–9

Year	Acquired	Location	Activity	Acquirer	Location	Activity	Stake (%)
1993	Psygnosis	UK	PD	Sony Corp.	JP	HW, PD	100
1995	Rare	UK	PD	Nintendo	JP	HW, PD	25
1995	Bullfrog	UK	PD	Electronic Arts (EA)	UK	PD	100
1995	Domark	UK	PD	Eidos	UK	PD	100
1995	CentreGold Group (inc. Core Design)	UK	PD	Eidos	UK	PD	100
1996	Ocean	UK	PD	Infogrames	FR	PD	100
1996	Probe	UK	PD	Acclaim	US	PD	100
1996	Iguana	UK	PD	Acclaim	UK	PD	100
1997	DMA	UK	D	Gremlin	UK	PD	100
1997	Mainstream Interactive	AU	PD	Gremlin	UK	PD	100
1997	Spidersoft	UK	D	Take 2 Interactive	UK	PD	100
1997	Millennium	UK	D	Sony Computer Entertainment Europe (SCEE)	UK (JP)	PD	100
1998	Rare	UK	PD	Nintendo	JP	HW, PD	25
1998	Crystal Dynamics	US	D	Eidos	UK	PD	100
1998	Centresoft	UK	DR	Activision	US	PD	100
1998	Reflections	UK	D	GT Interactive	US	PD	100
1999	Virgin (VIE)	UK	PD	Interplay	US	PD	44
1999	Gremlin	UK	PD	Infogrames	FR	PD	100

Key: HW = hardware; D = developer; DR = distributor; PD = publisher/developer
Source: Author's research

Time discipline is important for publishers for a number of reasons. First, it relates to the seasonal nature of the games market where the immediate Christmas period, although less important than previously, still regularly accounts for between 20 and 35 per cent of yearly sales. Second, many of the licences commonly attached to games are time-specific, such as those relating to sports events (e.g. the World Cup) or movie tie-ins where release schedules have to be synchronised with the film openings (e.g. *Star Wars*). Finally, time discipline helps to ensure consistent revenue flow by shipping products on time. More stable revenue streams have assumed greater importance within the industry as the major publishers have become publicly quoted companies. A stock listing presents a different set of financial pressures for publishers to work to, one that revolves around posting positive quarterly results and generating shareholder value. The delay or 'slippage' of key titles jeopardises these and can trigger financial headaches for even the largest publishers.[8]

As Table 5.1 indicates, consolidation within the games industry has been a key feature of the 1990s, and it should be stressed that this is a global process of restructuring in which the mergers and acquisitions have grown steadily larger, with unprecedented deals taking place during 1998. In particular, the big US interactive publisher The Learning Company (TLC) spent most of 1998 in acquisition mode, first buying reference/'edutainment'/games publisher Mindscape, in a deal worth $130 million, followed swiftly by the acquisition of 'edutainment' and games publisher Brøderbund for $420 million. However, by December, The Learning Company had itself become a target for acquisition and announced a massive $3.8 billion deal with toy giant Mattel, in what has been described as a 'merger', although TLC will now be a division of Mattel Inc.

Globally, then, the industry is thus increasingly structured around a core of between 10 and 20 major publishers. Table 5.2 lists what are, arguably, the ten biggest companies measured purely in terms of software sales. Given the difficulties in providing accurate like-for-like firm comparisons,[9] and the fact that turnover measured in any one year will be overly influenced by the release of a few key titles, we would also add the names of Konami (JP), Namco (JP), Capcom (JP), Eidos (UK), Microsoft (US), Hasbro/MicroProse (US) and Ubi-Soft (FR) to the list, in no particular order. All of the major publishers have their own in-house development teams, surrounded by a fringe of third-party or 'independent' developers. Even these 'independents' are often closely tied to an individual publisher by equity, retainers and output deals - what have been called 'one-point-five' or 'second-party' developers, as opposed to true 'third-party' developers (cf. similar scenarios for independent television production – Robins and Cornford 1992).[10]

Table 5.2 also illustrates the extent of vertical integration among the three main console manufacturers – Sony, Nintendo and Sega. In-house development and publishing has either been started afresh, as with Sony, or expanded in the case of their rivals, while each has invested heavily in acquiring stakes in external developers and publisher-developers. For these hardware producers, the rationale behind increasing their involvement with publishing and development activities is simple. The rising power and sophistication of dedicated games hardware has increased the cost of production beyond the level that consumers are prepared to pay. Under highly competitive conditions set by market leader Sony, prices have tumbled such that manufacturers are currently having to sell consoles either at cost or, in the case of the Nintendo64, at a loss – in order to achieve a pricing point attractive enough to build critical mass in the marketplace.[11] Given that revenues derived from games software represent the only real profit centres for hardware

TABLE 5.2: WORLDWIDE LEADERS IN COMPUTER AND
VIDEO GAMES SOFTWARE, BASED ON 1997 TURNOVER

Company	Turnover (US $m)
Nintendo (JP)	835
Sony (JP)	800
Electronic Arts (US)	673
GT Interactive (US)	530
Cendant Software (US)	490
Midway (US)	390
Sega (JP)	300
Square (JP)	295
The Learning Company (US)	270
Infogrames (FR)	270
Activision (US)	250

Source: Adapted from Paribase European Equity Research cited in Doward and Islam, 1999

manufacturers, then, it is unsurprising that Sony, Nintendo and Sega are all among the biggest publishers worldwide, under either their own names or the imprimaturs of subsidiaries such as Sony's Psygnosis.

THE DEMISE OF BRITSOFT

The overriding picture that emerges from the experience of the UK games industry in the last six years is one of a transition from indigenous to external ownership. As Table 5.1 details, of the major UK games companies of the 1990s (Eidos, Psygnosis, Rare, Virgin, Ocean, Gremlin, Bullfrog and Codemasters), only Eidos and Codemasters are not either fully or partially externally owned. The games industry in the UK now resembles the UK film industry: essentially a strong talent pool and a collection of production facilities, available for less than standard US rates. While in 1999 UK games companies may be responsible for the creation of titles that generate vast revenues, claimed to be in excess of $5 billion, only a fraction of those revenues will flow back to the UK (Barrie 1999). Equity to fund the level of growth required to succeed in a growing and globalising industry has been hard to come by for indigenous companies. The industry is considered rightly to be 'high-risk' by the traditionally cautious UK investment market, placing domestic companies at a distinct disadvantage relative to their US or even French rivals (Barrie, ibid.). Additionally, the lack of autonomy resulting from external ownership can, as in other industries, bring with it unforeseen difficulties that can have less than benign consequences for the subsidiary enterprise, as the case of Virgin Interactive

Entertainment (VIE) clearly demonstrates. VIE, then part of Richard Branson's Virgin group, was the first conglomerate to enter the UK games market in 1983. After significant and relatively lasting success, the company merged with fellow BritSoft company Mastertronic in 1987. VIE was subsequently acquired, first by Sega in 1991, and then by the video rental chain Blockbuster in 1994. Soon after, Blockbuster itself was bought by Spelling Entertainment, which is, in turn, a subsidiary of Viacom Inc.

The shift in corporate priorities and strategy that the acquisition of Blockbuster entailed proved disastrous for VIE. When Viacom ran into financial difficulties after its expensive purchase of Paramount Studios, it sought to amortise the purchase through the sale of 'non-core' assets and, with a change in Blockbuster's priorities (after the Spelling buyout), this included VIE. Thus began a long and drawn-out divestment process, lasting nearly two years, as Viacom sought an owner for VIE. As time dragged on, Viacom came under increasing pressure from US financial regulators to sell VIE because the company had posted VIE as 'discontinued' (which it clearly was not), in order for it not to appear on Viacom's full accounts.

After an eleventh-hour buyout fell through in June 1998, Viacom lost patience and sold off VIE's main asset (Westwood Studios in Las Vegas) piecemeal, while the ongoing instability resulted in VIE also losing their major European distribution deal with LucasArts. In the end, VIE's future was saved only when the remaining European operations were the subject of a management buyout at the end of 1998. Predictably, in trying to rebuild the company, VIE's new owners quickly struck a deal with the US publisher Interplay for mutual distribution of titles in their respective markets, a deal that has subsequently seen Interplay buy nearly half of VIE's stock.[12]

THE GEOGRAPHY OF COMPUTER AND VIDEO GAMES IN THE UK

How does this changing of industrial structure relate to the geographical organisation of the UK's computer and video games industry? We have established a database of 204 computer and video games *establishments* in the UK in 1999, covering 195 discrete companies, with five multi-site firms. This database is fairly comprehensive given that estimates from trade sources indicate that there were some 150 computer and video games development companies in the UK last year (ELSPA 1998). We have not yet been able consistently to identify the employment associated with each of these establishments, so some caution must be shown in interpreting these figures. Nevertheless, they do give a reasonably accurate indication of the geography of computer and video games activity in the UK.

In Table 5.3, we have categorised the games establishments according to four exclusive activities – 'pure' publishing, 'pure' development, publishing and development, and 'other', a category that includes recruitment agencies, specialist distributors, and producers of games software tools and games peripherals, etc.

TABLE 5.3: LOCATIONAL PROFILES OF COMPUTER AND VIDEO GAMES ESTABLISHMENTS IN THE UK, BY ACTIVITY, 1999

	Publishing only	Development only	Publishing & development	'Other'	All VAT-registered firms*
Total number of firms in UK	20	126	25	33	—
Percentage by region:					
Greater London	80	17	28	15	16
Rest of South-East (ROSE)	10	23	36	42	20
South-East (London + ROSE)	90	40	64	58	36
Rest of UK	10	60	36	42	64
Total	100	100	100	100	100

* These figures are for 1996 and are provided for comparison only

Source: Authors' research

Figures 5.1 to 5.3 show the distribution of establishments in three categories: development activity without associated publishing; publishing activity (whether co-located with development or not); and other games-related activity.

The data in tabular form also concentrate on the numbers of establishments in three geographical areas – London, the rest of the South-East (ROSE) and the rest of the UK. As is immediately apparent, the patterns of distribution for the establishments varies between the four classifications, with games development establishments the most widely distributed, pure publishing activity concentrated primarily in Greater London, and tools and other support services being disproportionately located in the rest of the South-East. It should be noted however that two of the UK's larger publisher-developers, Psygnosis and Codemasters, are headquartered in Liverpool and rural Warwickshire respectively – both geographical arrangements that are extremely surprising in the context of the locations of other media industries in the country.

As can be seen by comparing the distribution of establishments with the latest data for VAT registered firms as a whole, the computer and video games industry, and in particular development activity, is only slightly more concentrated in the South-East than in the UK economy as a whole. This pattern is particularly significant given that development is by far the most labour-intensive element of the value chain and therefore accounts for the bulk of the employment in the industry.

It should also be noted that, at a finer geographical scale, most games developers shun the 'downtown' locations and cultural ambience of city centres typical of both

FIGURE 5.1: THE LOCATION OF 126 'PURE' COMPUTER
AND VIDEO GAMES DEVELOPMENT ESTABLISHMENTS
IN THE UK, 1998

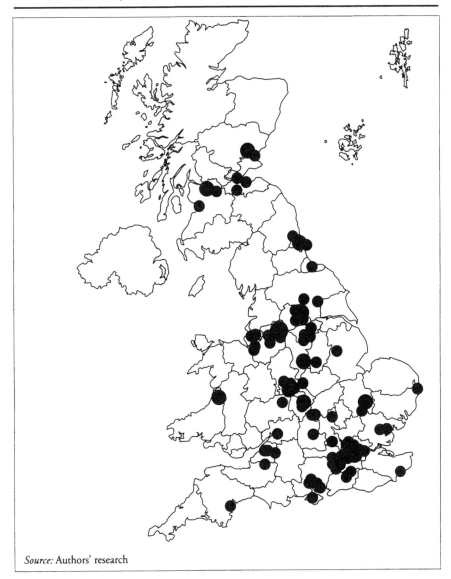

Source: Authors' research

'old' media such as television production and many segments of the wider
multimedia sector in the US (cf. Egan 1997: 20–1; Brail and Gertler 1997: 9–10).
Rather, developers typically favour the outlying urban fringe, often in the form of
business parks or industrial estates, with a select few choosing to locate in semi-
rural settings in converted farm houses that are much coveted within the industry.[13]

FIGURE 5.2: THE LOCATION OF 44 COMPUTER AND
VIDEO GAMES PUBLISHING ESTABLISHMENTS IN THE
UK, 1998 (INSET: THE SOUTH-EAST)

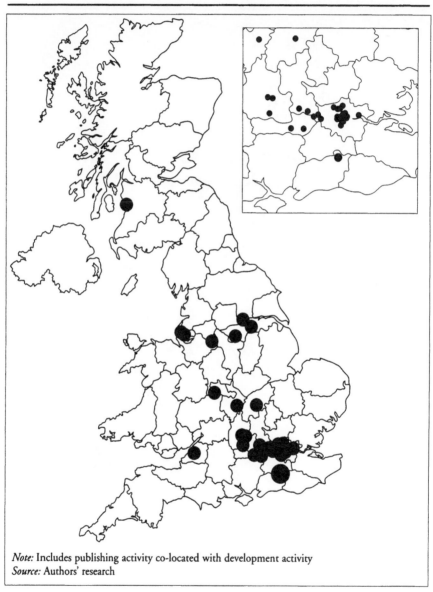

Note: Includes publishing activity co-located with development activity
Source: Authors' research

CLUSTERS?

With the possible exception of Guildford and the wider Surrey area, no particular
tightly knit clusters emerge from the database. Interviews with computer and
video games developers in the UK also reveal little inclination by managers for
their firms to cluster. Nevertheless, some recent developments would seem to
indicate that the co-location of firms may become a more significant feature of the
future UK computer and video games industry. In these instances, however,

FIGURE 5.3: THE LOCATION OF 33 'OTHER' COMPUTER
AND VIDEO GAMES RELATED ESTABLISHMENTS IN THE
UK, 1998 (INSET: THE SOUTH-EAST)

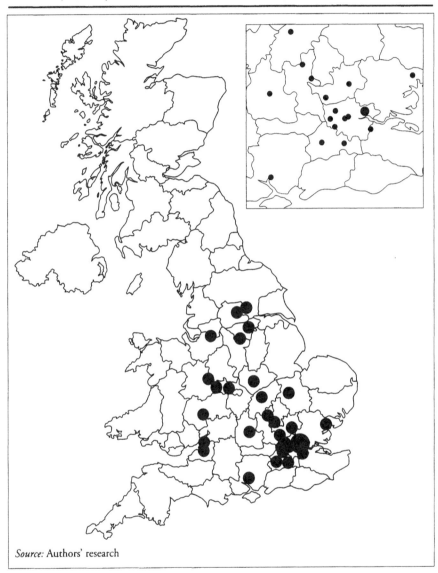

Source: Authors' research

co-location is not the result of the clustering of many and various small producers
to benefit from localised externalities. Rather, it tends to be the geographical
expression of the continually contested relationship between developers and
publishers that lies at the heart of the industry. This perpetual struggle – which is
also stereotyped as the battle between creativity and economics – promotes two
characteristic processes within the industry.

Firstly, tensions between developers and their immediate employers (usually publishers), can result in the phenomenon referred to as 'breakaway' or 'spin-off' developers whereby development staff of an existing publisher-developer or developer leave to seek greater creative freedom and/or greater financial reward by founding their own enterprise or enterprises. The blueprint for this spin-off activity was established in 1979 when four of Atari's leading games designers walked out to form Activision. After successfully fighting a lawsuit filed by Atari, Activision created the now widespread business model of third-party publishing and development and, despite intermittent setbacks, has remained one of the major players in the industry. More regularly, the fallout from the tensions between developers and publishers/marketeers is vertical and horizontal integration on the part of major publishers (as outlined above).

The Guildford/Surrey 'cluster', then, is a manifestation of the former process where the steady growth in the number of game companies has been instigated by new firms spinning off from Guildford's one large games company, Bullfrog, now owned by Electronic Arts (EA). This breakaway activity began when Bullfrog's former creative driving force, Peter Molyneux, left to form a new developer-publisher with two other ex-Bullfrog staff after the buyout by EA. Given that individuals rarely migrate in order to start their own businesses (Reynolds 1989), it is unsurprising that Molyneux's new enterprise, Lionhead, was founded in Guildford. Lionhead's recent investment scheme for small start-ups, named Lionhead Satellites, has provided an additional spur to cluster activity in the area.

However, the fate of Molyneux's previous company ably demonstrates the geographical dimensions of the opposing trends for corporate rationalisation and consolidation. Bullfrog and EA's co-located in-house development staff relocated to Chertsey in early 2000, where their new premises are shared with EA Europe's publishing and marketing operations. Chertsey was chosen primarily on the basis that it was virtually equidistant from EA's two existing operations, representing an equitable distribution of the commuting burden. Chertsey also represented one of the few locations where a purpose-built site that will eventually house 1,000 staff could be obtained 'cost effectively'.

Similarly, what appears to be an emerging cluster in and around Crawley, West Sussex, is in fact largely the fallout from the rationalisation and acquisition policy of The Learning Company (TLC), as outlined in the previous section. In late 1998, TLC moved to co-locate their UK operations with those of their recent acquisitions, Mindscape and Brøderbund. This horizontal integration embodied a transfer of jobs from Egham, Surrey in the case of Brøderbund; from Wimbledon, London for TLC UK staff; and from nearby Burgess Hill for Mindscape UK staff. In effect, the three companies are one; their individual names have been kept solely for their brand values.[14]

THE 'COMPULSION OF PROXIMITY' AND FUNCTIONAL 'FOOTLOOSENESS'

Leaving aside the examples above – where geographical concentration has been driven essentially by rationalisation, reduced overheads and the search for synergies and economies of scale – both the data contained in Table 5.3 and interview findings suggest that there are distinct benefits for publishers to cluster, but specifically to cluster in London. In addition to close proximity to the financial community, the key advantages of a location in the capital relate to securing the optimum 'channel to market', summarised succinctly by one small publisher-developer based in the North-East region of England looking in from afar:

> If you want to really capture the UK market, which is a reasonably-sized market – but it's a very difficult market to penetrate – you've got to be in the London area. Most of the buyers, the Virgins, the Comets etc. [major games retailers in the UK] are all in the London area and unless you visit them on a, literally, weekly/monthly basis, you don't get their ear. That has been one of our downfalls – not being able to get into the UK market. (Colin Courtenay, Managing Director of Microvalue-Flair – authors' interview 1998).

With games *publishing*, then, it would seem that the 'compulsion of proximity' (Boden and Molotch 1994) remains a strong factor in locational preferences. Importantly though, these companies are not clustering around each other – rather, they are clustering around their clients (the retail buyers). In this respect, games publishers can be said to be 'client-facing', that is, in a position where success depends upon maintaining regular, extensive and intensive interaction with their clients.

However, in terms of games development, where one might expect to find (according to Scott), tightly knit clusters based upon dense and localised social divisions of labour, the compulsion of proximity seems considerably weaker. Why is this? Firstly, developers are far less client-facing than publishers. For developers, their clients are the publishers, and frequently a developer will work only for one publisher at any given point in time. While being less extensive, client relationships for developers are also less intensive as, beyond the initial commissioning of a game, interaction with publishers is geared primarily around monthly/two monthly milestones, much of which consists of transmitting work-in-progress (screenshots, demo levels etc.), either as hard copy or over a network.

Secondly, computer and video games developers are now very much part of a global filière. Indeed, it is the primacy of securing access to *internationally* sourced technology, publishing, distribution and finance that would appear to lessen the need for localised production complexes. Interaction between both a developer's clients (publishers) and their main suppliers (specialist hardware and software vendors) is mediated through the major worldwide annual trade shows that form the key dates in the industry calendar. By far the most important of these is E3, the Electronic Entertainment Exposition, held every May in the US, followed by September's ECTS (European Computer Trade Show) in London and the twice-yearly Tokyo Game Show held every spring and autumn. Networking with their peers at these pivotal events is only a secondary motivation for developer attendance, compared with the real business of vying with rivals for the attention of publishers and technology companies.

While the globalisation of the computer and video games industry may appear to have introduced a degree of, at least, functional 'footlooseness' in the location of development activity, the articulation of these global linkages with local circumstances is a complex and contingent process. First of all – given the comparative youth of the industry – in many cases a firm's present base is still most likely to be one or other of the founder's home town or city, so companies often remain bound to their territories by strong personal and familial ties in the first instance. Although some companies that originate from outside London have since established operations in the capital (e.g. Rage and Codemasters), they have been reluctant to move and their headquarters remain, for the time being at least, located in their home territories.

Secondly, differential factor endowments are very important. Beyond the consideration of the availability of relatively low-cost, physical space that leads many developers to locate in business parks and industrial estates, sites outside London also help to depress labour costs for development. Wages in the UK games industry are significantly higher within the capital – by anything up to a factor of three – as there is a much greater demand from other sectors in general, and financial services in particular, for many of the generic skills utilised in games (specifically, programming).

In addition, the looser labour markets that tend to prevail in dispersed locations also aid recruitment while inhibiting the poaching of existing staff, as well as discouraging the copying of ideas and techniques. Further, with long development cycles for individual products, the loss of continuity on a title that the departure of (key) staff can cause further increases the risk of market failure, through the loss of creative and technical focus and/or through a more routine delay in the release date. The geographical distribution of games development in the UK, then, suggests that we should be wary of place-based accounts that tend to promote totalising readings of the nature and location of creativity, or the functioning of external labour markets in new media activity.

CONCLUSION

This chapter has demonstrated the necessity for analysis to remain sensitive to the particular sub-sectoral composition of what has become known as 'new media'. In the task of understanding the interaction between technological change and processes of industrial, commercial and geographical restructuring in the new media industries, it is also important to bear in mind historical trajectories of development. That is to say, given its maturity relative to other elements of the new media, the games industry should alert us to the importance of an industry life cycle.

As we have argued, the days of BritSoft in the early 1980s – though far removed from the reality of the UK games industry in the late 1990s – are an uncanny echo of Negroponte's somewhat misguided contemporary visions of a boutique/cottage industry. Similarly, although the development of the games industry in the UK has, to date, been almost bereft of what might be described as 'institutional thickness' (Amin and Thrift 1994), there are some indications that this may yet change.[15]

Lack of sensitivity to such historical phases of development has been identified as one of the shortcomings of the industrial districts literature. As Appold (1998) notes, research has focused on a relatively late stage of development of such clusters or districts, 'after industries and agglomerations have matured' (1998: 446). Consequently their accounts of the workings of external labour markets, reduced transaction costs and inter-firm networking may be 'a by-product rather than a cause of agglomeration' (Appold, ibid.).

The example of the present-day UK computer and video games industry clearly demonstrates that there can be no *automatic* association of successful new media industries with the spatial agglomeration of *production* activity. While the characteristics foregrounded by the institutionalist approach may yet rise to prominence in the future development of the games industry in the UK, they are not a significant feature of its present. Instead, the current commercial, industrial and geographical organisation of computer and video games production in the UK primarily reflects specific processes of market competition based on the need for portfolio strategies, strong financial backing, information exchange at global nodes (trade fairs), risk assessment and the (contested) dominant position of 'gatekeeper' firms executing strong vertical control.

NOTES

1. This section is based on initial research findings generated from interviews with games publishers, developers and trade associations, together with material from the trade press, undertaken for the ongoing UK Economic and Social Research Council (ESRC) project, New Media and Urban and Regional Development Opportunities in the UK (Grant No. R000237747).

2. The main exceptions to this are the handful of titles known as 'flagship' games. These are big-budget productions that are exclusively available on a particular console, produced in-house and primarily designed to drive-up sales of the console itself. Given their importance, such products now tend to have massive production teams. For instance, a team of over 100 full-time staff produced Sega's *Sonic Adventure*, which was released to drive sales of their own recently launched Dreamcast console in January 1999 in Japan.

3. For instance, while exact figures are hard to come by, Nintendo's flagship 1998 release, *Zelda: Ocarina of Time* was rumoured in trade press circles to have cost in the region of a staggering $22 million.

4. Quote from an interview feature, 'One-to-One with Bruno Bonnell', in the weekly trade magazine *MCV (the Market for Home Computing and Video Games)*, issue 7, 16 October 1998, 14–18.

5. Development licences for the various games platforms are a considerable cost burden for developers. For instance, in 1994 US developers had to pay $7 per cartridge in order to develop for the Sega Saturn console (Schuyler 1995: 45). So-called game 'engines' are also very expensive to purchase. Although the licensee pays only a one-off fee, the most recently licensed 3D engines from games such as *Quake II* and *Unreal* have commanded figures of $1 million each.

6. For more details regarding the history of this practice see David Jenkins' column 'Cover Mount War Strikes Britain', Gamasutra, *Industry Analysis* 3(3), 22 January 1999, at <http://www.gamasutra.com>.

7. For a lively and detailed diary account of the difficulties faced by new developers, see 'The trials of a start-up developer' by Demis Hassabis, founder of Elixir Studios, that begins in *Edge*, issue 63. The column in *Edge*, issue 65 deals specifically with the problem of raising initial finance and the pros and cons of venture capital versus publisher advances.

8. For instance, the big US publisher GT Interactive (GTI) announced earlier this year that it expects an operating loss for the fourth fiscal quarter of 1999 of some $50–55 million, only $25–30 million of which is attributed to one-off costs related to corporate reorganisation and relocation. As GTI's press release states, 'this loss is primarily a result of a delay in the shipment of five front-line titles', 8 April 1999 at <http://www.gtinteractive.com/>.

9. As implied, there are a number of discrepancies in the original Paribas figures, and this is the reason that the table has been 'adapted'. For instance, the original table quotes EA's 1997 turnover as $908 million, but this is in fact EA's 1998 turnover. Elsewhere, UK company Eidos originally appeared as the 10th firm in the table, with a turnover of $231 million. Given that this is less than Activision's turnover – and is once again inaccurate (it should be £137 million or *c.* $218 million) – Activision has been included in place of Eidos.

10. This is currently the favoured strategy of the UK's biggest publisher Eidos. After Eidos's initial entry into the games market, from a background in proprietary video technologies, the company bought troubled publisher-developers Domark and CentreGold. Since this time, Eidos has focused largely upon establishing exclusive output deals, such as the industry-first 10-year deal struck with US developer Ion Storm. More typically, Eidos has established these exclusive output deals in combination with the purchase of a minority equity stake in development companies, such as UK developers Pure (25 per cent), Hothouse Holdings (25 per cent), Tigon (30 per cent) and Sports Interactive (25 per cent), and 25 per cent in French developer Lankhor (Eidos page at Games Investor UK, <http://www.gamesinvestor.co.uk/>).

11. Sega has learnt the lesson to its cost. One of the reasons for the failure of the Sega Saturn console outside of Japan – where it has gained a modicum of success – was a prohibitively high launch price. In the UK, the first Saturns retailed at £400 in 1995, compared to Sony's PlayStation that arrived in the same year for £100 less. Sega's next console, the 128-bit Dreamcast launched in Japan in November 1998 for the equivalent of a loss-making £145. Keen not to make the same mistake twice, Sega promises that the machine will stay under the £200 barrier for its European launch in 1999 – even though it is more than four times as powerful as Sony's ageing £100 PlayStation.

12. This condensed narrative of VIE's rise and fall has been garnered from a collection of trade sources (online and offline) and through an interview with Joss Ellis, Vice President of Production, VIE, 12 January 1999.

13. The prototypical 'farmhouse' games companies are the very successful rural Warwickshire duo of Codemasters in Stoneythorpe, and Rare in Twycross. Rare's website <http://www.rare.co.uk/affairs/today/> proudly displays a photo of their farmhouse and the accompanying text eulogises this rural idyll.

14. Story from trade magazine *CTW*, 19 October 1998: 5.

15. For instance, Scottish Enterprise has established the Scottish Games Alliance to support and promote games companies in Scotland (<http://www.scottigames.org/>) and higher education is also increasingly seeking to support the industry with nine UK universities currently offering relevant courses, most of which are based in peripheral areas. For details, see 'Gaming Graduates' in *Edge* magazine, issue 58, May: 67–72, and 'Study Area', *Edge*'s special supplement on careers in the games industry, from issue 73, July 1999.

6 Globalisation and the Portuguese Textile and Clothing Filière in the Post-GATT Climate

INTRODUCTION

Clothing manufacturing and the related textile industries can be considered among the most paradigmatic cases in the ongoing debates within Europe in the current era of globalisation. Owing to its labour-intensive nature and low barriers of entry into industrial production, garment production appears to be one of the most threatened economic sectors likely to disappear from a post-industrial 'high-wage' Europe. However, such a unidimensional and linear approach towards industrial development runs the risk of overlooking the complexity and profound territoriality of the globalisation process that is occurring in the businesses concerned with fashion.

This chapter seeks to examine the impact of the increasing integration of different economies into the international clothing filière. It begins with a discussion of the nature of this process of globalisation, and considers it as a profound structural change in the overall filière. An analysis is then conducted of the ongoing integration experience of the Portuguese textile and clothing (T&C) filière. An outline of the historical process of this integration is presented and the current situation of the Portuguese T&C-filière is considered from two different perspectives. On the one hand, a view is given of the external role the country has in the filière; on the other, internal political and entrepreneurial actions and reactions of the Portuguese are examined.

THE WORLD OF FASHION TURNED INSIDE OUT: THE COMPLEX TERRITORIALITY OF THE GLOBALISATION PROCESS

Despite a clearly negative evolution of employment figures and the increasingly internationalised sourcing strategies of European clothing manufacturers,[1] it would be misleading to characterise the globalisation of clothing industries as a simple process of diffusion away from industrialised countries. There are, above all, three important reasons that imply the need for a more complex analysis of this particular 'global shift': first, the globalisation of the fashion business is much more than a simple relocation process on the part of clothing manufacturing firms. It can only be understood as a structural reorganisation of the overall T&C-filière, including new forms of both institutional and spatial divisions of labour. Second, the tendency towards decentralisation outside Europe is not the only active force in the process of territorial restructuring. Likewise there are counter-forces which imply a 're-Europeanisation' of clothing production; and third, from its very beginning garment manufacturing has tended to cluster locally owing to its need for flexible input–output transactions. This characteristic is also being reflected in the ongoing globalisation process.

This section focuses on the first two aspects in order to shed some light on the profound structural changes in the overall filière of the clothing business before leading to the actual cases. We shall thus attempt to discover the roots of this change and how it is increasingly having paradoxical impacts on the geographical structure of garment production.

Garment manufacturing has historically been one of the most flexible economic sectors, in both spatial and organisational terms (Dicken 1998). Two aspects have been especially important in this context: first, the need to respond to a changing seasonal market and, second, the requirement to access relatively low-cost workforces. As the clothing industry paid and still pays by far the lowest wages of all industrial sectors, labour market saturation and rising wage inflation in the 1950s forced it to leave the metropolitan regions in Europe. This gave rise to a series of rural garment clusters within central Europe, which benefited from the ease with which new production facilities could be established at the national and then international scale (Commission of the European Communities 1993). With the first wave of internationalisation in the late 1960s, these low territorial barriers underpinned the clothing industry in its role as a pioneer activity in the newly industrialising countries (NICs).

However, this process cannot be interpreted as being triggered solely by those in control of production. 'In fact, trade in clothing and textiles appears more to be masterminded by agents in the importing countries' (Scheffer 1994: 11). In other words, firms from Europe – in concert with often indigenous distribution networks – have been variously involved in the establishment of productive capacities in the Far East and elsewhere. This influx of new competitors has basically been due to a search for cheap products, probably on the part of the clients of domestic clothing suppliers in both the wholesale and retail sectors. Consequently, the process of increasing competition has been coupled with a gradual 'power shift' (Glasmeier and Kibler 1996) in the overall filière as buyers of assembled apparel were able to bypass their traditional suppliers in the value chain through their new international linkages. The fact that about two-thirds of total EU-imports are directed to retailers, either carried out by themselves or by their own or contracted agents (as highlighted by a study carried out by the

German company KSA Consult (Müller 1995)) demonstrates that the European manufacturers have meanwhile been excluded from the majority of international transactions.

However, the major changes in garment manufacturing have not only occurred on the supply side. The second dimension of flexibility that traditionally characterised the sector, namely the ability to deal with a cyclical market, has undergone a severe process of restructuring. This has mainly been caused by the substantially increasing diversity of consumption patterns in Western societies (Harvey 1989).

This shift – whatever its explanation – is mirrored in the fashion market in two ways. First, the traditional mass middle markets are tending to disappear, making way for a patchwork of different sub-markets. These are determined on one hand by lifestyle-oriented variables such as age, educational level and taste, and on the other hand by an increasing polarisation of income thereby creating a needs-orientated low-end market (Grüßen and Pohl 1994).

Second, the seasonality of the 'classic' fashion year, with its basic spring/summer and autumn/winter collections constituting the basic elements, is being substantially accelerated and gradually substituted by a pattern of differentiated seasonalities according to demographics and lifestyle perception (Crewe and Lowe 1996: 277). However, one must not run the risk of exaggerating the meaning of this increasing pace of change. Instead of substituting the traditional cycles, the acceleration process has rather been superimposed upon them. As a knitwear producer stated, the proportion of quick-response orders in their sector will never reach more than 30 per cent of the total volume of production (authors' interview 1997).

These major changes, to both the supply and demand logics of garment manufacturing, have had significant repercussions in the organisational and territorial structure of the overall value chain. In the case of the former, the diversification of consumption has reinforced the power shift originally caused by new purchasing strategies on the part of retailers. As a result, the interface between the production and commercialisation of clothing has become the pivotal point in the filière since from there both upstream and downstream activities can be controlled effectively. Thus, success stories, of which Benetton is the most widely quoted and enduring one (see *inter alia* Crewe and Lowe 1996; Pires 1994), display well-functioning control mechanisms at the industry-retail interface. In the case of Benetton, this occurs through creation of a new (global) product image, a refined just-in-time system and a risk-minimising network of franchised stores in more than a hundred countries across the world. Although nowadays the economic success of Benetton's clothing commercialisation has slowed substantially, the existing widely diversified holding is still benefiting from its 'McDonalds-of-fashion' image (Crewe and Lowe 1996: 275).

More recent success stories, such as Hennes and Moritz (H&M) and Marks & Spencer, are, unlike Benetton, giving preference to owning their shops rather than franchising in order to achieve economies of scale. Yet, both firms differ in their sourcing structures. Whereas H&M try to buy as cheaply as possible and employ their own sourcing agencies all over the world, the British market-leader, Marks & Spencer, has tended to pressurise its domestic suppliers. Only from the beginning of the 1990s did it focus on shifting purchasing abroad, using its 'preferred' or first-tier suppliers as a quality control mechanism for foreign sourcing (Crewe and Davenport 1992: 193). Hence, despite the emergence of a crucial interface in the filière, a variety of cases can be found in the fashion business that differ, according to country of origin, quality level, market segment and so on. As yet, it appears difficult to discern generalisable industry-wide trends. The focus on the retailer-supplier interface merely constitutes a framework that helps provide a better understanding of what is going on.

Whereas changing supply and demand patterns are having similar impacts on the filière in terms of organisation, resulting in an ongoing concentration process, they are impinging on the locational structure in a somewhat paradoxical way. Thus on the one hand there is a centrifugal dynamic underpinning the search for the lowest-cost production sites globally, while on the other hand, as market uncertainty has substantially increased because of shortened fashion cycles and reduced batches, a simultaneous centripetal dynamic is evident that implies a tendency to return and get closer to their core markets; 'Given that ordering from India has to be done three to six months in advance, and that distribution from the Far East takes on average six weeks, the pressure is clearly on for alternative, more localised and responsive sourcing arrangements' (Crewe and Lowe 1996: 277). Thus, the organisational and geographical structures of the firms reflect this trade-off between low cost and responsiveness that shapes the territorial pattern of the fashion business.

Therefore, since there is not only the simplistic and binary choice between the Far East and a localised sourcing structure, the reality is even more complex. The general trade-off pattern is distorted by a series of economic and non-economic dimensions, such as the quality level of the respective sourcing operation and the internal structure of the supplying country concerning capital availability and firm structure, trade regulation and so on. In the case of trade regulation, besides GATT and the more recent WTO developments, one policy instrument in particular has played a major role in Europe, namely the EU legislation on outwear processing traffic (OPT).[2] This measure gives EU producers the opportunity to export EU fabrics and re-import garments, paying customs duty only on the value added by the production. This special tool has underpinned the substantial internationalisation of EU manufacturers, whilst at the same time supporting their competitiveness and thereby contributing to their survival.

Given that the territorial dynamic of the clothing trade cannot be conceived as a simple competition between the industrial countries and NICs but rather as a complex pattern constituted between different agents and forces, the total phase-out of the GATT quota system may be expected to have diverse effects on the territorial structure of garment production. Whereas internationalisation will be reinforced by the centrifugal dynamic discussed above, the 'Back to Europe' tendency is to a large extent independent from trade policy. Thus, the European periphery appears likely to benefit from future changes, since it is able to combine the factors of proximity and low cost. In the following section, we shall outline how a peripheral country of Europe has performed as a textile and clothing producer and how recent shifts have influenced the performance of its production systems.

THE INTEGRATION OF PORTUGAL IN INTERNATIONAL CLOTHING PRODUCTION NETWORKS: FROM THE 'WORKBENCH PARADIGM' TO THE 'EXTENSIVE MODEL'

Portugal has been chosen for its unique recent history in terms of interaction with the wider economy, for its position on the periphery of Europe and for the major importance of the textile and clothing filière in the country's economy. Unlike many other European countries, Portugal has only relatively recently become involved in extensive external trade – after a long period of somewhat closed economic activity mainly confined to national and colonial markets. Two important steps of market liberalisation have occurred in Portugal's integration into the European Free Trade Association (EFTA) in 1960 and her accession to the European Community in 1986. After both stages of liberalisation, the two basic pillars of the present Portuguese filière were being established. The 1960s cemented the country's role as a low-wage 'workbench' for European companies, whereas accession to the EU gave rise to the so-called 'extensive model' which underpinned the boom in garment manufacturing on the basis of low assembly costs.

At the end of the 1950s, textiles accounted for 19 per cent of the total manufacturing workforce and clothing for less than 10 per cent. The filière was composed of only a few but relatively large textile firms, mostly located in the rural hinterland of Oporto, that specialised in yarn and cotton fabrics and benefited from cheap colonial cotton and protected markets. In 1950, 60 per cent of cotton fabric exports went to the Portuguese colonies. Clothing manufacturing was limited to myriad small enterprises geared toward satisfying the national domestic demand. In the 1960s the first foreign investments were attracted, marking the first shift in the filière in favour of clothing production. Large factories were established in the metropolitan areas of Oporto and Lisbon, owned by American, European and Japanese companies and producing the ready-to-wear garments for European middle-class consumers (Martins 1976). In that period international capital also provided the establishment of more technology-intensive upstream activities such as production of synthetic fibres, following significant investments by ICI (UK), AKZO (The Netherlands) and Mitsubishi (Japan).

In the period of uncertainty subsequent to the 1974 revolution and the establishment of the *Estado Novo* these activities were temporarily halted but they never stopped completely. However, the decolonisation, which took place as a consequence of the 25 April revolution, caused another change within the filière. This affected the large cotton enterprises in the hinterland of Oporto and forced them into a severe process of restructuring. Formerly integrated textile–clothing enterprises that had previously constituted the most important players in the North Portuguese context of diffuse industrialisation lost their formerly protected colonial markets. As a consequence they began to externalise mainly the cost-intensive assembly of garments or home textiles. Subcontractors were spun off from parent companies, thereby making the former textile workers into a new class of entrepreneurs (Sá Marques 1986; Domingues and Sá Marques 1987).

In the mid-1980s the Portuguese T&C filière was confronted with the country's accession into the European Community. This new phase of development is associated with direct investments that increased largely with the encouragement of European regional policy funding, support and subcontracting that brought Portuguese and European firms into a wide range of relations. International trade has kept growing since then, finally replacing national and colonial markets with the European market (Pires 1998).[3] By late 1986, more than 90 per cent of both knitwear and other clothing exports went to EU and EFTA countries (Dudleston and Pires 1996).

In this context of 'Europeanisation', the importance of the industry to the Portuguese economy kept growing. The workforce of the T&C filière increased from just under 300,000 in 1981 to 431,000 in 1991. In 1981, employment in T&C was 8.1 per cent of total employment in Portugal and 30.4 per cent of total manufacturing employment. This proportion had increased to 10.8 per cent of total employment and 40.8 per cent of manufacturing employment by 1991 (INE 1991). Between 1985 and 1993, the number of enterprises increased from 5,570 in 1989, to 9,171 in 1993. This kind of rapid growth still remained, based upon the 'workbench paradigm' established in the 1960s, and was frequently described as the 'extensive model' to characterise the growth process as a simple expansion of the existing production system (Taveira and De Sousa 1990; Reis 1998).

A look at the changes in the firm size structure of T&C industry appears to confirm the basic assumptions of the extensive model; the primacy of SMEs was reinforced after 1986. Firms with less than 100 employees increased their share of the total number of firms from 88.6 per cent in 1985 to 92.58 per cent in 1993. Those with more than 500 employees reduced their share in the same years from 1.7 to 0.8 per cent over the same period, while the average number of employees per enterprise decreased from 51.2 to 35.6 (Pires 1995).

Yet it may lead to serious misunderstandings to interpret this extension as a single and uniform dynamic. The process of integration into the global production network impinged upon the Portuguese filière in different ways in both sectoral and regional terms. Concerning the former it is clear that the relative importance of textiles is decreasing in favour of clothing and footwear. The textile sector accounted for 56.6 per cent of T&C companies in 1985 but only 39.9 per cent in 1993. On the other hand, the clothing sector increased its share from 28.6 per cent to 39.7 per cent and leather and footwear from 14.8 per cent to 20.4 per cent over the same period. These tendencies are mirrored in terms of both gross added value and external trade where textile industries have shown a negative tendency while clothing and footwear production were growing significantly. In other words: only the more labour-intensive segments of the filière benefited from the general market boom. This selective growth process not only increased the external dependence of the filière, it also affected the existing inter-firm linkages, since the Portuguese CMT (cut, make and trim) factories mainly assembled fabrics provided by their foreign clients.

Regarding the regional structure of the filière, the unprecedented expansion after 1986 appears to have affected it in an uneven and selective way. There has always been a significant variance in regional employment, but since entry into the European Community, the regions which traditionally specialised in wool and regions without any importance in T&C filière have shown a decline. Contrary to this, employment has increased greatly in the North, particularly in the Nomenclature of territorial units for statistics (NUTs) level-III regions Ave, Tâmega and Cávado – that is, the rural hinterland of Oporto that has consequently reinforced its prominent position in the national filière. Between 1993 and 1995, the Norte region's share of national T&C firms and of employment increased from 67 per cent to 70 per cent and from 78 to 79 per cent respectively. That is, international capital entered and participated in restructuring the system of diffuse rural industrialisation described above. This revealed, on the one hand, flexible subcontracting networks originating from the internal process of vertical disintegration and covering a wide range of textile-related activities, including spinning, weaving, dyeing and so on.[4] On the other hand, wages for CMT activities were low, a situation guaranteed by the household-centred economies still prevailing in the rural environment.[5]

Although the above account presents a generalised and simplified view of the 'extensive model', this selective expansion of the filière in regional and sectoral terms reveals that the hypothesis of a mere extension of the existing structure is generally sound. The shift in the Portuguese T&C filière towards clothing manufacturing and towards regional concentration suggests the maintenance and enhancement of the 'workbench' paradigm rather than the successful international market penetration on the part of Portuguese exporters. In 1987, for instance, 50 per cent of the clothing exports (excluding knitwear) from Portugal came under the OPT legislation (Marques 1992). Knitwear export, despite displaying higher growth rates than woven clothing (Domingues 1993), more strongly relies upon supply of local cotton yarn and therefore is not visible in OPT statistics.

Thus, the substantial growth in importance of the T&C filière in the Portuguese national economy is accompanied by a growing degree of 'passive dependence' (Quaternaire Portugal 1995: 111) and increasing vulnerability. Subcontracting and CMT processing is uncertain and subject to rapid changes. Customers could, for example, easily switch to using the relatively lower labour costs enjoyed by producers in Eastern Europe as they also share Portugal's advantage of geographical proximity. In the case of many German garment manufacturers, this evolution has already occurred. During 1992 and 1993 alone, OPT exports from Portugal to Germany fell by 47 per cent. Similarly, inward investment levels in Portugal in the T&C filière declined after 1991 and also employment decreased from 431,000 in 1991 to 332,500 in the middle of 1995. These contractions are likely to be reinforced by the opening of the Asian textile markets in the course of the last round of GATT liberalisation.

However, this period of contraction should not be seen as a total decline in the fortunes of the clothing production system, particularly in northern Portugal. Rather, the general changes can be considered as the end of the period associated with the extensive model. The critical question will be how Portugal is able to deal with this new, more challenging situation and attempt to promote competitiveness across the dimensions that fit more easily with the position it endeavours to assume in the EU. The next sections take two different perspectives on the current situation and future evolution of the filière. The present position of Portuguese enterprises in global production networks is discussed in tandem with an examination of the reactions inside Portugal in terms of political intervention and entrepreneurial strategies.

NORTHERN PORTUGAL IN THE FASHION FILIÈRE: THE SOPHISTICATION OF THE WORKBENCH PARADIGM?

The following case study focuses on the commercial interface between Portugal and Germany for two reasons. First, Germany was – along with France – the European country with the highest proportion of OPT in the total imports from Portugal in 1986 (Marques 1992). Second, the dramatic losses in OPT exports to Germany reveal that this interface was particularly affected by the opening up of Eastern Europe. The case studies therefore try to unravel how the logic of garment production for the German market in northern Portugal is evolving in a period of rapid change.

Taking an initially static analysis, our research sought to examine how responsibility for the product is distributed among the agents involved in the particular production chain and the criteria that are utilised to determine that responsibility. Hence, the agents involved comprise the client (who is the agent selling the fashion products into the German market), the Portuguese producer and an intermediate agent who establishes the link between them.

A general finding from this case study research is that the crucial variable for the distribution of responsibility is the quality or design level of the product. As the quality level increases, the responsibility taken by the Portuguese agent decreases (Table 6.1). Thus, at the high-quality end of the market, the factories only carry out CMT operations. Brands associated with a famous global designer such as Cerutti, Armani or Lagerfeld, or brands associated with enterprises operating at a high-quality level, such as Escada or MaxMara, do place orders for important batches of production from Portugal. However, these brands follow closely the process of assembly either in their own plants or in co-operation with an agent

TABLE 6.1: ROLE OF AGENTS INVOLVED REGARDING THE QUALITY LEVEL OF THE PRODUCED GARMENTS

Quality	Role of agents involved		
	Client	*Intermediate agent*	*Factory*
High	• management of the garment/design or design translation		• CMT operation in a client-owned enterprise
	• foreign investment		
	• management of the garment/design or design translation	• selection of factories • technical assistance • quality control	• subcontracted CMT operation
Medium	• design and purchase	• organisation of purchase of raw material • quality control at all stages of production • maintenance of subcontracting network	• full-price operation with several factories involved in one product
	• design and purchase	• quality control final product	• full-price operation • purchase of raw material • maintenance of subcontracting works
	• purchase	• design • maintenance of subcontracting network • purchase of raw material • quality control generally at all stages of production	• full-price operations or CMT, depending on stage of production • several factories involved
Low	• purchase		• management of the garment/design

Source: Authors' research

who guarantees quality control and the reliability of the enterprises in the subcontracting network. The degree of co-operation density can change as the story of an Italian agent responsible for Armani, among others, shows. For several years the agent himself owned a share in one of the factories, as it was claimed that otherwise he was not able to guarantee the required quality level. Furthermore, the agent temporarily provided the factories with Italian technicians for training and technical assistance (authors' interview 1997).

At the medium quality level, Portuguese manufacturers contribute with a 'full-price operation'. The client only provides the design pattern, while the intermediate agent generally undertakes the organisation and co-ordination of the production process, including the translation of design patterns into production. The notion of 'full price' means that the total financial responsibility is borne by the manufacturer. Thus, a full-price operation is a normal market transaction in financial terms, although it entails a dense co-operation in terms of product development. This level displays both the greatest regularity in all the operations that occur within it and the highest degree of differentiation among them. Such differentiation depends on the involvement of the agent, which in some cases even undertakes product development independently.

At the lower end of the market, the Portuguese enterprise tends to take full responsibility for the garment, with the clients buying final products according to their needs. There is little necessity for intensive quality control and the role of the intermediate agent in the value chain is redundant. The tenth-largest German mail order retailer Klingel, for instance, buys from Portugal in this way (authors' interview 1996).

It is clear that this systematic typology tends to overgeneralise. For instance, the knitted clothing is one of the most important segments within Portuguese garment manufacturing and is almost exclusively a full-price operation, independent from the quality level, owing to the local tradition in cotton and related yarn production. However, this classification scheme provides a useful insight and means of analysing the general structure of the logic of the spatial division of labour within the clothing filière.

Taking now the dynamic perspective, our case study research sought to examine how the current dynamics identified earlier in the overall filière are manifest in Portugal. The case studies highlight that Portugal is affected substantially by both centrifugal and centripetal dynamics, thereby at the same time attracting new and losing old activities.

Therefore, on the one hand, there exists a tendency to attribute a more sophisticated role to Portugal because of external and internal reasons. Fashion enterprises in the Western European markets are seeking cost savings by externalising more complex tasks to their suppliers in low-wage countries. Simultaneously, the production system in Portugal has undergone a process of upgrading, in response to the pressure of strong competition from other low-wage producers in Europe. In the case of knitwear manufacturing, for example, Portugal's quality levels are now considered comparable with Italy (authors' interview 1997). In this sense, the purchase of garments 'designed in Portugal' by retailers in the German lower middle market represents this 'centrifugal logic' not only through bypassing the agent in the value chain, but also by replacing the retailer's own design department through establishing subcontractors and design functions in the buying department (authors' interview 1996). Likewise, the gradual substitution of domestic production by production in Portugal on the part of German manufacturing firms, including the collection of models, quick-response orders and the establishment of logistical hubs (e.g. MaxMara), can be considered a step towards greater sophistication.

Whereas northern Portugal reveals its notable gains in the high-quality end of the market, the centrifugal dynamic appears to have disadvantaged the medium-quality level. Here, the competition with other low-wage producers clearly has repercussions in the production system. The loss of the majority of OPT operations in this segment has been a first step in this direction. The shift of the knitwear middle market to Africa is likely to occur in future years; first experiences with Portuguese-based agencies are already occurring with T-shirt production in Zimbabwe and the former Portuguese colonies (authors' interview 1996).

In the middle market, on the other hand, Portugal is benefiting from a centripetal, 'back-to-the-markets' dynamic. Many of the big retail chains, which until recently had sourced exclusively from the Far East, have attempted to take advantage of Portugal's proximity by relocating their production activities. Up to the end of the 1980s, Esprit, for example, exclusively ordered from Asian countries. Owing to the changing nature and pressure of markets demand, they were finally forced to 're-Europeanise' their buying policy. In the knitwear sector, European manufacturers have in the meantime obtained a 30 per cent share of the total Esprit garments, half of which are sourced from Portugal. Esprit buyers stressed the importance of quality as the central advantage of Portuguese producers in comparison with similarly located competitors (authors' interview 1996).

This example reveals the 'double role' that the northern Portuguese production system tends to play in the map of clothing production and knitwear is probably the paradigmatic example for this tendency. Quick responses to market changes entail a certain degree of design orientation. This combination of quality with proximity to Western European markets due to the concurrence of current centrifugal and centripetal dynamics in the fashion filière appears to make Portugal particularly apt to assume a role as a relatively high-quality, quick-response producer. A possible future scenario for garment production in Portugal, at least at the medium-quality level, could be a combination of different roles, with quick-response operations being carried out there and long lead-time orders (three to four months) sourced from northern or central Africa (authors' interview 1997). However, further developments are problematic to foresee due to the turbulent rapidly changing and uncertain environment in which changes in clothing production occur.

'INTERNAL' POLITICAL AND ENTREPRENEURIAL STRATEGIES: REDEFINING THE EXTENSIVE MODEL?

This section examines the strategies of government and industry that have attempted to create and maintain the competitiveness and redefine the position of Portuguese T&C in the wider economy. It focuses on two levels: the programmes and support mechanisms provided by the Ministry of Industry, and the reactions and priorities of the entrepreneurs within the T&C filière.

To assist manufacturing industry face the challenges related to its integration into the European Union, the Ministry of Industry created the Specific Programme to Develop Portuguese Industry (PEDIP). It was designed as an attempt to overcome a wide range of shortcomings in the Portuguese industrial infrastructure. The main objective was to set in train a modernisation process that was made difficult by the outdated equipment and low levels of investment in the last few decades. With the support of European structural funds, it became the most important instrument of modernisation of the economic structure. PEDIP was established to run between 1988 and 1992, but its budget (228 billion escudos) was exhausted before the end of this period.

While PEDIP targeted the manufacturing sector as a whole, the T&C industries benefited greatly in terms of investment from the programme. They represented almost 24 per cent of the approved projects and 18 per cent of the total investments in the manufacturing sector during this period. However it is quite clear that from a wide range of items which include infrastructures, qualification of labour, product innovation and so on, firms concentrated their strategy on modernisation of the production equipment supported by the sub-programme SINPEDIP. The majority (56 per cent) of PEDIP investments in the T&C industry were concentrated on the acquisition of equipment while only 1 per cent went towards the development of research and product development.

It is also evident that PEDIP was unevenly distributed among T&C firms in terms of sector, size and region. In 1989, although clothing firms accounted for half the firms in the T&C sector, textile companies benefited from 63 per cent of the projects and 77 per cent of investments made in the remit of PEDIP I. This is due mainly to the capital-intensiveness of spinning and weaving activities as well as the high degree of obsolescence of productive equipment in textile manufacturing. PEDIP investments were also disproportionately concentrated among the larger firms, which are in a better position to prepare projects, to access funds and to contract better loan conditions with the private banks. Small-firm owners were frequently unable either to manage the complexity of the process or to provide their own financial contribution to the investment. In terms of regional distribution, PEDIP investment has exacerbated the existing concentration of the filière. Two *distritos*, Porto and Braga, accounted for more than 70 per cent of the total projects and 83 per cent of the investment – perhaps because the larger textile and clothing firms are located in these areas.

Therefore, although representing a crucial phase in the support of the modernisation of Portuguese manufacturing industries, PEDIP I was selective and only addressed the traditionally dominant and not necessarily most dynamic firms. That is, besides the strong focus on productive equipment that neglected the qualitative aspects of the necessary restructuring in research and product development, small garment manufacturing firms only benefited from the financial support in a limited way. In addition, the massive regional concentration implied that the necessary diversification of industrial structure in those regions that specialised in the T&C filière did not happen, and the 'industrial monoculture' was sustained (Quaternaire Portugal 1995: 234). Last, the policy programmes did not address the increasing diversity within the filière reflected in the case studies discussed above. The fashion business in northern Portugal in the meantime consists of a growing diversity of various types of organisations, products and positions in international networks.

Some elements of recognition of these evident weaknesses can be seen in the programmes following PEDIP I. Most importantly, PEDIP II represents a qualitative shift from a primary focus on technological equipment towards a more strategic approach. It includes programmes designed to improve the strategies of the enterprises including marketing and the transfer of technology. PEDIP II also seeks to facilitate the design and development of new products, improve quality, preserve the environment and improve working conditions.

Similarly, in response to Portugal's structural fragility and the probable scenarios of the evolution of the T&C industries in Europe, the government created the Modernisation Program for Textile and Clothing Industries (PMIT) included in the Community Support Framework of European Policy for Portugal between 1995 and 1999. The Community Initiative for the Textiles and Clothing Industry (RETEX) is one of the most important instruments in this program, contributing both to the restructuring of T&C industries and also to the diversification of the industrial structure of the regions heavily dependent upon them. RETEX is a community initiative funded with 500 million ECUs, of which Portugal will receive 38 per cent.

The introduction of the Programme to Support Internationalisation of Portuguese Firms (PAIEP) can be seen as a reaction to the increasing external dependence of the clothing industry, as mirrored not only in subcontracting activities but also in the increasing penetration of the home market by international fashion chains. Thus, the government is actively supporting those firms that reveal an intent to set up operations abroad or to export their own brands from Portugal.

The reactions and strategies of the Portuguese entrepreneurs in the T&C filière were examined through postal survey research. Despite a small sample, it is possible to draw out some key issues from the findings. The research sought to gather information from the owners and/or managers of a sample of T&C companies in Portugal concerning their managerial and operational strategies, the use of technology within their organisations and their perceptions of their priorities and difficulties in the context of increased competition. Many of the firms were aware of the necessary strategies and actions to redefine Portugal's position – many cited the need for specialisation, improved quality and updating managerial and technological systems as crucial.

However, the ways in which the changing attitudes among the T&C filière entrepreneurs will be transformed into improved economic performance may to a large extent depend upon their size, region and position in the subcontracting chain. This is particularly true in terms of access to information and funds from the policy instruments discussed above. As can be seen from the case studies, each firm endeavours to obtain a position in the international production network which corresponds to its specific capability or capabilities. In this context development trajectories are uneven and unequal. Whereas there is a clearly evident general tendency towards upgrading within the filière, there also appears to be potential evidence of business failure (e.g. a high number of the questionnaires were 'returned to sender') and the further diffusion of garment manufacturing into low-wage rural markets (Dudleston and Pires 1996).

The case studies have also revealed that intermediate agencies tend to play a decisive role in the modernisation of the sector, not only by establishing the manufacturers' link to external markets but also by actively contributing to the sophistication of the Portuguese part in the production chain. Thus, while acting as mere buying agencies in the extensive model-period, they have nowadays frequently transformed themselves into complex order managers (Domingues 1993: 388) that have even begun in some cases to launch their own designs for Western European markets. Also, some of the larger T&C manufacturers are taking the initiative and setting up or expanding operations abroad. A notable example of the success of this is Maconde, one of Portugal's leading T&C companies, which has started to set up franchise stores in Spain.

It is evident that policy-makers and industrialists have undertaken strategies to redefine Portugal's position in the EU and the role of the Portuguese T&C activities in the global filière. There has been a clear change of attitudes amongst policy-makers and the economic agents as they identify their competitive edge and key success factors, like quality, product innovation and quick response to improve delivery time. Nevertheless, many problems remain in the T&C industry and it is still unclear how it will be possible to transform a traditionally rural industrial sector into a competitive cluster successfully involved in international clothing networks. The extensive model brought a relatively short period of such a successful involvement, but at the same time created severe problems of external dependence and precariousness. At present, policy instruments and programmes seriously need to take into account the internal and external dynamics of the filière as well as the structural diversity of the sector in order to develop appropriate intervention.

CONCLUSION: SEMI-PERIPHERAL RESTRUCTURING IN GLOBAL FILIÈRES

This chapter has sought to show how the 'global shift' of the textile and clothing filière both interacts with and changes national and local/regional productive systems. We started our case study of Portugal with the assumption that the current changes in the global filière may benefit the European Periphery since it has a combination of relatively low production costs and a high degree of responsiveness to Western European markets. That is, we argued that semi-peripheral countries appear to be particularly suited to cope with the opposing forces characterising the spatial dynamic of the fashion value chain.

At first glance, our arguments have been confirmed by the empirical cases. Both centrifugal and centripetal dynamics are clearly visible in the production system in Portugal. Yet the case studies also provide a more detailed view of how these conflicting dynamics have been interacting within the national filière and demonstrate that by no means are there only positive impacts.

Thus, in relation to the theoretical terms developed in section two, Portugal was affected by a first wave of the centrifugal dynamic after its economy was opened in the 1960s. The inward investment attracted at that time, along with the restructuring of the traditional textile industry in the 1970s, constituted the basis for the extensive growth model of clothing manufacturing in the rural hinterland of Oporto, which started with Portugal's accession to the European Community in 1986. At present, the centrifugal tendency in the global filière is continuing to shape the regional production system, but at the same time these changes are being overlaid by the opposing centripetal dynamic. Both trends challenge the extensive model of 'growth without modernisation', since they have caused the loss of purely low-cost-based activities and the demand for a more sophisticated involvement of Portuguese firms in international transactions.

Hence, northern Portuguese clothing manufacturers are forced to adapt their activities to this new situation, either through finding more demanding roles in existing subcontracting networks or even by placing their own products on international markets, the latter being more likely in low design quality segments. Success stories such as Maconde – although important for the development of the overall sector – may remain exceptions, at least over the medium term. The main change may be that there is no longer any single best way or model for economic co-ordination that could guarantee competitiveness and could be pursued as part of a guaranteed growth process in the second half of the 1980s.

Policy, however, is also diversifying its support activities. After an exclusively technology-oriented PEDIP I that accompanied the extensive-model period, current support programmes are following a more qualitative approach, focusing upon diversification of the regional economic base, assistance in internationalisation, product development and so on. What is clearly missing is an explicit commitment to the sophistication of subcontracting activities, or, in other words, an approach that addresses upgrading across all the constituent dimensions of the prevailing development trajectory. So far, this huge subcontracting segment is dealt with through private intermediaries that play a decisive role in the modernisation of Portuguese garment producers.

Apart from the fact that the global fashion map is a dynamic field and the general future of the filière in Portugal is therefore hardly foreseeable, the regional impact of the ongoing modernisation processes in the rural hinterland of Oporto remains unclear. That is, the increasing sophistication of enterprises' involvement in global networks requires a growing degree of professionalism not compatible with the strong integration of manufacturing within a rural, household-based and diffuse territorial structure. Recent consultancy studies of the sector even call for an 'urban recentring' (Quaternaire Portugal 1995: 248), supported by a centralising infrastructure policy. At the same time, however, the diffusion into the relatively low-wage labour markets is continuing in an attempt to keep assembly costs down. Thus, further detailed research of the social environment of clothing manufacturing is needed so as to unravel the logic through which the rural environment is adapting to the new challenges.

NOTES

1. Between 1980 and 1989, employment in clothing manufacturing in all statistically comparable OECD countries decreased by 20.9 per cent (Audet 1996). According to Scheffer (1994), the 'produced abroad' or sub-contracted part of the overall clothing production in six studied EU countries, increased from 28 per cent to 40 per cent between 1983 and 1992.

2. There is similar legislation in the US covering the Maquiladors operation on the USA–Mexico border that has fostered the emergence of millions of jobs particularly in the assembly of cars, electronic components and apparel (Glasmeier et al. 1993).

3. Portugal's total exports to the EU 15 increased between 1960 and 1990 from 37.3 per cent to 73.9 per cent, while exports to the former colonies decreased from 25.6 per cent to 3.4 per cent (Freund 1995: 287).

4. However, these more 'qualitative' preconditions for internationalisation were at that time mainly limited to the knitwear sector, which could make use of the traditional cotton production system.

5. For a profound insight into the interplay between diffuse territorial structure and economic development in the North-West of Portugal, see Domingues and Sá Marques (1987) among others.

PART III:
INDUSTRIAL AND REGIONAL INSTITUTIONS AND POLICY

7 Local Institutional Responses for Innovation and Technology: Comparative Evidence from the UK and Germany

INTRODUCTION

The aim of this chapter is to provide a comparative analysis of some of the institutional responses for innovation and technology (I&T) in two European localities. They are South-West Wales in the UK, and the eastern part of the Ruhrgebiet situated in North Rhine Westphalia in Germany. Both of these localities continue to face economic problems associated with the decline of traditional industries and have attempted to address these issues through the introduction of new growth strategies based in part on innovation and technology (see DTI 1998b; National Assembly for Wales 1999). Commentators claim increasingly that regional or local institutions, particularly those of the public sector (Gregersen 1992), are central to the effective provision of such strategies (see, for example, Landabaso 1995; Callon 1995).

The chapter explores the institutional approaches to innovation and technology in South-West Wales and the eastern Ruhrgebiet, as part of the wider debate (see Jessop 1992; Jessop and Hay 1995; Painter and Goodwin 1995).[1] As this debate has been based primarily in the context of developments in the UK, it is necessary to determine the extent to which the shift towards *governance* is evident in the German case. This chapter draws on empirical evidence from an intensive, interview-based study of local governance in South-West Wales conducted in 1995,[2] and studies of regional policy and innovation networks in Germany (Ache 1994, 1998). Although each of the two country studies was undertaken to a different research agenda, they provide evidence to enable a comparative analysis of the local institutional structures and processes for economic development and, more specifically, innovation and technology. The argument in this chapter is structured as follows. First, the conceptual context for the analysis is established, based on a discussion of the perceived shift from government to governance for local economic development. Second, the organisational structures, policy processes and economic strategies adopted in each locality are presented, focusing on the innovation and technology elements of each approach. Last, the summary and conclusions are outlined.

LOCAL GOVERNANCE FOR INNOVATION AND TECHNOLOGY (I&T)

Interest in 'local economic governance' in the UK in particular has developed particularly since the 1980s and lies with several interlocking developments. First, the role of local government in undertaking local economic development initiatives has increased and expanded (Cochrane 1990). Second, there has been an increase in the number and range of Non-Departmental Public Bodies (NDBPs) or 'quangos' in the area of economic development (Morgan and Roberts 1993). Third, the devolution agenda has raised issues concerning the nature of subnational governance (Leach 1994; Osmond 1994; Murphy and Caborn 1995).

Conceptually, such developments have been expressed in terms of a fundamental change in local economic governance, including: a shift from 'government' to 'governance' with the increased responsibility of non-elected, local agencies for the delivery and management of services; a reordering of relationships between government and their agencies; and a reduction in the role of central government together with an increase in the role of local partnerships (Jessop and Hay 1995: 22).

Given the needs for comparative analysis of the UK and Germany, such developments in local economic governance must be seen in the context of the national system of governance. It is well established that there are different country models with respect to their mode of regulation, just as there are different national systems of innovation (Nelson 1993; Braczyk *et al.* 1998). In terms of regulation models, the capitalism evident in the UK is regarded as neo-liberal and centralised, while that in West-Germany is seen as negotiated, close to the 'Kalmarian' system of Sweden (Rogers *et al.* 1994; Berger and Dore 1996; Hodgson 1999). Critical to the discussion of regulation models have been their respective 'technological-institutional systems', which are evident in particular historical phases and geographical areas (see Storper and Scott 1992). In particular, the mode of regulation that is claimed to provide 'the best possible political shell' for *contemporary* economic structures of post-Fordism is that of the Schumpetarian workfare state (SWS), (Peck and Tickell 1995: 293; Jessop 1992). Again, this is characterised according to different country models. Critically for this chapter is the central role for innovation and technology (I&T) in this mode of regulation, as suggested by the Schumpetarian label. The SWS framework has received criticism because of

its preliminary and rather speculative status, [the concerns] about the precise theoretical character of the arguments so far deployed in defense of the SWS, the dangers of operating with a simple dualistic contrast between the KWS (Keynesian welfare state) and the SWS, and the issue of the real empirical and practical scope of the overall argument. (Jessop 1992: 20)

Despite this uncertainty and current flux in the precise nature of future forms of governance, it does appear clear that *local governance* is strategically significant in the provision and support of *innovation and technology* activities. In functional terms, such activities may include: the provision of infrastructure (especially new information and communication technologies); support for innovation and training; place marketing for inward investment (part of which involves supporting the R&D requirements of foreign firms); the development of 'local (I&T) capacity' and the formation of networks for I&T (based on Table 6.1 in Painter *et al.* 1995: 10).

Such strategic developments including the local governance structure appear to be compatible with the requirements of contemporary, post-Fordist forms of capital accumulation. In many countries, attempting to repeat the localised innovation and technology of Silicon Valley has become a popular strategy (Keeble and Wilkinson 1999). However, the success of such simple 'duplication' methods is far from apparent (see Markusen, Chapter 2 in this volume). Indeed it has been suggested that a key factor inhibiting this translation and adaptation process may be the *different 'local governance' structures* that exist within the *different state forms of regulation in different local economies.*[3] In order to gain a better understanding of the role of governance structures and the particular institutional responses to I&T evident in different localities, it is therefore important to undertake more specific empirical investigation. The remainder of this chapter takes up this focus of analysis.

THE TWO CASE STUDY LOCALITIES

The focus of the UK case is the locality of South-West Wales. This is compared with the German study of the eastern part of the Ruhrgebiet (comprising the city of Dortmund, the county of Unna and the city of Hamm – henceforth DUH). Both of these localities are important components of wider 'regions' that have been the focus for a number of studies upon which the following account is based (for South-West Wales see Cooke 1995; Morgan and Roberts 1993, Painter *et al.* 1995; for North Rhine Westphalia (NRW) Ruhrgebiet see Kilper 1994; Ache 1994, 1998). Although each of the authors' studies were conducted separately and to different agendas, they provide some insight into the conceptual nature of local governance for I&T and enable a comparative discussion about the concrete experience in two localities.

South-West Wales is defined here as including three of the unitary authorities which emerged as a result of the reorganisation of local government in Wales in 1995 (see Boyne *et al.* 1995). The area includes the County of Swansea, Neath and Port Talbot County Borough, and the County of Bridgend. In turn, the boundaries of DUH are constituted by the two cities of Dortmund and Hamm and by the county of Unna, all located at the eastern end of the Ruhrgebiet. The region was established as one of 15 during the latest phase of regional policy in NRW. The boundaries of this territory cover the area of the local Chamber of Industry and Commerce (Kruse 1991).

There are important economic differences between the two regions and localities (see Tables 7.1 and 7.2). The first difference is their size. South-West Wales is much smaller in terms of area and population, with a lower GDP and higher unemployment rate than DUH (Table 7.1). However, the activity rates and the *proportion* of the population which is of a working age are similar.

TABLE 7.1: COMPARISON OF BASIC ECONOMIC INDICATORS AT THE LEVEL OF THE REGION AND THE CASE STUDY LOCALITY

Region	Population	Population of working age (%)	Unemployment rate (%)	GDP (ecus m)
Wales	2.9m	63	9.6	27.4
NRW	17m	41	10.3	340 000
Locality:				
South-West Wales	c. 360 000 (population of working age c. 256 000)	61	c. 10–12	c. 85% of the national UK average
DUH	1.2m	65.7	13.8	114.4

Various sources and various years, including: 1991 Census; Regional Trends CSO; Department of Employment 1994; 1991 Regional Planning Report of the Federal Republic of Germany; 1996, March, Regional information Ruhrgebiet, KVR; 1991/92 West Glamorgan County Guide 1992; EC 1994 A study of prospects in the Atlantic regions; 1995 Annual Report, Chamber of Industry and Commerce, Dortmund; Figures for July 1997 range between 12.9% for Hamm, Unna, and 16.6% for Dortmund; EC 1994b Periodic Report, EC, the figure covers the Regierungspräsidium Arnsberg, of which DUH forms only one part.

TABLE 7.2: COMPARISON OF BASIC ECONOMIC INDICATORS FOR NORDRHEIN-WESTFALEN AND WALES

Region	Ages 15–64 as % of population[1]	Activity rate[1] (%)	Unemployment rate[2] (%)	GDP/per inhabitant[3]
Wales	64.4	47.3	9.7	83.2
Nordrhein-Westfalen	69.9	46	6.6	110.8

Source: EC 1994b *Competitiveness and Cohesion in the Regions* (Table A27: 198–202)

Notes: 1 Figures are for 1990; 2 Figures are for 1993; 3 The 3-year average for 1989–91 in the EUR12 was 100.

South-West Wales has experienced a major restructuring of its industrial base, which has accelerated in recent decades. The long-run demise of the 'capitalism' of coal-mining, steel-making and heavy engineering that propelled growth from the late 19th century has been replaced to an extent by recent waves of inward investment (Painter *et al.* 1995: 15). The steel industry is still in existence, albeit in a rationalised form, and British Steel (now Corus) remains the largest single employer at its Port Talbot site. Recent inward investment has been concentrated in the automotive components and electronics sectors although overall the public and private service sector has become the main source of economic activity in the locality. Despite such activities, there remain significant economic problems associated with the adjustment to large-scale economic restructuring experienced in recent decades.

The picture in DUH is rather more mixed. Between 1980 and 1994 the total labour force fell by about 4.2 per cent in the region as a whole, with Dortmund losing jobs, while Unna and Hamm experienced slight job gains (KVR 1996). The production and processing sector revealed the steepest declines, while services increased. In common with South-West Wales, such changes may be indicative of a structural change towards a service economy. Compared with other German cities, especially those with similar functions or roles in the urban hierarchy, the respective structural change remains relatively lower than that experienced in the leading centres. Such cities have higher and faster-growing shares of service activity. As a result, relatively high unemployment remains a problem in Dortmund (15 per cent) and Unna (11 per cent), with long-term unemployment becoming more significant (Ache 1994). These developments have to be understood in the context of the major structural changes experienced by the Ruhrgebiet in recent decades. The downturn of the coal and steel industries and the high degree of dependency on those industries has affected jobs in almost every sector and branch of the regional economy. Between 1964 and 1992, nearly 600,000 jobs were lost in industry, with half of them in the mining and steel sector. Consequently, unemployment rates in the Ruhrgebiet are among the highest in Germany including the new former East German Länder.

A COMPARATIVE ANALYSIS OF LOCAL GOVERNANCE FOR I&T

Although there are economic differences between the two localities then, they both face similar economic problems and have both sought to address the question of regional renewal through reorganisation of the local governance structures for I&T. This is evident in recent key policy documents, where the National Assembly for Wales (1999) suggests that initiatives 'should build upon existing domestic programmes such as the Regional Technology Plan, which has the aim of improving the innovation and technology performance of the Welsh economy'. The focus on the role of local governance structures in delivering such I&T objectives forms the basis for the subsequent discussion using evidence from the two localities. Here, the term 'local governance' not only refers to organisational or institutional structures, but also describes the relationships between organisations and the processes through which strategies may be delivered. As such, this comparative discussion of the two localities not only focuses on the organisational composition of local governance, but also explores the key strategies and processes of delivery.

ORGANISATIONAL STRUCTURE FOR I&T

The Institutional Structure in Wales

The Welsh Office (recently replaced by the National Assembly for Wales) played a central and distinctive role in the governance of South-West Wales (Boyne *et al.* 1991, 1995; Madgwick and James 1980; Morgan and Roberts 1993). Formerly, there were departments of the Welsh Office relating specifically to the innovation and technology aspects of economic development, including: the Industrial Development Division, among whose responsibilities were the Regional Enterprise Grants and Innovation Grants aimed at small firms wishing to invest or innovate, and the Business Services Division whose functions included the areas of technology transfer and R&D.

The Welsh Office's role was complemented by the Welsh Development Agency (WDA), which was central to economic development in Wales, although I&T activities are a fairly recent addition to its role, co-ordinated and delivered through its Technology and Innovation Group. The increased emphasis on I&T was prompted by massive cuts in UK regional aid throughout the 1980s in particular, and a growing competition throughout Europe to attract inward investment. As Morgan (1995: 27) points out, 'The WDA set about revising its traditional strategy to set a higher premium on the "soft" infrastructure of business support services, technology transfer, [and] skills development' for both small and medium enterprises (SMEs) and foreign-owned firms. The WDA has been decentralised to three main regional offices, including the West Wales Development Agency, which is currently based in Swansea in South-West Wales. This implies a potentially *local* presence 'thereby bringing the Agency closer to its customers in the field' (Morgan 1994a: 9).

There are a number of other local organisations which operate mainly in the area of economic development. Among these are West Wales TEC and the further education (FE) colleges, that are involved in training and education, as well as the universities and technical centres that have R&D and technical expertise and involvement. Local government provides some more general economic development and business-related services that overlap and complement I&T activities. The WDA Technology and Innovation Group works with the universities in the development of 'centres of expertise'. There are also several local innovation and technology counsellors (ITCs) working with the Business Connect business support agencies, for example in Neath and Swansea. However, although there seems to be growing involvement by some organisations in the provision of I&T support, there is limited evidence of any local organisation in South-West Wales developing an explicit function in terms of I&T.

State Organisations in Germany

The South-West Wales situation can be contrasted with the experience in Germany, where there is a distinct structure of state organisations from the *Land* government of NRW through to the local level of DUH. Each level has a functional remit that is clearly set out. First and most important is the *Land* government level, where technological issues are constantly on the agenda. Since the introduction of the first programmes aimed at structural change in the region, technology was of major importance, including for example the establishment of the regional universities in the late 1960s. Subsequently, an extended technology infrastructure has been established, particularly since the early 1980s. The importance of the government in this respect is epitomised by the landmark speech of the Ministerpresident of 1990 entitled 'Managing Ecological and Economic Renewal', that launched the discussion and scientific work on the importance of environmental industries and strategies to develop clusters in this sector (Nordhause-Janz and Rehfeld 1991).

In addition to the *Land* government, the main actor in the field of I&T is the Ministry for Economy, SMEs, Technology and Traffic (MWMTV), which is responsible for formulating final programmes in detail and delivering services. Here, in-house policies are designed, co-ordinated and managed, and financial subsidies – EU, Federal and *Land* – co-ordinated. Other important arms of government are the Science and Education Ministry, responsible for the universities, and especially the Ministry for Social Matters, Gender and Qualification (previously MAGS, since 1998 MSKSS). MSKSS provides the labour-related programmes in the system, aimed at improving the skills and qualifications of the labour force.

At the local level, the organisations operating I&T policies are the regional conferences and the local authority departments that are responsible for economic promotion. The regional conferences are the most recent institutions in the structure of designing and discussing the policies in this field. Regional conferences and local authorities both have to be considered as independent from the first, ministerial layer, as local authorities have a constitutional right to design their own economic promotion strategies. However, in the final instance local authorities remain dependent upon the resources available at the *Land* level.

Alongside the public sector institutions are a number of other organisations, forming the Network of Technology Infrastructure that encompasses, at the *Land* level, 150 different institutes, offices and initiatives (MWMT 1993a).

The core of this network consists of about 60 technology centres, 50 transfer offices, 26 technology agencies, 31 R&D centres, 34 higher education institutes, and 12 technology initiatives. Within this complex, ZENIT plays a somewhat exceptional role as a centre for innovation and technology, market research unit, business consultant and technology 'expert'. Being a public–private partnership between the *Land* government, the house bank of the *Land* and about 100 SMEs, ZENIT, which was established in the early 1980s, is responsible for the assessment of I&T projects suggested under the I&T related programmes in NRW. The network also incorporates the Technology Consultancy NRW (TBNW), with private consultants and university academics giving technology advice to SMEs. All of these institutes are spread throughout NRW but concentrate their activities on the Ruhrgebiet. DUH can, in turn, be seen as a marked local concentration of that Network of Technology Infrastructure, thanks especially to the University of Dortmund with its neighbouring technology centre and technology park that accommodates approximately 40 R&D institutions.

At first glance, the Network of Technology Infrastructure seems to be functionally and geographically comprehensive. However, its decentralised structure has led to problems of duplication where there may be an excess of activities and institutions with no clear-cut agenda nor any quality control in service delivery. This critical concern has been partly reflected in the *Land* government's new policy approach, which focused more on network building, creating synergy and enhancing specialism amongst the existing organisations.

COMPARISON BETWEEN WALES AND GERMANY

What is most evident from the case of Germany, for example, is that a number of organisations are explicitly involved in innovation and technology functions. This is a clear point of departure from the locality in Wales, where there are few organisations which have an explicit role in terms of I&T. Innovation and technology issues, at best, form part of their wider economic development remit.

Second, there are clear differences between the two cases in terms of the geographic distribution of organisations with an I&T function. In Wales, the issue of reaching all localities via the current organisational structure is made difficult by the lack of congruity between the geographic boundaries of the TECs and the West Wales Development Agency. The experience is different in the German case, where at an operational level – although there are some gaps in provision – there appears to be a fairly even distribution of organisations involved in I&T throughout the Ruhrgebiet and DUH, notwithstanding the recent political changes.

PROCESSES FOR THE PROVISION OF I&T SUPPORT AND STRATEGIES

Having examined the organisational structures, we now focus on the main processes used in the provision of strategies and support to address I&T needs in the two European localities.

Formal Delivery Systems in Wales

At a broad level of analysis in Wales, there appears to be a comprehensive system for the delivery of certain economic development services at the local level. However, based on discussions with representatives from a range of organisations, the evidence suggests that some activities, such as European grant applications, are duplicated in the overall pattern of service provision with organisations competing to provide particular services:

> There is a real danger when you have enterprise agencies, the careers service, education-business partnerships, all the local authorities – that we all go off and reinvent the wheel, we all do our own thing which will waste resources. Somewhere there needs to be a strategic view. (Authors' interview 1997)

Elsewhere, other activities such as those relating to small firms have been less well represented in the overall pattern of service provision. For example, support for the promotion of 'enterprise' amongst small firms in particular has, until recently, been deficient – as one WDA representative, again from the South-West Wales study, suggested 'one of the problems with the TEC is that the "enterprise" hasn't come through in Wales, we rely on the enterprise agencies to fill that need' (authors' interview 1995). The lack of provision of I&T services in particular was also clearly evident in Wales until recently. This is now being addressed through a range of events and activities prompted by introduction of the part EU-funded Regional Innovation and Technology Transfer Strategy (RITTS) and Regional Technology Plan for Wales (WDA 1996; Morgan 1997).

Some commentators see the introduction of the Welsh Assembly (Osmond 1994) as potentially providing the necessary strategic co-ordination and management for service provision, such as for economic development and, more specifically, I&T. Although the National Assembly for Wales was instituted in 1999, its success may depend on both an economic development strategy and processes for implementing such a policy. As Murphy and Caborn (1995) have argued in their analysis in the English regions,

> unless we weave some regional economic realities into the political structures we propose, those political structures will not produce results: [w]hat we need in Wales, therefore, is not a regional policy geared to reproducing the past (with low skill, low paid jobs), but an innovation strategy that can begin to chart a more rewarding form of economic development in the future.

Indeed, part of the National Assembly's Single Programming Document for West Wales and the Valleys (<http://www.wales.gov.uk> 1999) is a measure to 'encourage and develop innovation and R&D'. Thus, the Assembly may provide these necessary strategic-level mechanisms to respond to I&T needs and to modernise the existing organisational structures outlined earlier – although, until the National Assembly has been in place long enough to prove itself, it is too early to say whether it is up to the task.

Formal Delivery Systems in Germany

In contrast to the Welsh case, rather more formal delivery mechanisms for services exist in NRW. As described above, a variety of governmental and local authority, as well as public–private, institutions exist which support and define I&T strategies and services to differing degrees. The MWMTV is the central actor in the system, setting up the programmes and defining the concrete aims according to political decisions, and providing higher-level services. The most important means in this context are programmes. Up to the beginning of 1990, the overall landscape of programmes amounted to 120 or so different programmes and initiatives. At the beginning of the 1990, the *Land* government started a major reorganisation, primarily because this abundance of programmes was detrimental to transparency. Now, through *Impulse für die Wirtschaft*, an umbrella programme has been established to substitute and reduce old programmes and provide more focus. The programme is financed through federal, EU and *Land* level sources, and consists of several elements necessary to support economic production including economic promotion for SMEs, start-up funding and subsidies, and energy technologies and efficiency measures. A separate activity among these is innovation and technology. The technical side of project appraisal and accounting has existed since 1975, when the first Technology for the Economy programme was established. Accountability within this system is a matter of parliamentary debate and subject to rigid rules and scrutiny by the *Rechnungshof* (Audit Office).

Partnerships, Collaboration and Networking

Collaboration provides a point of similarity in relation to the local governance of I&T in South-West Wales and DUH. This is critical to I&T activities, as the European Commission claims that (CEC 1991 cited in Morgan 1995: 18):

> it is not simply the presence of units of research and technological development (RTD) infrastructure, but of the degree of interaction between them which is the most significant factor in local innovation. The quality of the linkage and the presence of local synergy is the key element. Therefore a systems or network approach provides the best basis for understanding and promoting regional RTD-based innovation.

South-West Wales

It appears that partnerships, collaboration and networks in South-West Wales have tended to be based on local activities and interpersonal relationships between local agents. The promotion of 'active partnerships' for economic development is evident in the 'Team Wales' approach, promoted by the former Welsh Office, in concert with the WDA, the local authorities, TECs and enterprise agencies. Swansea County also proposes that collaboration for the provision of TEC-funded courses and integration with the Wales Business Connect Network are central to business service plans (County of Swansea 1995: 22–3). More recently, the RTP is seen to rely on 'organisations working in partnership' in order to implement the main innovation priorities in Wales (WDA 1996; Morgan 1997).

More specifically in terms of I&T, one of the most recent partnership initiatives is the European-funded Wales 'Relay Centre'. This was established by the WDA and the former Welsh Office and is a means of conveying information to firms about EU-funded science and technology exploitation opportunities. Additionally, there are 'Innovative Training' partnerships for the engineering industries, and the Engineering Centre, a partnership between a number of agencies including the former Welsh Office, the WDA, local government, TECs, firms, FE colleges and UK-level engineering bodies. The aim is to boost the number of recruits in the engineering profession (see Cooke 1995: 47). The network approach is also mentioned, as the WDA 'has sought to enhance the technology-support infrastructure in the region by promoting a network of centres of technical expertise' – these are largely university-based (Morgan 1995: 30). A Business Connect (a Welsh version of Business Link in England) has also recently been established as a network of service providers in eight localities, providing services such as 'innovation counselling' and 'innovation credits' (Cooke 1995). In terms of the use of computer-based networks, there is increasing use of the Internet and the WDA-funded EDI Awareness Centre has been established to assist Welsh companies understand and adopt EDI and Electronic Commerce.

In addition, the formation of clusters has been promoted through the WDA's Source Wales programme which supports local sourcing as part of 'a strategy designed to encourage high calibre local suppliers' (Morgan 1995: 29). It has been argued by Cooke (1995: 12), that 'there are pronounced signs in Wales that associative thinking, partnership building and encouragement of policy networks to facilitate the emergence of new industrial clusters are developing'. These include, in particular, industrial clusters in the automotive and electronics engineering industries (Cooke 1998b). While perhaps limited and not solely I&T focused, there is at least some evidence that partnerships, collaboration and networking are emerging in the local governance structure for I&T in Wales.

North Rhine Westphalia

In NRW, the remit of the network between the various technology organisations has been established to set up and extend co-operation activities and to create synergy between institutions. The tools utilised to target and concentrate the available services are the initiatives (like VIA and MEDIA) that in turn promote network formation. Co-operation and collaboration, especially between SMEs, have only entered daily practice on a slow and limited basis. In response, the *Land* government launched the Forum Zukunft Mittelstand to promote the idea of extensive co-operation not only between companies, but between companies and public bodies (Ache 1997).

However, the most explicit form of partnership and dialogue has been established at the local level in 15 regions throughout NRW, which have all been asked to set up regional conferences and regional dialogue. In DUH, the regional conference has more than 70 members. Representatives come from the main social partners with the aim of developing the regional development strategy through working groups, co-ordinated by a steering group that also manages the regional conference (REK DO 1993).

A closer look at the Regionalkonferenz Dortmund/Kreis Unna/Hamm (the Regional Conference – REK DO) and the respective *Regionales Entwicklungs-konzept* (Regional Development Strategy) provides an example of this new form of decentralised Regional Structural Policy. In the case of DUH, 23 projects constitute the priority list of activities, and of these 18 projects have been financed until now (authors' interview 1998). I&T measures, although a central element of the strategy, are embedded in a more complex set of general guidelines focused on the mobilisation of real estate, infrastructure, innovation and technology, labour market/gender/qualification, and ecological renewal/ sustainability. These areas are derived directly from a proposal provided by the ministry at the beginning of the 1990s to inform the regions about the possible content or areas with specific importance.

With respect to concrete I&T projects, the focus in DUH is developed around three priority projects: to establish a technology-based development trajectory; to create a network of centres of excellence; and to start a new industrial dialogue between the universities, further education, and consultants. While the relocation of the Dortmund polytechnic, part of the first priority project, has been denied by the ministry, the network of centres of excellence is well under way and there have been extensions of the technology centre and new initiatives at the university. The main event in terms of dialogue took the form of the Dortmund Conference in 1995. However, this meeting only included Dortmund and the regional dimension has yet to be seen.

The regional networking process has, at least for the time being, come to a halt. Dortmund, for example, departed from the network to establish its own dialogue and to develop a media industry cluster. Another activity has been set up in the field of city marketing, including European relations. The recently established media working group has been constituted around representatives from the department for economic promotion and the representatives of companies working in the media field. The Ministry, which financed a preparatory study for the city of Dortmund, is now keen to see the regional content of this new venture that has as yet to be demonstrated (authors' interview 1998). Such an independent initiative also marks a clear division between the discussion in the regional assembly on technology and innovation, and the current approach taken by individual agents towards the topic. For example, the group working on the I&T sections of the REK did not meet for more than a year. Notwithstanding the apparent success with respect to the number of projects that have already received financing, clear signs of visible change remain to be seen. Additionally, some organisations are not represented in the process of dialogue, notably the citizens' groupings and environmental movements. The results of this new form of designing and delivering regional structural policy has been assessed and widely debated (Fürst and Kilper 1995; MWMT 1993b). Division exists between those who see it as the *Land* government's incentive to retain control over the regions, and others who see it as a more positive example of partnership and dialogue.

Alongside the streamlining of programmes outlined above, another recent change has been a further refinement of programme content and structure with the general aim of encouraging *Verbund und Kooperationsansatz* (cluster and co-operation). The idea behind this is to develop industrial cluster in several areas. The most advanced initiatives are VIA for automotive suppliers and MEDIA for the information and communication industries with local foci in Cologne, Dusseldorf and, probably, in Dortmund. These initiatives are managed in a slightly different style, introducing private consultancies as the main actors responsible for spreading information, attracting project proposals, assessing and selecting projects. The *Land* government expects that the co-operation part of the initiatives will result in a renewed dialogue between industry and policy-makers, although there are fears in industry that these developments would bring further regulation. But, the *Land* government has stressed that its intention is to launch dialogue between the social partners, not to introduce further regulation. At a broad level, dialogue has become central to policy-making and delivery processes in NRW. This is reflected at the local level in DUH with the Dortmund Conference, where a priority project (*Leitprojekt*) of the regional development strategy in the field of I&T was to 'extend dialogue between universities, industry, and society'. In general, the search for dialogue does not imply that no competition exists among organisations. In fact, there is competition in the bidding for funds for specific projects. This may be seen as a positive feature in order to ensure the quality and content of the projects undertaken by particular organisations and that the customer receives the necessary availability of services.

In summary, the main evidence from NRW indicates that strategies for I&T are based on a historic experience and are characterised by learning and constant adjustment. At the local level, the picture might seem to be more complex and difficult. Here, there is clear evidence of the utilisation of regional level initiatives, but with a local concentration on local needs and assets. The resulting abundance of strategies at the local level may be detrimental with respect to focus, efficiency and inter-municipal competition in the longer term.

CONCLUSIONS: 'LOCAL GOVERNANCE' FOR I&T?

This chapter has explored the approach toward innovation and technology as part of the 'local economic governance' of two European localities – South-West Wales and the eastern part of the Ruhrgebiet, in Germany. The aim was to compare whether there are different local and regional approaches to I&T within two different national governance systems. The discussion explored some of the current developments in local governance, focusing in particular on the organisations, processes and strategies used to support I&T activities at a local level. The analysis was based on primary empirical evidence, obtained from different studies, although with common concerns and foci.

There appears to be a fundamental difference between the case studies, grounded in the different constitutional form of the two nation states. In Germany, there is an elaborate federal system while the UK retains a centrally organised and dominated system that has fundamentally shaped the Welsh system of governance. These different national governance structures have profound influence upon the organisational composition, processes and policies for economic development and I&T in the two localities studied here.

First, to focus on organisations involved in the provision of support for I&T, although there are a number of organisations in South-West Wales involved in I&T there are no *explicit* organisations for I&T. This contrasts with the DUH where there are several organisations specifically and explicitly responsible for I&T activities. In Germany there is a more formalised structure of state and other public organisations involved directly in the area of innovation and technology. Second, in terms of processes for delivering I&T support and strategies, in South-West Wales this was limited until the recent introduction of the Regional Technology Plan (RTP) and Regional Innovation and Technology Transfer Strategy (RITTS). In contrast, I&T initiatives in NRW have evolved to create the more comprehensive Network of Technology Centres, the regional conferences and regional development programmes as part of integrated approaches to structural policy. The RTP appears to have addressed the lack of an explicit I&T strategy in Wales, although the results have been relatively small scale, limited and recent, while NRW has, arguably, had a long-standing experience of focus upon I&T activities as part of regional renewal strategies.

From the preliminary view of recent developments in South-West Wales and NRW outlined in this chapter, it appears that institutions, including local agents, have experienced increased demands for their involvement in the support and development of I&T. This is evident to some extent in South-West Wales and is more embedded in the case of NRW. In NRW, the delivery of policy is based on local dialogue, which provides the ideas and projects rooted in a comprehensive strategy. In turn, the more focused initiatives are run by private consultants with technical and accounting expertise.

Thus, at first glance, there have been some shifts evident in the nature of local governance for I&T in both localities. In both cases, emphasis has been placed on the importance of partnerships, collaboration and networking between different types of government and governance agency for I&T activities. This has involved local agents – to some extent in South-West Wales, although based on a Wales-wide approach, and to a greater degree in NRW – perhaps reflecting the different economic geographies and approaches in the two areas of concern. The institution of the National Assembly for Wales may herald a shift to a more local, or at least regional and sub-national (UK), agenda. However, evidence presented here suggests that claims of a wholesale shift from government to governance are at worst overgeneralised and at best inconclusive. This is particularly true in the case of Wales, given that recent emphasis on I&T as a means for improving economic competitiveness seems to be driven heavily by central UK government through its competitiveness strategies and programming documents. The flavour of such strategies is also reflected in the Single Programming Document of the National Assembly for Wales. Further analysis is evidently required to distinguish the real nature of networking relationships and the impact of the collaborative approaches from the rhetoric of such strategy documents. Evidence from the German case suggests a still more government-shaped approach, where policy is formulated by the state at the *Land* level with explicit I&T content, and the regional conferences integrate I&T elements into their wider development strategies. Thus, the evidence explored in this chapter suggests that the role of central government in the local governance of I&T in both countries remains significant.

NOTES

1. See, in particular, work in the UK under the ESRC's 'Local Governance' Programme 1994–96.

2 South-West Wales was selected as one of three localities which formed the empirical basis for an investigation into 'British Local Governance in the Transition from Fordism' (see Painter *et al.* 1995).

3 This has been addressed in the industrial district literature (see, for example, Lagendijk 1996; Mayer 1996) which discusses the role of local regulation.

Acknowledgements
An earlier draft of this paper was presented at the 'Territorial Dimensions of Innovation' EUNIT seminar in Dortmund, 22–24 May 1996. The South-West Wales case study was based on empirical research carried out for a project under the Economic and Social Research Council's Local Governance Programme. That project was entitled 'British Local Governance in the Transition from Fordism' (grant number L311253011) (see Painter *et al.* 1995).

8 Industrial Policy in the Basque Country

INTRODUCTION

Like South-West Wales and the eastern Ruhrgebiet, the Basque Country is an old industrial region that has been struggling for decades to find a new economic role. Moreover, like the Ruhr area, the Basque Country is a European region with a high institutional density and long-standing tradition of innovation policies. This has turned the region into a laboratory for examining in detail the evolution of regional innovation policies. Where the region differs from the case studies in the previous chapter is the political dimension. In many respects, the Basque Country has a governance system typical for southern Europe. The regional state intervenes in a top-down way, only allowing for selective participation from businesses and civil groups. Institutional links and policy processes are highly politicised. That is, they are strongly informed by the particular interests and power positions of parties and individuals involved. However, this particular political culture does not prevent many policy initiatives from having a strong impact on the regional development process. Despite some radical shifts in the political complexion of the regional government, the Basque Country has been able to develop a potent technology infrastructure and powerful planning machinery that perhaps serve as an example for other European countries and beyond. Within Europe, the Basque Country presents a meeting point for researchers and policy-makers on regional innovation that appears to matched only by some German and Italian regions. Even the most critical observers of this region cannot ignore the region's appeal in this respect.

The purpose of this chapter is to review recent developments in industrial and technology policy against the background of the Basque Country's specific industrial and political history. On the one hand, the discussion will focus on the way innovation policies have changed over time, stressing the capacity of policy actors to learn from previous initiatives as well as from abroad. Particular attention will be paid to the cluster initiatives developed over the 1990s, which present an innovative approach at the intersection of technology and industry policies. On the other hand, the question is how these initiatives have been governed, and who has benefited. How and through whom were new policies conceived, developed and implemented? What has been the impact in terms of business groups, sectors and geography? While no detailed answers can be provided for all these issues, their discussion provides a more critical outlook on how innovation policy has evolved. Material for this chapter was in part provided by interviews with local experts held in September 1997.

The chapter starts by introducing the regional context for industrial and technology policy, and identifies distinct phases in policy evolution. The next two sections address the development and evaluation of the Competitiveness (cluster) programme, then comes a discussion of its links with technology policy. In the latter section, specific attention is paid to the way the 'regional innovation systems' debate has influenced thinking on regional policy in the area. The final section provides the conclusion.

THE CHALLENGE: CHANGING INDUSTRIAL AND POLITICAL CULTURE

The Basque Country entered a phase of serious industrial decline in the 1970s, and since then the region has seen a continuous flow of industrial closures, of direct support for mature industrial sectors and of regional plans geared to improving the regional economic structure. While the severity of the crisis and its persistent impact should not be understated – certain sectors and areas continue to suffer from high levels of unemployment, it is important to note that the region has undergone massive change since the 1970s. Indeed, while industry is still a prominent economic sector (Table 8.1), the Basque Country no longer fits easily into the image of a 'rustbelt ' (Cooke 1995). Not only has

TABLE 8.1: DISTRIBUTION OF EMPLOYMENT PER ACTIVITY IN 1995 (%)

Sector	EUR15	Spain	Basque C.
Agriculture	5.3	9.3	3.4
Industry	30.2	30.2	37.9
Services	64.5	60.5	58.7
Total	100.0	100.0	100.0
Unemployment (1998)	10.7	21.1	18.8

Source: EUROSTAT (1996, 1998).

the region always had strong and competitive activities outside heavy industrial sectors, such as finance and the food and drinks industry (e.g. Rioja wine), it has also managed to diversify and specialise both in industrial and non-industrial sectors. Strong industrial sectors are metallurgy and metallic products, machinery, petrol refining, food, rubber and plastic and transportation equipment (Basque Institute of Statistics 1995). Non-industrial sectors include finance and insurance, producer services, commerce and building.

Through the 1980s and 1990s, moreover, the physical infrastructure has received massive investment, especially in roads and local public transport, with more investment planned in high-speed train lines, for example. More significantly, a network of technology centres (EITE) and related business support agencies has been developed to create the Basque Network of Technology. This has made the Basque Country a leading example of good practice in regional innovation support in Europe (Table 8.2). As a result, the region's economic fabric at present can be described as more solid, competitive and outward-looking than in the years before the crisis.

These regeneration developments are also manifested in terms of wealth creation. Whereas in the 1980s the Basque Country almost hit the bottom of the league of Spanish regions in terms of growth and unemployment figures,

TABLE 8.2: COMPOSITION OF THE BASQUE TECHNOLOGY NETWORK, 1996

Network members	Employees	Turnover*	Sectors/activities	
Technology Centres (EITE)	1 021	8 579	• automotive • aeronautics • machine tools • electro-informatics • telecommunication	• environment • heavy metal • capital goods • construction • consumer goods
Sectoral and University Business R&D Centres	381	3 053	• steel/metal • agro-alimentation/fishery • automotive • energy	• electrical appliances • wood and furniture • machine tools • aeronautics
European Centres	115	1 472	• engineering software	• telecommunication software
University Research (science only)	892	3 656	• applied physics • engineering • chemistry • environment	• informatics • bio-technology • electronics • telecommunication • biotechnology
Public centres		n.a.	• agriculture • cattle breeding • fishery	• oceanographic science

* million pesetas
Source: Gobierno Vasco (1997)

now most indicators point at the reverse, and even show signs of an economically thriving region. In 1998 unemployment fell below the Spanish average (Table 8.1). The gross regional product per capita was 2,128,579 pesetas in 1996, that is 85.6 per cent of the EU average. The economy expanded by an annual average growth rate of 4 per cent between 1994 and 1998. While one should not ignore the fact that there are some spatial pockets showing continuing problems (for example the left bank of the Nervión around Bilbao), overall results suggest that the Basque Country has ceased to be an old industrial area in decline.

The role and development of innovation policies needs to be understood against the process of reconversion and renewal the region has witnessed over the last two decades. It is also important to dig deeper into the industrial and political cultures that have guided, and sometimes obstructed, the process of change. Indeed, one task for the Basque Country has been to move its economic anchor from mature to growth sectors, accompanied with technological improvements. Another, more difficult task has been to change habits, routines and 'mindsets'. In effect, while much has been achieved within the structural and technological areas, the latter tasks are still posing a major challenge. The major achievement of the last decade in the Basque Country has been a growing acknowledgement of the cultural and institutional dimensions of economic regeneration. As will be shown below, the change in innovation policy in this period can be explained partly in terms of such insights.

So what challenges has the Basque country been facing? An influential study carried out in the early 1990s as part of the development of the cluster policy pointed at several deeply rooted problems in the Basque business sector (Monitor Company 1991). The most serious defect detected was that the level of technological expertise and efficiency was not matched by marketing efforts. Especially in foreign markets, high-quality products were sold cheaply or indirectly through foreign retailers. Many advanced machine tools made and largely designed in the Basque Country have been sold under German brand names. Food products are sold via French or Italian retail chains. One of the reasons for the poor selling capabilities in foreign markets is that the Spanish market only opened to external markets from the early 1960s; exports had been very limited before that. Moreover, during the years of economic isolation the domestic market had also been heavily regulated. This lack of competitive experience has had a great impact in shaping business attitudes in the post-war period. In most sectors, notably those dominated by smaller firms, the business culture can be characterised as individualistic but not competitive, not really entrepreneurial and not keen on modernisation (Gómez Uranga and Ozerin 1997). The Monitor report thus concludes on this issue:

> Therefore, the general perception of academics, politicians and business people that the Basque is entrepreneurial is not fully supported by the facts. In effect, it seems that perseverance and extreme independence is misinterpreted as

entrepreneurialism. Improvement of management education, streamlined regulation for start-ups and a fiscal environment favourable to risk-taking will help to invigorate the authentic Basque entrepreneurs. (Monitor Company 1991: 187–8, our translation)

Another weakness identified in the regional economy is the lack of linkages between the business and science and education sector (Intxaurburu and Olaskaoga 1998). In particular, university courses and research tend to be theoretical and basic, unconnected to applied forms of research. The technology centre network seeks to provide some compensation here, but only in a very focused way. The only exception is the Mondragón Corporación Cooperativa (MCC), the industrial co-operative conglomerate in the middle of the Basque Country, which recently established its own university with a strong industrial focus. It should be noted, however, that Mondragón represents an almost unique co-operative form of capitalist development (Moye 1996). Changing business attitudes has been a major theme for Basque development agencies in the 1990s and will remain so in the 2000s. Even more daunting are the political and institutional challenges. Interestingly, contrary opinions exist that illustrate the capacity of the region to produce very different images. A positive picture can be found for instance in the work of Rhodes (1995), which regards the regional institutional system in the Basque Country as coherent, flexible and effective. This perception is grafted upon the existence of a powerful regional government with a strong planning culture, and the creation of the technology centres and other support organisations. A negative image emanates from the work of Cooke and Morgan (1998), who postulate the notion of a 'Basque Conundrum'. This conundrum, in their view, lies in the combination of a strong regional government and a weak overall strategic capacity in the area of regional development. A primary reason for the conundrum is political, residing in the fact that 'the potential of the regional state apparatus has been compromised by ideological conflicts between socialists and nationalists on the one hand and between rival nationalist parties on the others' (Cooke and Morgan 1998: 191). As a result, the region is rich in institutions, but these often fail to co-operate and create a corresponding network of institutional interaction (see also Gómez Uranga and Ozerin 1997).

The political culture, accordingly, can be characterised as being short on collaborative attitudes, lacking open participatory approaches in policy-making, and being dominated by political party-based lobbying and manipulation. This also translates into a highly politicised public sector. Political interests and strategies penetrate deeply into the local public system and its institutional affiliates. Infused by this culture, industrial and technological policies rely heavily on top-down approaches. In particular, there is a tendency to develop new initiatives around a single dominant concept or approach, generally imported from abroad such as technology centres, clusters and leader or 'tractor' firms. While such concepts allow for changes in direction and for the exploration of new opportunities, they tend to be implemented with relatively little analysis and adaptation to the local situation. Also, the engagement with other actors, including the wider business community, is generally low (Cooke and Morgan 1998). Hence, while potentially highly innovative and supportive, new initiatives often fail to meet expectations because of the way they are managed and implemented in practice. In addition, shifts in the political composition of the regional government have generally been accompanied by changes in perspective, in regulation and the role of organisations, as will be shown below. It is to the historical search for concepts that our discussion now turns, starting with industrial policy in the post-Franco period after 1975.

TECHNOLOGY AND INDUSTRIAL POLICY PHASES: THE EVOLUTION OF CONCEPTS 1975–90

Thinking about regional industrial planning started in the late 1970s when the depth and severity of the industrial crisis became apparent, and the political situation had stabilised somewhat. In particular, the transfer of planning competencies to the newly formed autonomous regional government provided a new organisational basis for industrial policy-making. In the first phase, running to the mid-1980s, the dominant concept was economic *reconversion*, linked with concepts of restructuring and rationalisation. This was translated into practical ideas about improving production processes, the search for new markets and technological innovations. The primary goal of these measures was to mitigate the economic and social effects of the industrial crisis, itself largely attributed to structural factors such as the nature of economic specialisation and technological backwardness.

While the technological aspects were addressed by the regional government and development agencies, industrial restructuring of the most affected sectors – iron and steel, special steel and ship-building – remained the responsibility of the central government in Madrid. The reason for continued central involvement was the high level of public ownership in these sectors. The industrial restructuring initiatives resulted in massive investments geared to the modernisation of the sectors which had been hit especially by competition from South-East Asia. The fact that support was heavily biased towards what can perhaps be interpreted as mature sectors may be attributed to the large concentrations of employment in these industries, combined with fear of the social and political consequences of further decline and massive redundancies. Another factor is labour power. The labour force was protected by some of the most favourable employment conditions found in Europe which made redundancies prohibitively expensive; it was also well organised, unionised and capable of strong resistance to attempts at rationalisation.

Complementary to the central state restructuring policies, the Basque Government developed a series of initiatives under the Plan of Exceptional Relaunch (PRE), which came into operation between 1985 and 1987. PRE explicitly targeted sectors dominated by middle-sized firms: machine tools, metal construction and metal products. This selection was rather arbitrary, reflecting the personal interests of the actors involved and, as a result, received considerable criticism. Nevertheless, it provided a welcome and in many respects effective addition to the central state's focus on large-scale, mature industries.

Technology policy took off at the regional level in the early 1980s, with specific support for high-tech applications in mature as well as 'emerging' sectors (Table 8.3). The first programme, launched in 1982, was CN-100 (converted to ECTA – Systems of Advanced Technology Concepts – in 1985). These programmes helped the machine tool sector with applying and developing numerical control technologies. The next year, IMI (Introduction of Micro-electronics in Industry) aimed at promoting the use of micro-electronics among industry in general. In 1987, furthermore, the use and development of telematics was encouraged through the programme SPRITEL. Also in the mid-1980s, the concept of technology parks became fashionable. The first such park – the Parque Tecnológico–Teknologi Elkartegia, SA – opened in 1985 and was followed by a technology park in the village of Zamudio, six kilometres from Bilbao, which welcomed its first company in 1989. This technology park has now pooled 81 high-tech enterprises employing 2,800 people and is evolving as a new technology area in the Basque Country (Table 8.4). Both indigenous and foreign firms (e.g. ITP, Air Liquide) have

TABLE 8.3: BUSINESS SUPPORT PROGRAMMES IN THE BASQUE COUNTRY, 1985–95

Period	Programme	Aim	Initiating institution	No. of firms involved	Investment (Ptas m)
1985–87	PRE	To promote actions among enterprises, innovation in process and products	Basque Government	206	24 986
1982–83	CN-100	Introduction of machines with numerical control	SPRI	112	1 157
1984–89	ECTA	To introduce equipment of advanced technological conception	SPRI	598	7 587
1983–91	IMI	Introduction of microelectronics in industry (promotion)	SPRI	--	1 531
1988–92	SPRITEL	To promote the use of telematics	SPRI	2 000	

Source: Torres (1995)

TABLE 8.4: BUSINESS ESTABLISHMENTS IN THE
TECHNOLOGY PARK OF ZAMUDIO BY SECTOR,
MAY 1999

Sector	No. of firms	%
Aeronautics	4	4.9
Electronics	8	9.9
Automation	1	1.2
Telecommunication	14	17.3
Information technology	11	13.6
Engineering	13	16.1
Environment	3	3.7
Research & Development consultancy	6	7.4
Other services	4	4.9
Producer services	16	19.8
Health	1	1.2
Total	81	100.0

Source: Technology Park of Zamudio

established plants here, which has also helped to foster interaction between these two sectors.[1] While the technology parks had some significant successes, it should also be recognised that, within the Basque Country as a whole, they remain as enclaves of innovative activities. At present the parks face two challenges: first, to interconnect, for instance by nurturing inter-firm relations, and second to create innovative atmospheres, for instance in areas such as the Deba Valley where the MCC started.

During the 1980s, technology initiatives were co-ordinated primarily through the regional development agency Society for Industrial Promotion and Restructuring (SPRI), which was established in 1981. In this period, SPRI, which worked in tandem with but independently from the Ministry of Industry, could be regarded as one of the most proactive development agencies in Europe.

Whereas the early 1980s was dominated by ambitions to revitalise existing industries and to build a regional high-tech focus, the perspective changed gradually in the mid-1980s. While existing activities were never out of focus, more attention was paid to issues of diversification and the overall economic environment. Diversification was seen as the only route to compensate for the inevitable loss of employment in current industrial activities. Such compensation could take place either by upgrading the industrial profile of existing firms or by nurturing new activities. Improving the economic environment was the objective of a range of 'horizontal' measures. These included broader measures to improve generic business capabilities (accounting, marketing, R&D, management, and training) and to improve technological standards. Through providing information and enhancing business capabilities with an emphasis on skill development, the regional government aspired not only to facilitate technology transfer but also to create an environment conducive to the emergence of new economic activities (Velasco *et al.* 1990).

The 1980s, as a result, paved the way for the more proactive forms of industrial policy that have emerged in the 1990s. From an initial focus on assisting existing activities, the agenda broadened with the ambition of modifying the regional economic structure. Departing from a strong technological orientation, other dimensions of business development also started to receive attention. However, what did not really change was the way the business community was approached. Little attention was paid to small firms (with fewer than 50 employees), and even business associations were often (only) involved at the margin. Large national firms (with more than 250 employees), through national support schemes, and established middle-sized Basque firms (51–250 employees), through their connections with regional authorities, remained the principal beneficiaries of the various policy initiatives and support schemes.

What is more, the political changes in the early 1990s may even have aggravated this situation. Whereas in the 1980s a part of the technology and industrial policy implementation went through SPRI, this changed with the transfer of the responsibility for industrial policy from the socialist to the nationalist party in 1991.

The nationalist party ministers reclaimed much of the territory previously handed over to SPRI, effectively reducing the latter's role to responsibility for high-quality business support and policy implementation. One result was an even closer alliance between the regional government and dominant business players to the detriment of other actors in the region.

THE COMPETITIVENESS PROGRAMME

The cluster approach was the key concept that inspired the government-based policy in the 1990s. The early 1990s thus ushered in a new period in Basque structural policy in which the sector-oriented approach that existed before was further developed. The cluster approach, however, provided a more systematic basis for a sector-oriented structural policy. The concept of clusters had been introduced by Porter through his influential work on the 'competitiveness of nations' (Porter 1990). While clusters presented a new approach, in the Basque Country its introduction followed naturally from developments in the decade before, in which both old and new sectors had already received target support. So why was the cluster policy adopted?

First, 'clusters' responded to the demand for concepts to underpin structural interventions in the regional economy. In particular, clusters suited the double objective of assisting established mature industrial activities while providing incentives to nurture new activities, within the overall aim of improving 'regional competitiveness'. To develop the cluster orientation, a study was carried out by Monitor, the consultancy organisation established by Porter and a group of students at the Harvard Business School in the early 1980s. The study made an important contribution to highlighting the deeper weaknesses in the regional economy, notably in the areas of business culture and entrepreneurial attitudes. The report also identified existing sectoral strengths and opportunities, setting out a cluster-based route of improving competitiveness. The report defined clusters as industrial systems marked by vertical (supply chains) and horizontal relationships: to customers, common resources and, particularly, technology.

Second, supported by its technology component, the cluster approach presented a welcome step in the process of moving towards a more demand-oriented style of technology policy. In the view of the ministry, a prime function of the cluster initiatives was to articulate technology demands and to relay those to the technology centres in the region. Clusters thus helped to build a 'complete' model of technology support. Whereas the technology centres presented the supply side of technology development and transfer, the clusters could now organise the demand side.

Third, clusters played into the hands of the new protagonists of industrial policy in the early 1990s. The Monitor report stated explicitly that a cluster-oriented policy required a strong role for the state. However, such a role should not be read as state intervention directly at the business level, as had been the case so far, but rather as acting as an orchestrator and catalyst. One of the outcomes of the Monitor research was the detection of weak co-ordination among businesses in the region, and the recommendation of public action to improve business attitudes in this area. Obviously, such advice dovetailed neatly with the ambitions of the Ministry for Industrial Development to become the major player in regional industrial policy.

The new position and aspirations of the Ministry were first laid down in the 'Industrial Policy – General Framework 1991–1995'. Through this document the basic priorities of the new government in the field of industrial policy were made public. Besides the cluster-oriented programme (the competitiveness programme), nine other thematic priorities were listed, including:

- the drafting of a regional economic development policy within the Basque Country;

- promoting new investments;

- financial subsidies for investments in SMEs;

- horizontal measures (technology, innovation, ICT);

- industrial management;

- energy conservation and environmental protection;

- planning of the mining sector;

- support to internationalisation and exporting;

- education, training, and industrial relations.

With the presentation of the plan, the government practised openness and mustered support. Nevertheless, in its totality, the plan repeated a series of mistakes that had also characterised earlier phases of policy-making. The plan was too ambitious, lacked focus, and introduced too many novel concepts and new institutional entities. Some also argued that the programme reflected too much the political aspiration of gaining broad results quickly, turning a blind eye to the fact that most policy initiatives would only show impact on the medium-to-long term. Admittedly, this critique applies not so much to single initiatives but rather to the plan as a whole. It does indicate, though, the crowded environment in which each initiative, including that of clusters, had to be developed. The only advantage in the case of the cluster programme has been that, because the programme acquired a status close to that of a flagship project, it managed to receive considerable support and resources.

The cluster project was developed in three phases: analysis and cluster identification, the establishment of working groups, and implementation of policy actions. In the first phase, the analysis resulted in an initial list of prioritised clusters (Table 8.5), in which two kinds of activities were distinguished: activities with strong presence in the Basque economy and with international growth potential, and smaller sectors which due to their level of specialisation and position in the regional economic system have strong future potential (the latter sectors are marked with an asterisk in Table 8.5). This first selection, however, hardly corresponded to how clusters had been defined in the Monitor document:

> International competition rises frequently in clusters of co-located industries. Industries that are competitive at a global scale are often concentrated in tightly limited geographical zones and have developed a crucial accumulation of links between suppliers and between firms with similar activities. (Monitor Company 1991: 165–6, our translation)

The Basque Country can clearly be marked as an industrial region. Yet this does not justify the inclusion of so many industries as prioritised sectors. As a result, the whole procedure of auditing, mapping and selection of clusters incurred considerable criticism. Not only organisations which had been side-lined, such as SPRI and the technology centres, but also business representatives revolted against the lack of consultation and the top-down imposition of the cluster policy. In the words of Cooke and Morgan (1998: 245), it was felt that the cluster auditing was carried out in a 'rather secretive fashion'. So, responding to these criticisms, the plan was revised. The decision was taken to drop several sectors, while adding various sectors with a stronger service orientation.

TABLE 8.5: ADAPTATION OF THE LIST OF PRIORITISED CLUSTERS

Cluster analysis	Policy priorities	Adapted policy priorities	Cluster associations	Technology plan 1997–2000 (clusters with PTCs)
Industrial cooling*				
Fishery*				
Rioja wine*				
Value added steel	Value-added steel	Value-added steel		
Machine tools	Machine tools	Machine tools	AFM	Machine tools
Appliances	Appliances	Appliances	ACEDE	Appliances
Sports accessories*	Leisure industry			
Hunting and fishing*				
Travel and leisure				
	Food-agriculture			
Industrial pipework*	Industrial pipework			
Port handling*	Port handling	Port activities	Cluster del Puerto de Bilbao (CPB)	
	Pulp and paper	Paper	CLUSPAP	
	Automobile industry and parts	Automotive industry	ACICAE	Automotive industry
	Aeronautics	Aeronautics		Aeronautics
	Environment	ALCIMA	Environment	
		Business management and knowledge	Cluster de Conocimiento en Gestión Empresarial	Business management and knowledge
		Telecommunication	GAIA	Telecommunication
		Energy	Agrupación de Cluster de la Energía	Energy

Note: * sectors identified as promising in the Monitor cluster analysis
Sources: Monitor Company, 1991; Boletín Informativo sobre los Clusters del Pais Vasco

The result of the adaptation is shown in Table 8.5. Three new sectors, 'environment', 'business management and knowledge' and 'telecommunication' were introduced to reflect the ambition to support a more diversified economy. They can be classed under the category of 'new strengths' for which the region was seen as having potential but currently low levels of activity. Each cluster developed a strategic business plan, generally developed around a Porter-inspired analysis of the sector and a detailed assessment of its international competitive position.

The second phase concerns the implementation of the cluster policy, which varied from sector to sector. The linchpin of most clusters is a newly established working group, dominated by the lead firms in the industry. The working groups are steered by a board on which sit representatives of the government, lead firms and selected business organisations and technology centres. They are administered by a secretariat appointed by the government. Exceptions to this general model are the machine-tool clusters and the new constituted 'environment', 'business management and knowledge' and 'telecommunication' sectors. The cluster initiative in the machine-tool sector is managed by the business association Asociación de Fabricantes Máquinas Herramientas (AFM). The composition of the working groups for the new sectors depended on the kind of local expertise available. The telecommunications sector initiative revolves around a single telecommunication company, and the other initiatives combine a variety of actors from different backgrounds. What all workshops share, however, with the exception of machine tools, is that they consist of closed networks. Following the idea that the workshops should act in some way as 'mentors' for the wider sector by embodying the best available expertise, they employ strict membership rules and nurture strong profiles to show to the outside world. The outcome of this stage was the establishment of various cluster associations (Table 8.5).

The third phase shows different lines of development for each cluster. Each is expected to produce plans and activities in three areas: technological innovation, quality management and human resource development. Under the supervision of Monitor, sub-groups were formed that focused on these issues and produced recommendations for the cluster as well as regional policymaking. The results of these exercises were laid down in the Cluster Technology Plans (PTCs) (Monitor 1996). Most cluster groups have submitted their PTCs and developed a variety of initiatives in their sector (Table 8.5). The Cluster Technology Plans, in addition, have been an input to the most recent regional technology plan (see below).

EVALUATION OF THE CLUSTER PROGRAMME

Within the recent history of technology and structural policy in the Basque Country, the cluster programme promised to fulfil a vital role in improving support to Basque firms. Whereas in the past policies had largely followed a technology-push model, the cluster approach provided a strategy to shift towards a stronger demand orientation. In the view of the responsible Department of Industry, Agriculture and Fishery, clusters were seen as complementary to the existing network of technology centres. While the regional technology network embodied the *supply* side of business support, clusters were supposed to articulate the *demand* side. In principle, thus, the cluster approach had the potential to fill an important gap in the support infrastructure of the region.

In reality, results have been somewhat disappointing (cf. Cooke and Morgan 1998). Owing to the elitist nature of the cluster working groups, the articulation of demand has been restricted to the small group of leading firms and actors participating in the groups. Indeed, it cannot be denied that businesses had now come to play a more important role in policy design and implementation. However, owing to the way the cluster initiatives had been developed, no basis was provided for communication with other firms, notably SMEs, or business associations, with the exception of machine tools. Hence, the initiative had still not managed to overcome the problem of selectivity and isolation that had also characterised previous policies. Some observers pointed to the fact that a sector like appliances was included. Since this is a sector dominated by large firms, this means assistance to SMEs is reduced. The overall attention to SMEs in the programmes remained weak.

Perhaps a more fundamental point of discussion is to what extent clusters provide the most appropriate template for structuring support. While some local experts shared Monitor's advocacy of a sector-oriented approach, other experts, notably those addressing issues of innovation, cast doubt on this standpoint. Rather than a sectoral angle, critical observers preferred to take the more general business environment as the starting point of support. They sought to promote a more cross-sectoral, horizontal approach around themes such as R&D, management, training and marketing. It was especially felt that the sectoral approach would lead to strong and undue biases in the way the Basque business sector would be targeted and therefore to ineffective allocation of public resources. To quote one observer:

> The core of industrial policy, which is understood as the policy of improving competitiveness, needs to be horizontal. This is the most adequate approach to prevent that the interventions, which in the end are geared to addressing market failures, give rise to government failures. (Martín 1993: 11)

Experts in favour of the sectoral approach, in turn, claimed that purely horizontal approaches, which lacked any sectoral focus or customisation, presented a waste of efforts. In particular, they saw a sectoral approach as an indispensable tool to strengthen the structure and specialisation of the Basque economy and its regional competitiveness. Those in favour of sector-oriented policies highlight the limited effectiveness of horizontal policies and the high costs of reaching critical mass (Ferraro 1997: 144). In addition, the advocates of sectoral approaches pointed at the already existing infrastructure of horizontal support in the form of institutions (e.g. SPRI, the technology network) and the SPRI support programmes such as RETO (efficiency improvement among SMEs), Organisation and Strategy (SME strategy improvement), Inter-firm Co-operation and Industrial Land (site preparation and provision for all types of firms).

A point of debate within the sector-oriented approach is the role of domestic versus foreign companies. Clearly, the cluster approach followed meant that the success of the Basque initiatives depended on the quality of the 'mentor' firms selected. However, not all lead firms in the region, some observers claimed, match their international competitors. This casts doubt on their role as coaches of sectoral improvement. This debate focused especially on the issue of foreign investors. In other Spanish regions foreign investors have come to play the role of 'demanding customers', which is regarded as one of the pillars of cluster development – for instance, the car industry is considered a sector in which foreign investors have helped to improve local supplier networks (Lagendijk 1993). While there were programmes for attracting foreign investors in the Basque Country, such as Garapen (1991–5) and through the establishment of the 'Office of Strategic Investments', their impact has been limited. In 1998, the Basque Country received 6.3 per cent of the foreign investments in Spain, ranking third after Madrid (50 per cent) and Cataluña (28 per cent). Most of the investments however are geared to acquiring local firms rather than establishing greenfields (the latter only accounted for 2.25 per cent between 1988 and 1996). The data thus suggest that the region could improve its attractiveness (Ferreiro 1997: 151–2). In this respect, at the time of writing, the end of terrorist actions resulting from the truce between the separatist movement ETA and the government in September 1998 provided a significant step forward in removing obstacles to attracting foreign investment.

THE IMPACT OF THE CLUSTER PROGRAMME ON RECENT TECHNOLOGY POLICY: TOWARDS A BASQUE INNOVATION SYSTEM

However the final verdict on the cluster initiatives may read, the programme has at least left its footprints on other policy strands. In particular, the Technology Plan developed in the early 1990s manifested some substantial changes, which can be partly attributed to the introduction of the cluster approach. The plan, Plan de Tecnología Industrial 1993–1996, was marked by:

- an emphasis on technological co-operation through concerted action by a variety of actors;

- an emphasis on multi-sectoral and flexible approaches;

- selection and targeting of certain strands for technology;

- rationalisation of the technology provision from the Basque Technology Network by stronger demand orientation;

- relating to the cluster initiatives by supporting the articulation of technology demand through the cluster working groups;

- promoting synergy between R&D activities and education;

- integration of R&D activities in Spanish and European programmes.

These intentions reflect clearly the wish to strengthen the role of clusters as intermediary chains between businesses and the technology support infrastructure as part of the ambition to make technology support more demand-oriented. They also reflect the stronger emphasis on co-operation and the engagement with a variety of actors involved in technology development and application. In practice, to meet its various goals, the plan prescribed three types of projects:

- generic projects proposed by the technology centres, to improve or change their technology profile;

- generic projects proposed by the cluster organisations or other sectoral groupings to meet future technology needs;

- individual projects presented by individual R&D units of firms, possibly in co-operation with the technology centres or the universities.

Overall, this new direction of technology policy presents some important advantages compared with past policies. Through encouraging interaction between technology suppliers and users, and offering more transparency, it has promoted a more structured provision and dissemination of technology support. One result is that technology centres have developed clearer priorities and reduced overlaps. Businesses are more engaged in setting the strategic orientation of technology policies, while they also interact with the technology centres on a daily basis. Support for the customisation of technology supply was also provided by the EU initiative under article 10 of the Regional Development Fund (ERDF) Regional Innovations Strategies (RIS). Being one of the RIS areas, the Basque Country used the European assistance for technological audits and forums in which both business representatives of the cluster companies (demand) and technology centres (supply) participated. The RIS were thus meant to contribute to the formulation of cluster technology strategies.

The stronger link between technology policy and cluster development also brought some disadvantages, however. To start with, firms active in sectors that were not part of the prioritised clusters now have much less opportunity to find technology support. Another sensitive issue is the appropriation of benefits, especially those stemming from the generic projects. To what extent and against which conditions should new technologies developed within certain firms, generally in collaboration with a technology centre, be disseminated to other firms in a cluster? A related question must be how the external applicability of new technology is to be secured and managed.

Another point of debate is the position of the technology centres. In operational terms, these centres acquired central positions in the shaping and implementation of technology policy. According to recent survey work, however, firms are still not satisfied with the way the centres respond to their needs, while the services are also considered as expensive (Buesa 1998). For direct contact with businesses, accordingly, the pivotal role of the technology centres remains a problem, and one may question their ability to become more demand-orientated.

The most recent technology plan, Plan de Ciencia y Tecnologia 1997–2000 (Science and Technology Plan), introduced another major innovation. Whereas in the past technology promotion and science development had been completely separated, now they had been integrated through the collaboration of the two responsible departments: the Department of Industry, Agriculture and Fishery and the Department of Education, Universities and Research. The promotion of collaborative attitudes introduced in the previous plan continued, but now the ambition became to nurture interaction within a systemic approach to innovation. This shift was inspired by recent ideas on regional innovation systems and their application at the regional level, and followed similar trends elsewhere in the western world (Cooke *et al.* 1997; Cooke 1998b; Asheim 1996). In the Basque context, the development of an innovation system called for the integration of all relevant agents and institution: businesses, the technology support infrastructure, universities, research centres, authorities etc., in an enlarged technology network. The integration of universities in the Basque Technology Network presented a novelty, thus responding to the wish to make the university more oriented to regional needs. The plan thus aimed at infusing the economy as well as society at large with a culture of innovation, and even at changing attitudes within the administrative sector. More specifically, the plan followed the following aims:

- Promoting the role of technology agents in a systematic manner; this meant the creation of a consolidated and coherent network which facilitated and advanced the interaction between firms, the technology infrastructure, universities and government.

- Promoting process of technological innovation in non-linear ways, by structuring the interaction of technology demand and supply in the innovation system.

- Linking the demand-side to the technology needs of clusters (restricted to the clusters for which PTCs have been developed, see Table 8.5).

- Securing an optimal and balanced contribution (also financial) from each of the agents involved, by improving business engagement, adapting the technology infrastructure and increasing the involvement of universities.

With the exception of the merger with science policy, this latest plan can in many ways be seen as a continuation of the previous plan. It further strengthened the demand orientation and the link with clusters. It also further explored the integration with technology initiatives at National and European levels. In addition, two new aspects are worth mentioning. First, the fact that the adjective 'industrial' had now been dropped, reflecting the already ongoing trend of extending technology support to service sectors. Second, an ongoing monitoring and evaluation system with quantitative indicators has been designed. According to a recent study, one of the contributions of the support to the local innovation system has been an improvement in technology management by Basque enterprises. For instance, various local companies have established a policy of technological co-operation with national and international technological agents, while others have involved clients and suppliers in their innovation projects (SPRI 1998: 33–4).

While the improvements should not to be underplayed, one should also note that the plan carried along some of the weaknesses of its predecessor. This included the core position of the technology centres as part of different strands of the programme, giving rise to certain conflicts of interest (Buesa 1998). Another problem is the exclusion of certain types of firms as a result of the selective cluster orientation. Also, two new points of controversy can be mentioned. First, while evaluation has become more important, the reliance on purely quantitative indicators may not do justice to the strong qualitative dimensions of the programme's intentions such as instilling more innovative forms of behaviour. Second, despite the inclusion of universities and a systematic approach to innovation, the programme failed to come up with a strategy to link basic and applied forms of research. This will be an issue which may need to be addressed in the next technology plan.

CONCLUSION

The Basque Country presents a rich study ground to examine industrial and technology policy. The region presents its own interesting and informative history of policy development and change. Plans followed after plans, often in an attempt to respond to the shortcomings of previous policies. The region also presents a case of the implementation of new concepts that have dominated regional structural policy over the last decades, such as technology centres, technology parks, clusters and innovation systems.

The Basque Country has been innovative, in particular, in the way it has integrated cluster-oriented policies and the innovation system approach. The new approach appears to fulfil a double aim. The adoption of a cluster approach contained a method to address what was seen as one of the key problems of the Basque economy: the lack of collaboration and inter-firm interaction. In addition, the new approach was geared to remedy failures observed in the technology and industrial policies of the 1980s, notably a poor identification of and response to actual business needs. Clusters were especially intended to facilitate the latter, to provide a sounding board for the articulation of technology demands. Together, the innovation system approach and technology policy have shaped a proactive form of structural policy for the Basque Country, that is expected to help further with the shedding of its 'rustbelt' identity.

While the changes in policy-making are impressive, and may provide guide-lines for other regions, it is also clear that the region is still struggling with some negative sides of its political culture. Indeed, there are various aspects of this culture that are seriously hampering the effectiveness of technology policy. Perhaps our work does endorse Cooke and Morgan's notion of the 'Basque conundrum' – the coexistence of a strong regional government and a weak overall strategic capacity – but it also points at areas where communication and interaction with regional actors, notably the less dominating ones, are deficient. As a consequence, while the Basque Country turns out to be a good pupil in absorbing the innovation in regional development strategies – tech-nology parks, clusters, regional innovation systems – it presents a poor case of engagement and consultation in the phases of detailed policy design and implementation. The interesting question is to what extent the recent emphasis on collaboration and system integration will be able to do away with the somewhat mixed feelings observers are confronted with today.

NOTE

1. An example of a very successful enterprise located in this technological park is Ingemat, SA. Created in 1986 with local capital, it started with four workers in the field of automation. By 1999, it employed 90 people (3.3 per cent in R&D) and continued to be financed by local capital. The turnover in 1998 was between 1,000 and 5,000 million pesetas and it exported 50 to 75 per cent of its production. It has continued working in automation, especially car bodywork production. Its clients include multi-nationals such as General Motors and Mercedes. It maintains relations with a technological centre in the park, and has now begun opening markets in South America.

PART IV:
CONCLUSIONS

9 Territorial Integrity and Intermediate Institutions

INTRODUCTION

In this final chapter, pulling together the arguments and empirical evidence developed by the contributions to this volume, we would like to present some 'stylised facts' regarding the relations between restructuring processes in filières, territorial development and the role of regional institutions. After this introduction, the chapter is in two parts. The first of these provides an over-view of a central theme within this volume, namely, the tension between the contradictory processes of territorialisation and deterritorialisation resulting from the restructuring of filières within Europe's regions. These processes are set within the perspective of the interplay of territorial development and change at the level of specific filières. An important aspect associated with this interplay is the locus of control and command within the filières and the func-tional roles and status of individual localities in the less-favoured regions in Europe within the spatial division of labour. The overview affords the opportunity to propose some critical reflections on the notion of territorial integrity and external economies of localisation. More specifically, the question will be raised whether territorial integrity still can be considered as an appropriate concept for sustaining regional development, given the rapidly changing and uncertain conditions in markets, technologies and organisations. If so, the main issue is how, given these dynamics, such integrity can be regenerated over time (Varaldo and Ferruci 1997: 27).

The second section focuses on the analysis of the role played by intermediate institutions in the interplay of restructuring filières and territorial development. It is argued that the devolution of decision-making to intermediate institutions often at the regional level reflects a recognition on the part of the policy-makers that the institutional fabric of the region – with all its attendant historically constructed values, knowledge and customs – may constitute a substantive and material productive force in itself, one that combines and interrelates with other factors of production. On the other hand, such awareness is an indication too of just how strong the imitation effect is in local development policies. Intervention is often aimed solely at replicating, at least in name, the successful experiences of specific territorial agglomerations, the Italian industrial districts being the prime examples. The last part of this section discusses two policy concepts which have played a dominant role in guiding local action towards the shaping of the position of territories within wider filières, and which have featured within the practices of copying between regions: (1) clusters of firms in association with innovation policy; (2) foreign investments and local embeddedness. This discussion, which draws largely on the use of these concepts in the case studies mentioned in previous chapters, allows us to shed further light on the tensions between territorialisation–deterritorialisation and the concept of territorial integrity.

THE TERRITORIALITY OF RESTRUCTURING PROCESSES: AN OVERVIEW

A common feature running across most contributions in this volume is the spatial concentration of productive activities incorporating greater or lesser segments of filières. This concentration chimes with the view of recent commentators that 'although the manufacturing industry as a whole has been continuously decentralising, there is indeed a general process of spatial concentration taking place within almost all sectors of industry' (Maskell and Malmberg 1999a: 175). What is interesting is that this concentration goes hand-in-hand with the increased integration of markets, networks and business activities at a global level. The spatial pattern emerging from this interplay consists of networked nodes of industrial production, in which the sliced value chain, to use the expression coined by Krugman (1996), is connected through strings of beads. The principal drive behind much of these spatial–organisational changes derives from various types of processes of structuring. Indeed, many of the chapters in this book have taken structuring and/or restructuring as the starting point of their analysis, linking it to processes of territorialisation and deterritorialisation at the regional level. The phenomenon of deterritorialisation became manifest in chapters dealing with the impact of relocation resulting from the internationalisation of supplier relationships. This includes Thiel, Pires and Dudleston's analysis of the textiles and clothing development in Portugal (Chapter 6), Giunta's discussion of recent changes in the aeronautics industry in Italy's Mezzogiorno (Chapter 3), and Markusen's consideration of the transformation of industrial districts (Chapter 2). Processes of territorialisation, in turn, appeared in the case highlighting the embedding of foreign investments discussed by Pike, Lagendijk and Vale (Chapter 4), which revealed how productive specialisation can be built from scratch, customising the physical and social infrastructure in an attempt to match the specific requirements of particular private companies to broader regional development objectives. Another relevant case is that of the computer and video games industry in the UK (Cornford, Naylor and Driver, Chapter 5), where some small firms in the filière clustered for the sake of convenient physical proximity to the big distribution and financial centres. The twin processes of territorialisation and deterritorialisation running through these cases are now discussed in more detail.

DETERRITORIALISATION

In tension with the spatial concentration of productive activities mentioned above, stands the apparently contradictory process of deterritorialisation or delocalisation. Each filière appears to find its own fragile temporal resolutions to these inherently complicated processes. As one of the major manifestations of the internationalisation or even globalisation process, delocalisation is evident in the agency of individual firms, networks and even whole filières to differing degrees across and through a variety of territories. The chapters in this volume bear out the wider trends highlighted in various other studies: over the past twenty years, the rising integration of world markets has brought with it a disintegration of production process, in which manufacturing or services activities carried out abroad are increasingly closely combined with those performed at home (Feenstra 1998: 31). It is important, however, to apply a broad spatial perspective to the processes of (de)territorialisation. What manifests itself evidently as deterritorialisation at the regional level, for instance the shift from local sourcing to external sourcing, may be interpreted as spatial integration at a higher spatial level, such as the national or supranational, with significant consequences for territorial organisation at that level (reterritorialisation). A fundamental issue, thus, in the processes of (de)territorialisation is the aspect of scaling.

As we saw in the introduction to this volume (Chapter 1), the delocalisation process at the local level has been powerful enough to generate pressures for change even among the industrial districts of the 'Third Italy' – organisational models hitherto markedly self-contained and which, by valuing their territorial constitution as an integral part of the local production system, have come to stand as leading reference models (Amin 1993). While formerly the outside world had played a part in district life solely as a market outlet, the changes now occurring – transition from flexible to fixed exchange rates, keen competition from countries with relatively lower labour costs and so on – are now driving entire segments of the filières out of the districts. New power relations of competition and co-operation are developing between the various classes of firms – which we shall be returning to briefly later in this section – and today the formerly unthinkable is unfolding before our eyes, in that the territorial coherence of the district model appears to be unravelling and changing its nature.

At this point we may ask whether the centrifugal forces at work in the process of delocalisation have proved powerful enough to overwhelm the territorialising forces and downgrade the role of territories? The agglomerative forces behind the resurgence of regional economics have been extensively studied over the past 20 years. Various approaches have emerged but they concur in ascribing a central role to territorial proximity and coherence in economic performance. These include the classical stream of studies, originating with various Italian economists (Becattini 1987; Brusco 1989) and subsequently crossing with the branches of flexible specialisation (Piore and Sabel 1984) and *milieux innovateurs* (Camagni and Capello 1999), the Marshallian triad of location externalities, namely labour market pooling, technological spillovers and intermediate goods supply and demand linkages (Martin 1999). Subsequently, the theory of agglomeration was given new perspective by the neo-institutionalist school, according to which the geography of transaction costs helps explain agglomeration and the spatial division of labour (Storper 1999: 51). Finally, the more recent evolutionary approach attaches importance to the 'untraded interdependencies', notably when the technological trajectories are particularly open, that underpin the need for territorial agglomeration despite centrifugal forces (Maskell and Malmberg 1999: 172; Storper 1995: 206). The latter, traditionally associated with products and factor markets, operate to achieve static competition based on lower labour costs. In addition to these two factors, the spread of the new information and communication technology (ICT) has allegedly softened 'the friction of space' (Maskell 1999: 8), and reduced the need for colocation, substituting it with network proximity.

Another case pointed at the process where, after a process of territorial embedding of supply chains, changes in the filière brought about a dramatic shift towards local deterritorialisation. This example comes from the aeronautical filière, examined in this volume. The aeronautical industry is undoubtedly a high-tech industry and thus in theory, according to studies carried out in the *milieux innovateurs* (Camagni and Capello 1999) and by the Storper school, subject to a greater need for territorial agglomeration, given the role played by uncodifiability and tacitness of knowledge development. The contributions to this volume by Markusen and Giunta (Chapters 2 and 3) afford the opportunity to explore the dynamics at different levels of the aeronautical filière. Markusen analyses the case of Seattle, where Boeing, a prime manufacturer alongside Airbus in the global aeronautics duopoly, plays the leading role. Giunta evaluates the second layer of the value chain, which includes Alenia's operations in Campania, southern Italy, that are just one among Boeing's preferred suppliers. Recent restructuring processes at Boeing have given rise to a reorganisation of network relations, squeezing Alenia out of certain areas of manufacturing in favour of Japanese firms embedded in the more promising South-East Asian markets. The territorial implications of such restructuring in the two regions is in sharp contrast. The Seattle area enjoys sustained levels of growth, while in Campania, as Giunta points out, the competition of the Asian countries has forced Alenia to undertake an intensive reorganisation and production with dire territorial impact in terms both of workers made redundant by Alenia and the exit of many small local subcontracting firms from the market.

Slicing the value chain, it can be revealed that the different levels of growth shown by the two nodes of aeronautical production flow from the emerging scenario in which the leading agent, namely Boeing, is mediating the pressures of competition by reorganising its productive structures. In the aeronautical field, lower international transaction costs together with prospects of access to promising new markets imply, in concrete terms, the entry of a new geographical area – Japan – into the value chain and, the marginalisation of other territories formerly part of the network, namely Italy's Mezzogiorno. Again the pattern of networked nodes, in which the territorial process within the nodes evolves in conjunction with changes in the organisation of a global web, dominated by large firms, seems to be an appropriate description.

Turning now to the textile-clothing filière in Portugal, we can shift the focus to where price competition prevails and is thus, in principle, more exposed to the blast of centrifugal forces. In fact, Portugal offers a classic case of potential marginalisation, since Thiel, Dudleston and Pires (Chapter 6) argue that the labour-intensive nature of garment assembly and its low barriers of entry make it 'one of the most threatened sectors, likely to disappear from a post-industrial high wage Europe'. Here, the authors find low-quality level production decentralised to eastern Germany, while production marked by quality rather than price competition and by shortened fashion product cycles has been left to Oporto in northern Portugal.

Events in Portugal reflect fairly closely what has happened in Italy's textile clothing districts. In the early 1980s, the larger or leading firms from districts like Carpi or Prato launched a far-reaching de-localisation process for selected unskilled, labour-intensive stages of production. Again mirroring developments in Oporto in Portugal, the Italian textile clothing districts seem to have taken a development path concentrated on the higher value-added functions such as marketing, design and trademark promotion. International integration has changed the position of peripheral regions and districts in the international division of labour. In both cases the process has led to upgrading with apparently virtuous effects, at least over the short–medium period. For Portugal this has consisted of a shift to production activities aiming at a medium-quality segment of the market, while for the Italian districts – which already have a fairly long standing in the higher segment of the market – it has meant specialisation in the more profitable and less cost-sensitive functions such as marketing and design.

TERRITORIALISATION

Cases of territorialisation within the context of filière restructuring can be found in more recently developed local agglomerations like those in the North-East of England. The case of the automotive sectors described above (Pike, Lagendijk and Vale in Chapter 4) started from a critique of the ways in which embeddedness and embedding have been utilised in recent economic geography. The conclusions reached in the previous analyses are largely over-turned here, and the causal processes appear to be working in the opposite direction. The results of the analysis demonstrate that it is in fact precisely on account of its lack of history that the North-East of England became attractive as a local system of production for the Japanese transnational Nissan. Here local involvement was in fact the outcome of a restructuring process promoted by Nissan's 'globalisation–localisation' strategy and attempts to promote mechanisms for labour market governance and training within the regional industry. The story recounted by Pike, Lagendijk and Vale (Chapter 4) adds another piece of empirical evidence to the current debate on the emergence of 'embedded transnational investments', that scrutinises the extent to which footloose companies are now being tied to regional economies.

Finally, the case of the relatively youthful computer and video games industry in the UK provides a timely challenge to the current stories being told about the locational dynamics of the new media among the California School (Scott 1996). According to this branch of study, the specificities of this industry, namely the constant need for innovation coupled with the high risks involved with unstable markets and highly differentiated products, will result in a process of vertical disintegration and organisation of media production focused upon metropolitan 'industrial districts' comprised predominantly of small firms. In contrast, Cornford, Naylor and Driver (Chapter 5) convincingly demonstrate that in the case of the UK there is no automatic association between the new-media industry and the spatial agglomeration of production activity. An array of geographies of new media are evident. Indeed, if trends towards agglomeration do emerge, they should rather be explained in terms of the contested relationship between small production companies and the major publishers, as the political economy school of cultural industries analysis would suggest. It is through this case that we are perhaps directed most towards a scalar model of territorialisation that works across and between a range of levels rather than through a simplistic bipolarity of 'global' and 'local'.

This debate, in conclusion, points to a growing complexity and inter-dependency between territorialising and deterritorialising processes. The contributions to this volume suggest that the extent and nature of the temporal resolution between these conflicting processes is profoundly shaped by the role and position of particular regions within their constitutive filières. Hence, the contributions to the volume summarised above provide a consistent story that enables us to begin to understand some of the key influences that shape the balance between deterritorialising and territorialising processes in particular places. A significant part of this story consists of the historical construction of territorial economies and the changing relative roles and positions of territories within filières in the international division of labour. Prolonged temporal continuity can work both ways – in making disinvestment more expensive because of sunk costs or promoting disinvestment owing to the age of the capital stock. Similarly, the historical social relations of territorial economies may promote or inhibit the extent and nature of adaptation and change (Cooke and Morgan 1998). Such processes can be understood only when both economic and political dimensions are addressed. The extent and nature of power and control residing within filières and territorial economies shapes the form of restructuring processes through the increasingly complex interaction of shifting cores and peripheries in the international division of labour.

This very last point, also raised by Cornford, Naylor and Driver (Chapter 5) in their discussion of contested relationship between small production companies and large distribution and publishing firms, prompts some reflections on the relations developing within filières between the firms involved in the various stages of production and their consequent territoriality. In the face of internationalisation of productive processes, it is precisely the filières approach taken in this book that raises two questions of fundamental import. First, who holds the dominant positions within each specific filière? Second, how do positions change with the evolution of markets and technologies (Bellini 1996: 56)?

The second question goes beyond the scope of this volume, although some of its insights suggest areas for future research. On the other hand, we can attempt an at least partial answer to the first question by analysing what emerges from the contributions to this volume and drawing upon recent studies (Crestanello 1997; Rullani 1997) on the evolution of organisational patterns within the filières. Our understanding of the process of the internationalisation of production mechanism challenges the vision of competition and collaboration among small firms tending toward harmonious equilibrium and sustained competitiveness. This mechanism is thrown awry because the process of internationalisation is characterised not so much by collaboration between peers as by an unequal and contested arena often dependent upon the 'visible hand' of a governing regulatory structure or, more explicitly, leadership (Storper and Harrison 1991). This leadership is taken on by those parties which are in possession of the resources, skills and capacities to handle the functions of highest value added – research, engineering, design, marketing and so on – and to afford the international transaction costs, that is, 'obtaining information about market conditions of the final product, identifying appropriate trading patterns, enforcing contracts between parties, financing the transaction and bearing the risk of default' (Linsu et al. 1997: 105). The governing structures take on the semblance of lead firms that shape the governance of territorial economies and are revealed in the examples in this volume as Boeing, Nissan, Esprit and the distribution and finance centres of the British computer and video-games industry (see also Crestanello 1997; Varaldo and Ferrucci 1997).

It is, therefore, the large corporate groups that often retain control of the strategic functions of the filières and cascade the tasks, functions and hierarchies of the other units operating outside and within the same area, on a differentiated scale and at different levels of the filière. Control is also exerted and solidified by the setting of standards and processes of certification. This empirical finding does not represent an absolute novelty; in the early 1990s when 'district intègrisme' was in full swing, some scholars warned that 'the development prospects of the majority of localities in Europe will become more and more tied to their position in relation to different international corporate networks' (Amin 1993: 291–2). Whether this process entails a loss of territorial integrity, and whether such a loss ultimately constitutes a downgrading for the territory itself remain a matter of debate. As we explain below, territorial integrity does not necessarily imply an almost full overlap of governance structures at the territorial and filière level, as suggested by the ideal type of an industrial district. Rather, it resides in the capability at the regional level to create and regenerate appropriate institutions and strategic capacity to monitor and shape the regional position in respective filières.

Thus the contributions to this volume can perhaps help us towards a more detached, and at the same time less pessimistic position on territorial integrity. The exit of firms from territories and the emergence of leading firms have, it is true, entailed some loss in territorial integrity, but only if we use the term in a narrow sense. Actually, the development of a new way of belonging to the territory does not necessarily imply its impoverishment, at least over the medium term. Indeed, the presence of leading firms in the area can perhaps underpin employment levels, promote occupational upgrading, attract new firms, raise standards of living and, in short, open the way for development in new directions. The extent to which these changes spell out a different and, indeed, sustainable regional competitiveness depends on the interrelations attained between the territory and the power of leading firms. Within this dialectic we may find ample room for the actions of the intermediate institutions in local and regional governance, which we consider in the following section.

INSTITUTIONS AND TERRITORIES

The devolution of decision-making processes to the regional level is widely observed in many areas of Europe (Keating 1999), while the extent and nature of such regionalisation varies in each national context. For example, Germany with its sturdy and time-honoured federal experience stands in marked contrast to the much more centralised UK in this respect, as is rightly pointed out by Ache and Wood (Chapter 7). The political importance of the region is thus allegedly grown alongside the globalisation of economic, social and cultural relations and, in particular, along with the construction of a more integrated Europe (Lanzalaco 1999: 17). In fact, the Structural Funds are undoubtedly a strong stimulus for innovation in the design and implementation of regional policy. In many European regions where the regional institutions are weak (UK) or unaccountable (e.g. southern Italy), 'the existence of EU regional policy has been the catalyst to the development of local planning structures which are essential if regional structural problems are to be effectively tackled' (Amin and Tomaney 1995: 308). This point is borne out in the contributions to this volume by Thiel, Dudleston and Pires on Portugal (Chapter 6), Ache and Wood on NRW and Wales (Chapter 7), and Torres and Lagendijk on the Basque Country (Chapter 8).

According to a shrewd observer (Bellini 1996: 37) it would be reductive to term this phenomenon as the 'regionalisation of policies', that is the devolution of powers and competence organised by the central authorities and applied among the regions merely to serve the needs of reorganisation, reform and modernisation of the nation state. Another view is that delegation of decision-making to the regions perhaps derives from the policy-makers' – relatively rapid – acknowledgement of changes affecting the organisation of production. The perception of production as a territorialised process rooted in local contexts has now entered the lexicon of intermediate institutions at the local and regional level. It is today being implemented with its own tools, which are certainly not those typical of state intervention and do not correspond to purely market-based solutions. However, the new-found perspective adhered by policy-makers on the relations between the territory and new productive configurations, and the ability to translate these insights into workable policies, is questioned in many of the contributions. The close examination of the evolution shown by Torres and Lagendijk's analysis of industrial policy in the Basque Country (Chapter 8) offers a clear picture of the transition from traditional-style economic policy in the 1970s, geared to support the public enterprises operating in heavy industrial sectors, to a new style of policy in the 1990s inspired by the emerging concepts of cluster and innovation systems and technology centres.

In this process of regionalisation, the intermediate institutions – the peripheral state structures, local bodies, consortiums, associations and local banks – have taken on a substantial role as additional creators of local advantages. The task of these institutions is to supply at the local level differentiated public goods (for a particularly significant example, in relation to training and labour market governance, see Chapter 4 by Pike, Lagendijk and Vale), including professional training, information services and incentives for co-operation, aimed at specific economic parties in order to affect the relative prices of local resources (Arrighetti and Sezzavalli 1999).

A strategy of territorialisation underpinning regional competitiveness has thus become a fundamental ingredient of the repertoire of institutional intervention available both to the intermediate institutions and the broader regions.

Alongside this strategic turn, the basket of regional economic policy tools shows a strong orientation towards innovation, such as the Regional Planning Agreements or the Territorial Pacts in southern Italy described by Giunta (Chapter 3). They reflect a new intervention philosophy, or in other words the policy-makers' intention to substitute bilateral obligation for administrative acts. Thus, the relations between the local institutions and the beneficiaries of aid (transnational firms, consortiums of firms, large firms) is characterised by a process of negotiation between the parties designed to 'bend' the interests of the firms themselves to the purposes of local development as part of a territorialisation strategy.

Again, it can be argued that a generalised aim of such local policy intervention is to replicate the most dynamic and developmental characteristics of the 'Marshallian' agglomeration model. On approaching the issue in closer detail, however, and analysing specific cases, a rather different picture emerges. While the rhetoric of agglomeration and clustering is used for purposes of legitimisation and fund-raising, in reality policy strategies appear to be much more pragmatic (Lagendijk 1999). Many strategies are actually focused on creating points of leverage at the interface of local and non-local networks. For instance, to enhance the region's competitive performance, business support and learning policies facilitate the acquisition of external knowledge and intelligence to guide the development of locally established business and the innovation support sector. They also contribute to the opening up of external channels to promote business exports. Another, even more pragmatic process is the actual forging of linkages between and among local and externally owned firms. Territorial integrity, in this context, does not refer to the effective containment of a filière within a region, but to the coherence and effectiveness of a region's set of competitiveness-focused policies, and also includes the democratic control over policy design and implementation. An important source of coherence, for instance, stems from the relationship between, on the one hand, the promotion of business investment in a certain sector and, on the other, targeted skills policies (Cooke and Morgan 1998). Territorial integrity is thus understood more in a socio-political than a socioeconomic sense.

To illustrate the way the adoption of general concepts results in specific local applications, two themes are now further discussed here: first, favouring the clusters of firms and, within them, providing incentives to embrace innovation at the levels of process and product alike; second, attracting foreign investments and encouraging local embedding. Taking these two themes, the contributions to this volume provide some insights into the understanding and assessment of such regional policies.

Clusters of Firms and Innovation Policy

In many ways, Torres and Lagendijk's (Chapter 8) analysis of the Basque Country offers an emblematic picture of just how powerful the imitation effect can be in local development policy. Specific approaches forged in particular local contexts appear to have taken on the status of universal reference models and have thus been replicated in the most disparate geographical environments. In fact, the cluster approach adopted in the Basque Country takes explicit inspiration from the work of Porter (1990), who has also been making a direct contribution with his territorial advisory consultancy (Monitor) to effective implementation in building up a complete model of technology support. As for the efficacy of the intervention, Torres and Lagendijk document a sustained rate of growth in the region and relatively successful transformation of the economic structure. One complaint, however, is that the very spirit of local development policy is betrayed when it comes to implementation. In fact, the central institutions such as the Ministry of Industry and party-based lobbies have played the leading roles with very poor engagement of local institutions. This illustrates the lack of territorial integrity from a political perspective.

Much the same type of experience emerges in Chapter 7 by Ache and Wood. In South-West Wales in the UK and in the eastern Ruhrgebiet in Germany, local policy intervention has sought to enhance processes of technological innovation through local agencies devoted to the supply and management of services. Here, shift has been discernible from central government to local economic governance with the aim of duplicating localised innovation and technology clusters. In the case of South-West Wales, imitation proves disappointing precisely in those aspects involving the local institutions and their efficiency. Thus we find another confirmation for the working thesis that the representative institutions of local economic governance are to some extent conditioned by the national system of governance, which may compromise territorial integrity. While the German model is based on the combination of intensive central regulation together with an equally substantial supply of public goods at the local level, the United Kingdom shows poor intervention capacity at the level of the decentralised institutions, which undermines the potential of local economic governance.

Attracting Foreign Investments and Promoting Local Embedding

The arguments for and against attracting foreign investments to foster local development have been well rehearsed in a considerable literature (Hudson 1999). Significantly, the key new insight is the 'alleged replacement of hierarchy by networks which are changing the relationship between TNCs and localities' (Dicken *et al.* 1994: 24). This argument is that transnational companies are becoming more vertically disintegrated and thereby increasing organisational autonomy. In this context, the main aim of the institutions – and, as we shall see, various institutional levels are in play in this case – becomes that of embedding the transnational company. Pike, Lagendijk and Vale (Chapter 4) suggest that socio-spatial embedding can encompass a process of anchoring the firm to the territory, involving an array of intermediate institutions, some local, others regional or subregional, with a great variety of functions from management training and business support at the one end, to industry networking support for the delivery and management of public service at the other. Again, much depends on the shared and mutual coherence of ideas and activities between these organisations. The relative success of these ventures partly rebuts the theorem of the impotence of economic policy advanced by some (e.g. Dicken *et al.* 1994: 42), by revealing that there can in fact be margins of manoeuvre, albeit constrained and perhaps temporary, within which the agents may anchor transnational firms to territorial economies. And, indeed, it is here that the intermediate institutions display relative strength, perhaps because of the evolution of their role and competence.

In the cases of Portugal, the Basque Country and Italy's Mezzogiorno, the local institutions give less cause for optimism, pervaded as they are both by the central political interests and by historical weaknesses conditioning their effective and integral capacity for the decentralised management of resources. Here it is shown that the pace of institutional change is markedly slower than the process of economic transformation and there are no shortcuts to drive local institutions into the virtuous path of responsible decentralisation. These issues are not unknown in the literature, where different frameworks of actions such as 'institutional borrowing' (Storper 1995) 'institutional thickness' (Amin and Thrift 1994) and 'institutional redundancy' (Grabher 1993) have been discussed by researchers, although as yet they offer only partial and somewhat unsatisfactory solutions to the problem of building, maintaining and generating institutional capability in less-favoured regions.

The task is a complex one: this collection illustrates that firms can nurture interests that display both loyalty and indifference to territorial economies over time. The evidence in our volume suggests the changing nature of the district model and its attempted imitation and adaptation reinforce the critical point that there is no one best way nor any single institutional paradigm that is solely suited to bending the territorialising and deterritorialising dynamics of restructuring filières to the developmental advantage of particular localities. The work of social science in the cause of regional development remains unfinished.

REFERENCES

Ache, P (1994) *Wirtschaft im Ruhrgebiet* (Arbeitspapier 123). Dortmund: IRPUD.

Ache, P (1997) 'Forum Zukunft Mittelstand – an initiative to create (innovative) milieus amongst SME in North Rhine-Westphalia?', paper prepared for the EUNIT International Conference on Industry, Innovation and Territory, Lisbon, 20–22 March.

Ache, P (1998) 'Lokale innovative Milieus in altindustriellen Regionen – Theoretische Konzepte und empirische Befunde. Eine Untersuchung am Beispiel der Regionen Dortmund und Newcastle upon Tyne', dissertation, Fakultät Raumplanung, Universität Dortmund.

Adelman, MA (1955) 'Concept and statistical measurement of vertical integration', in G Stigler (ed.) *Concentration and Price Policy*. Princeton, NJ: Princeton University Press, 281–322.

Aerospace (1994) selected issues.

Aksoy, A and Robins, K (1992) 'Hollywood for the 21st century: global competition for critical mass in image markets', *Cambridge Journal of Economics* 16, 1–22.

Allen, J (1997) 'Economies of power and space', in R Lee and J Wills (eds) *Geographies of Economies*. New York: Wiley, 59-70.

Amin, A (1993) 'The globalisation of the economy: an erosion of regional networks', in G Grabher (ed.) *The Embedded Firm*. London: Routledge, 278–95.

Amin, A (1998) 'An institutionalist perspective on regional economic development', paper presented at the Economic Geography Research Group seminar 'Institutions and Governance', University College London, 3 July.

Amin, A and Malmberg, A (1992) 'Competing structural and institutional influences on the geography of production in Europe', *Environment and Planning* A24(3), 401–16.

Amin, A and Robins, K (1990) 'The re-emergence of regional economies? The mythical geography of flexible accumulation', *Environment and Planning D: Society and Space* 8(1), 7–34.

Amin, A and Thomas, D (1996) 'The negotiated economy–state and civil institutions in Denmark', *Economy and Society* 25(2), 255–81.

Amin, A and Thrift, N (1993) 'Globalization, institutional thickness and local prospects', *Revue d'Economie Régionale et Urbaine* (3), 405–27.

Amin, A and Thrift, N (eds) (1994) *Globalisation, Institutions and Regional Development in Europe*. Oxford: Oxford University Press.

Amin, A and Thrift, N (1995) 'Institutional issues for the European regions – from markets and plans to socioeconomics and powers of association', *Economy and Society* 24(1), 41–66.

Amin, A and Tomaney, J (1995) 'A framework for cohesion', in A Amin and J Tomaney (eds) *Behind the Myth of European Union*. London: Routledge, 307–21

Aoki, M (1984) 'Innovative adaptation through the quasi-tree structure: an emerging aspect of Japanese entrepreneurship', *Zeitschrift für Nationalokonomie* (suppl.), 177–98.

Aoki, M (1990) 'Toward an economic model of the Japanese firm', *Journal of Economic*

Literature, 28 March (1), 1–27.

Appold, SJ (1998) 'Labor market imperfection and the agglomeration of firms: evidence from the emergent period of the US semiconductor industry', *Environment and Planning* A(30), 439–62.

Arrighetti, A and Serravalli, G (eds) (1999) *Istituzioni intermedie e sviluppo locale*. Rome: Donzelli.

Asanuma, B (1992) 'Manufacturer–supplier relationship in Japan and the concept of relation-specific skill', *Journal of the Japanese and International Economies*, 3 March (1), 1–30.

Asheim, BT (1996) 'Location, agglomeration and innovation: towards regional innovation systems in Norway', paper presented at the International Geographical Congress, The Hague, 5–10 August.

ASSA (1998) Pledge Certificate. Washington, Tyne and Wear: ASSA.

Audet, D (1996) 'Globalisation in the clothing industry', in OECD (ed.) *Globalisation of Industry: Overview and Sector Reports*. Paris: OECD, 323–55.

Bagdakian, B (1983) *The Media Monopoly*. Boston, MA: Beacon Press.

Barnouw, E (1997) *Conglomerates and the Media*. New York: The New Press.

Barquero, AV, Garofoli, G and Gilly, JP (eds) (1997) *Gran empresa y desarrollo economico*. Madrid: Editorial Sintesis.

Barrie, C (1999) 'How the British lost the game', *The Guardian*, Online, 27 May.

Basile, R and Giunta, A (1993) 'Divisione del lavoro e proiezione internazionale: il comparto aerospaziale campano', *Quaderno d'Istituto ISVE*, no. 36.

Becattini, G (ed.) (1987) *Mercato e forze locali: il distretto industriale*. Bologna: Il Mulino.

Beckouche, P (1996) *La nouvelle géographie de l'industrie aeronautique européenne*. Paris: L'Harmattan.

Bellini, N (1996) *Stato e Industria*. Rome: Donzelli.

Berger, S and Dore, R (1996) *National Diversity and Global Capitalism*. Ithaca, NY: Cornell University Press.

Boden, D and Molotch, HL (1994) 'The compulsion of proximity', in R Friedland and D Boden (eds) *NowHere: Space, Time and Modernity*. Berkeley: University of California Press, 257–86.

Bolton, R (1992) 'Place prosperity vs. people prosperity revisited', *Urban Studies* 29, 2, 185–203.

Bolton, R (1998) 'A critical examination of the concept of social capital', paper presented at the AAG Annual Conference, Boston, March.

Boyer R (1997) 'L'Usine BOEING d'Everette: une reflexion sur les modèles productifs, leur evolution et leur diversité', *La Lettre du Gerpisa*, 113, 7–12.

Boyer, R and Drache, D (eds) (1996) *States Against Markets*. London: Routledge.

Boyne, G, Griffiths, P, Lawton, A and Law, J (1991) *Local Government in Wales*. York: Joseph Rowntree Foundation.

Boyne, G, Jordan, G and McVicar, M (1995) 'Local government reform: a review of the process in Scotland and Wales', final draft report to Joseph Rowntree Foundation, December 1994.

Bozdogan, K (1998) Supplier systems and relationship focus group, <http://lean.mit.edu/public/pubnews/Suppl_Pt_Paper.html>.

Braczyk, HJ, Cooke, P and Heidenreich, M (eds) (1998) *Regional Innovation Systems – The Role of Governance in a Globalized World*. London: UCL Press.

Brail, SG and Gertler, MS (1997) 'The digital regional economy: emergence and evolution of Toronto's multimedia cluster', paper presented at the International Workshop on Regional Economic Restructuring and Multimedia, Stuttgart, 8–11 October.

Brusco, S (1989) *Piccole imprese e distretti industriali*. Turin: Rosenberg & Sellier.

Brusco, S (1992) 'Small firms and the provision of real services', in F Pyke and W Sengenberger (eds) *Industrial districts and local economic regeneration*. Geneva: International Institute for Labour Studies, 177–96.

Brusco, S (1995) 'Italy – trust, social capital and local development: some lessons from the experience of the Italian districts', in *Networks of Enterprises and Local Development: Competing and Co-operating in Local Productive Systems*. Paris: OECD, 195–9.

Buesa, M (1998) 'La política tecnológica en el País Vasco: un análisis en la perspectiva de las empresas innovadoras', in *Jornadas RICTES Sistemas y políticas regionales de Ciencia y Tecnología*. Donostia: San Sebastián.

Callon, M (1995) 'Recent trends in French institutions for regional innovation policies: an appraisal', presentation to NISTEP International Workshop on Regional Science and Technology Policy Research RESTPOR '95, 13–16 February.

Camagni, R and Capello, R (1999) 'Milieux innovateurs and collective learning: from concepts to empirical findings', paper presented to the International Economic Conferences on 'Local Developments in Europe: New Paradigms and New Schemes of Economic Policy', Varese, 1–2 October.

Camagni, RP (1995) 'The concept of innovative milieu and its relevance for public policies in European lagging regions', *Papers in Regional Science* 74(4), 317–40

Cassell, J and Jenkins, H (eds) (1998) *From Barbie to Mortal Combat: Gender and Computer Games*. Cambridge, MA: MIT.

CEC (1991) 'Four motors for Europe: an analysis of cross-regional co-operation', *FAST Occasional Paper* 241, CEC (DGXII), vol. 17.

CEC (1993) *New Location Factors for Mobile Investment in Europe* (final report). Brussels: CEC.

CEC (1994a) *Regional Development Studies: Study of Prospects in the Atlantic Regions*. Luxembourg: CEC.

CEC (1994b) *Competitiveness and Cohesion: Trends in the Regions. Fifth Periodic Annual Report on the Social and Economic Situation and Development of the Regions in the Community*. Luxembourg: CEC.

CEC (1996) *First Report on Economic and Social Cohesion*. Luxembourg: Office for Official Publications of the European Communities.

CEC (1997a) *Sixth Periodic Report on the Social and Economic Situation and Development of the Regions of the European Union*. Brussels: CEC, DG XVI.

CEC (1997b) 'Green paper on the convergence of telecoms, media and IT sectors and implications for regulation: towards an information society approach', *COM(97)* 623, final, 3 December.

Checkland, S (1975) *The Upas Tree*. Glasgow: Glasgow University Press.

Chinitz, B (1961) 'Contrasts in agglomeration: New York and Pittsburgh', *American Economic Association, Papers and Proceedings* 40, 279–89.

Christopherson, S and Storper, M (1986) 'The city as studio; the world as back lot: the impact of vertical disintegration on the location of the motion-picture industry', *Environment and Planning D: Society and Space* 4(3), 305–20.

Clark, G (1997) 'The informational content of financial products and the spatial structure of the global finance industry', in K Cox (ed.) *Spaces of Globalisation: Reasserting the Power of the Local*. New York: Guildford Press, 89–114.

Cochrane, A (1990) 'Recent developments in local authority economic policy', in M Campbell (ed.) *Local Economic Policy*. London: Cassell, 156–73.

Coleman, J (1988) 'Social capital in the creation of human capital', *American Journal of Sociology* 94, S95–S120.

Cooke, P (ed.) (1995) *The Rise of the Rustbelt*. London: UCL Press.

Cooke, P (1998a) 'Introduction: origin of the concept', HJ Braczyk, P Cooke and M Heidenreich (eds) *Regional Innovation Systems – The Role of Governance in a Globalized World*. London: UCL Press, 2–25.

Cooke, P (1998b) 'Global clustering and regional innovation. Systemic integration in Wales', in HJ Braczyk, P Cooke, and M Heidenreich (eds) *Regional Innovation Systems – The Role of Governance in a Globalized World*. London: UCL Press, 245–62.

Cooke, P and Morgan, K (1993) 'Growth regions under duress: renewal strategies in Baden Wurtemburg and Emilia Romagna', in A Amin and N Thrift (eds) (1994) *Globalisation, Institutions and Regional Development in Europe*. Oxford: Oxford University Press, 91–117.

Cooke, P and Morgan, K (1998) *The Associational Economy: Firms, Regions and Innovation*. Oxford: Oxford University Press.

Cooke, P, Uranga, MG and Etxebarria, M (1997) 'Regional innovation systems: institutional and organisational dimensions', *Research Policy* 26, 475–91.

Cooke, P, Uranga, MG and Etxebarria, G (1998) 'Regional systems of innovation: an evolutionary perspective', *Environment and Planning* A30(9), 1563–84.

Coopers and Lybrand Consulting (1996) *New York New Media Survey: Opportunities and Challenges of New York's Emerging Cyber-Industry*. New York: New Media Association.

Coopers and Lybrand Consulting (1998) *Survey of the Interactive Media Industry in San Francisco*. San Francisco: MDG.org.

County of Swansea, The (1995) *Draft Service Delivery Plan 1996/97*. Swansea: The County of Swansea.

Cox, KR and Mair, A (1991) 'From localised social structures to localities as agents', *Environment and Planning* A23, 197–213.

Crestanello, P (1997) 'Le trasformazioni in dieci distretti industriali durante gli anni 1980', in R Varaldo and L Ferrucci (eds) *Il distretto industriale tra logiche di impresa e logiche di sistema*. Milan: Angeli, 243–74.

Crewe, L (1996) 'Material culture: embedded firms, organisational networks and the local economic development of a fashion quarter', *Regional Studies* 30, 3, 257–72.

Crewe, L and Davenport, E (1992) 'The puppet-show: changing buyer-supplier relationships within clothing retailing', *Transactions of the Institute of British Geographers* 17, 183–97.

Crewe, L and Lowe, M (1996) 'United colours? Globalization and localization tendencies in fashion retailing', in N Wrigley and M Lowe (eds) *Retailing, Consumption and Capital: Towards the New Retail Geography*. Harlow: Longman, 271–83.

De Fraja, G and Hartley, K (1996) 'Defence procurement: theory and UK policy', *Oxford Review of Economic Policy* 12, 4, 70–88.

Dicken, P (1998) *Global Shift: Transforming the World Economy* (third edition). London: Paul Chapman.

Dicken, P and Thrift, N (1992) 'The organisation of production and the production of organisation: why business enterprises matter in the study of geographical industrialisation', *Transactions of the Institute of British Geographers* 17, 279–91.

Dicken, P, Forsgren, M and Malmberg, A (1994) 'The local embeddedness of transnational corporations', in A Amin and N Thrift (eds) *Globalisation, Institutions and Regional Development in Europe*, Oxford: Blackwell, 23–45.

DiGiovanna, S (1996) 'Industrial districts and regional economic development: a regulation approach', *Regional Studies* 30, 4, 373–86.

Digital Media Alliance (1998) *Recommendations for Growth: UK Digital Media*. London: Digital Media Alliance.

Diniz, CC and Fabiana Borges, TS (1999) 'Manaus: vulnerability in a satellite platform', in A Markusen, YS Lee and S DiGiovanna (eds) *Second Tier Cities: Rapid Growth Outside the Metropole*. Minneapolis: University of Minnesota Press, 125–45.

Domingues, A (1993) 'Serviços às empresas – concentração metropolitana e desconcentração periférica', PhD thesis in Human Geography, Universidade do Porto.

Domingues, A and Sá Marques, T (1987) 'Produção industrial, reprodução social e território – materiais para uma tentativa de abordagem do médio Ave', *Revista Crítica de Ciências Sociais* 22, 125–42.

Doward, J and Islam, F (1999) 'Gaming gets ugly', *The Observer*, Business, 7 February.

Driver, S and Gillespie, A (1993a) 'Structural change in the cultural industries: British magazine publishing in the 1980s', *Media, Culture and Society* 15, 183–201.

Driver, S and Gillespie, AE (1993b) 'Information and communication technologies and the geography of magazine print publishing', *Regional Studies* 27(1), 53–64.

DTI (1998a) *Regulating Communications: Approaching Convergence in the Information Age*. London: TSO.

DTI (1998b) *Our Competitive Future: Building the Knowledge-Driven Economy* (White Paper). London: Department of Trade and Industry.

Dudleston, A and Pires, I (1996) *The Portuguese Textile and Clothing Industry in the Post-GATT Climate* (EUNIT Discussion paper 4). Newcastle upon Tyne: Centre for Urban and Regional Development Studies (CURDS).

Economist, The (1995) 'The death of distance', special supplement, 30 September.

Economist, The (1999) 'Airbusiness as usual', 19 June.

Egan, EA (1997) 'Becoming digital: sources of localisation in the Bay Area multimedia cluster', paper presented at the International Workshop on Regional Economic Restructuring and Multimedia, Stuttgart, Germany, 8–11 October.

ELSPA (1998) *Playing for Success: A White Paper on the UK Leisure Software Industry*. Offenham: European Leisure Software Publishers' Association (UK) Ltd.

Fagan, B (1996) 'The region as political discourse', unpublished paper, Macguire University.

Feenstra, R (1998) 'Integration of trade and disintegration of production in the global economy', *The Journal of Economic Perspectives* 12, 4, Fall, 31–50.

Ferraro, FJ (1997) 'Criterios para el diseño de la política industrial regional', *Economía Industrial*, 317, 141–52.

Ferreiro, J, Gálvez, J, Rodríguez, C (1997) *La inversión directa extranjera en la industria vasca durante la década de los noventa*. Bilbao: Círculo de Empresarios.

Finegold, D and Soskice, D (1988) 'The failure of training in Britain: analysis and prescription', *Oxford Review of Economic Policy*, 4, 21–53.

Florio, M and Giunta, A (1998) 'I contratti di programma 1986–1997: una valutazione preliminare', *Economia pubblica* 6, 53–90.

Freeman, C. and Soete, L (1994), *Work for All or Mass Unemployment: Computerised Technical Change into the 21st Century*. London: Pinter.

Freund, B (1995) 'Portugal's Industrie in der westeuropäischen Arbeitsteilung. Branchenspektrum und Standortstrukturen eines Niedriglohnlandes', *Geographische Rundschau* 47, 284–91.

Friedland, F and Alford, RA (1991) 'Bringing society back in: symbols, practices and institutional contradictions', in WW Powell and PJ DiMaggio (eds) *The New Institutionalism in Organisational Analysis*. Chicago: University of Chicago Press, 232–63.

Frith, S (1987) 'The industrialization of popular music', in J Lull (ed.) *Popular Music and Communication*. Newbury Park, CA: Sage, 53–77.

Fuchs, G and Wolf, HG (1997) 'Regional Rejuvenation with the Help of Multimedia?', position paper for the International Workshop on Regional Economic Restructuring and Multimedia, Stuttgart, 8–11 October.

Fürst, D and Kilper, H (1995) 'The innovative power of regional policy networks: a comparison of two approaches to political modernization in North Rhine-Westphalia', *European Planning Studies* 3, 3, 287–304.

Garnett, N (1985) 'Nissan's ray of hope in a grim landscape', *Financial Times*, 26 November.

Garnham, N (1990) *Capitalism and Communication: Global Culture and the Economics of Information*. London: Sage.

Garrahan, P and Stewart, P (1992) *The Nissan Enigma: Flexibility at Work in the Local Economy*. London: Mansell.

Gates, B (1995) *The Road Ahead.* London: Viking.

Giddens, A (1984) *The Constitution of Society: Outline of the Theory of Structuration.* Cambridge: Cambridge University Press.

Giddens, A (1994) *The Constitution of Society.* Cambridge: Polity Press.

Giunta, A (1997) *Restructuring processes in the Italian aeronautical industry: the case of Alenia* (Eunit discussion paper no. 14). Newcastle upon Tyne: Centre for Urban and Regional Development Studies (CURDS).

Giunta, A (1998) 'Gli esiti del processo di ristrutturazione delle grandi imprese: un'analisi comparata', in *CER-SVIMEZ (a cura di) Rapporto CER-SVIMEZ sull'industria meridionale e sulle politiche di industrializzazione.* Bologna: Il Mulino, 373–455.

Glasmeier, A and Kibler, J (1996) 'Power shift: the rising control of distributors and retailers in the supply chain for manufactured goods', *Urban Geography* 17, 740–57.

Glasmeier, A, Thompson, J and Kays, A (1993) 'The geography of trade policy: trade regimes and location decisions in the textile and apparel complex', *Transactions of the Institute of British Geographers* 18, 19–35.

Gobierno Vasco (1997) *Plan de Ciencia y Tecnología 1997–2000.* Vitorio: Gobierno.

Golob, E, Gray M, Ock-Park, S and Markusen, A (1999) 'Valley of the heart's delight: reconsidering Silicon Valley', in A Markusen, Y Sook Lee and S Di Giovanna (eds) *Second Tier Cities: Rapid Growth Outside the Metropole.* Minneapolis: University of Minnesota Press, 291–310.

Goodman, E and Bamford, J (eds) (1989) *Small Firms and Industrial Districts in Italy.* London: Routledge.

Gordon, D (1973) 'Why the movie majors are major', *Sight and Sound,* 42, 4, Autumn, 194–6.

Grabher, B (1993) *In Praise of Waste: Redundancy in Regional Development.* Berlin: Edition Sigma.

Grabher, G (ed.) (1993) *The Embedded Firm: On the Socioeconomics of Industrial Networks.* London and New York: Routledge.

Granovetter, M (1985) 'Economic action and social structure: the problem of embeddedness', *American Journal of Sociology* 91, 481–510.

Granovetter, M (1992) 'Problems of explanation in economic sociology', in N Nohria and R Eccles (eds) *Networks and Organisations: Structure, Form and Action.* Boston, MA: Westview Press.

Granovetter, M and Swedberg, R (1992) *The Sociology of Economic Life.* Boulder, Co: Westview Press, 25–56.

Gray, M and Markusen, A (1999) 'Recruit and parlay: creating comparative advantage in Colorado Springs', in A Markusen, YS Lee and S Di Giovanna (eds) *Second Tier Cities: Rapid Growth Outside the Metropole.* Minneapolis: University of Minnesota Press, 311–32.

Gray, M, Golob, E and Markusen, A (1996) 'Big firms, long arms, wide shoulders: the hub-and-spoke industrial districts in the Seattle region', *Regional Studies* 30, 7, 651–66.

Gregersen, B (1992) 'The public sector as a pacer in national systems of innovation', in B-A Lundvall (ed.) *National Systems of Innovation: Towards a Theory of Innovation and Interactive Learning.* London: Pinter, 129–44.

Groenewegen, J (1989) *Planning in een markteconomie: indicatieve planning, industriebeleid en de rol van de publieke onderneming in Frankrijk in de periode 1981–1986.* Delft: Eburon.

Grüßen, C and Pohl, I (1994) *Das endogene Entwicklungspotential der Modewirtschaft in den Städten und Regionen Nordrhein-Westfalens.* Düsseldorf: Ministerium für Wirtschaft, Mittelstand und Technologie des Landes Nordrhein-Westfalen.

Haddon, L (1993) 'Interactive games', in P Hayward and T Wollen (eds) *Future Visions: New technologies of the Screen.* London: BFI Publishing, 123–47.

Halford, S and Savage, M (1997) 'Rethinking restructuring: embodiment, agency and identity in organisational change', in R Lee and J Wills (eds) *Geographies of Economies.* New York: Wiley, 108–17.

Harrison, B (1992) 'Old wine in new bottles?', *Regional Studies* 26, 5, 469–83.

Harrison, B (1994) *Lean and Mean: The Changing Landscape of Corporate Power in the Age of Flexibility.* New York: Basic Books.

Harvey, D (1989) *The Condition of Post-Modernity.* Oxford: Blackwell.

Harvey, D (1996) *Industrial Districts: Justice, Nature and the Geography of Difference.* Oxford: Blackwell.

Hay, C and Watson, M (1998) 'The discourse of globalisation and the new logic of no alternative', in A Dobson and J Stanyer (eds) *Contemporary Political Studies* 1998. Nottingham: Political Studies Association, 812–22.

Heinze, RG and Schmid, J (1994) *Industrieller Strukturwandel und die Kontingenz politischer Steuerung: Mesokorporatische Strategien im Vergleich* (SIT working papers). Bochum: Ruhr-Univ, 94–102.

Held, D, McGrew, A, Goldblatt, D and Perraton, J (1999) *Global Transformations: Politics, Economics and Culture.* Cambridge: Polity Press.

Henning, K (1997) *Multimedia in the UK: Business Opportunities in the Digital Age.* London: Financial Times Telecomms and Media Publishing.

Hesmondhalgh, D (1996) 'Flexibility, post-Fordism and the music industries', *Media, Culture and Society* 18, 469–88.

Hesmondhalgh, D (1998) 'The British dance music industry: a case study of independent cultural production', *British Journal of Sociology* 49(2), 234–51.

Hirsch, PM (1972) 'Processing fads and fashions: an organisation-set analysis of cultural industry systems', *American Journal of Sociology* 77, 639–59.

Hirst, D and Thompson, G (1996) *Globalization in Question.* Cambridge, MA: Blackwell.

Hodgson, G (1999) *Economics and Utopia: Why the Learning Economy is Not the End of History.* London: Routledge.

Hollingsworth, JR, Schmitter, PC, and Streeck, W (1994) 'Capitalism, sectors, institutions and performance', in JR Hollingsworth, PC Schmitter and W Streeck (eds) *Governing Capitalist Economies – Performance and Control of Economic Sectors.* Oxford: Oxford University Press, 3–16.

Hudson, R (1999) 'The learning economy, the learning firm and the learning region: a sympathetic critique of the limits to learning', *European Urban and Regional Studies* 6 (1).

INE (1991) Recenseamento Geral da População, Instituto Nacional de Estatística: Lisboa.

Intxaurburu, G and Olaskaoga, J (1998) 'University–industry relations – some organisational issues: the case of the Basque country', in R Oakey and W During (eds) *New Technology-Based Firms in the 1990s* (vol. 5). London: Paul Chapman, 49–56.

Jacobs, J (1961) *The Death and Life of Great American Cities.* New York: Vintage, 112–40.

Jeong, JH (1995) 'Spin-offs formation and linkages in Taeduck Research Park', *Journal of Geography* 25, 57–80 (in Korean with English summary).

Jeong, JH and Ock Park, S (1999) 'Taeduck: a high-tech satellite platform', in A Markusen, YS Lee and S DiGiovanna (eds) *Second Tier Cities: Rapid Growth Outside the Metropole.* Minneapolis: University of Minnesota Press, 199–222.

Jessop, B (1992) 'Changing forms and functions of the state in an era of globalization and regionalization', paper presented to EAPE Conference, Paris, 4–7 November.

Jessop, B (1994) 'Post-Fordism and the state', in A Amin (ed.) *Post-Fordism.* Oxford: Blackwell, 251–79.

Jessop, B and Hay, C (1995) 'Local economic governance', paper presented at ESRC Local Governance Conference, Exeter, 19–20 September.

Keating, M (1997) 'Culture, collective identities and development', in *Regional Identity and Economic Development.* Brussels: Foundation Europe of Cultures 2002, 16–31.

Keating, M (1999) *The Political Economy of Regionalism in Europe.* London: Routledge.

Kechidi M (1996) 'Co-ordination inter-enterprises et relations de sous-traitance: le cas d'aerospatiale', *Revue d'Economie Regionale et Urbaine* (1), 99–120.

Keeble, D and Wilkinson, F (1999) 'Collective learning and knowledge development in the evolution of clusters and high-tech SMEs in Europe', *Regional Studies* 33, 4, 295.

Kenney, M and Florida, R (1993) *Beyond Mass Production: The Japanese System and its Transfer to the US.* New York: Oxford University Press.

Kilper, H (1994) *Das Ruhrgebiet im Umbruch: Strategien regionaler Verflechtung Schriften des Institute Arbeit und Technik.* Opladen: Leske & Budrich.

Kozul-Wright, R (1995) 'Transnational corporations and the nation state', in J Michie and J Grieve Smith (eds) *Managing the Global Economy.* Oxford: Oxford University Press, 135–71.

Kristensen, PH (1994) 'Strategies in a volatile world', *Economy and Society* 23(3), 305–34.

Krugman, P (1996) 'Does third-world growth hurt first-world prosperity?', *Harvard Business Review* 72, 113–21.

Kruse, H (1991) 'Eigenständige Regionalentwicklungspolitik im gemeinsamen Binnenmarkt – Das Beispiel Nordrhein-Westfalen' in HH Blotevogel (ed.) *Europäische Regionen im Wandel. Dortmund: Vertrieb für Bau-und Planungsliteratur,* 323–42.

KVR (1996) *Lokales Informations system Arbeitsmarkt Essen:* Kommunalverband Ruhrgebiet.

Lagendijk, A (1993) *The Internationalisation of the Spanish Automobile Industry and its Regional Impact: The Emergence of a Growth Periphery.* Amsterdam: Thesis Publishers.

Lagendijk, A (1996) 'Spatial clustering at the cross-roads of territorial and industrial development: a review', paper presented to the EUNIT Conference on 'Territorial development in Europe: the impact of innovation and restructuring', Dortmund, 22–24 May.

Lagendijk, A (1999a) 'Regional cluster policy in a global economy: from market competition to institutional anchoring: the cases of the North-East of England and Aragón', *European Planning Studies* 7 (6), 775–92.

Lagendijk, A (1999b) 'The emergence of knowledge-oriented forms of regional policy in Europe', *Tijdschrift voor Economische en Sociale Geografie* 90(1), 110–16.

Lagendijk, A (1999c) 'Regional anchoring and modernisation strategies in non-core regions: evidence from the UK and Germany', *European Planning Studies* 7(6), 775–92.

Lagendijk, A (2000) 'Regional paths of institutional anchoring in the global economy. The case of the North-East of England and Aragòn', in J Groenewegen and W Elsner (eds) *An Industrial Policy Agenda 2000 and Beyond – New Challenges to Industrial Policy.* Dordrecht: Kluwer Academic.

Landabaso, M (1995) 'The promotion of innovation in regional community policy: lessons and proposals for a regional innovation strategy', paper presented to NISTEP International Workshop on Regional Science and Technology Policy Research RESTPOR '95, Japan, 13–16 February.

Langlois, RN and Robertson, PL (1995) *Firms, Markets and Economic Change: A Dynamic Theory of Business Institutions.* London: Routledge.

Lanzalaco, L (1999) 'Tra micro e macro. Il ruolo delle istituzioni intermedie negli ordini regolativi', in A Arrighetti and G Serravalli (eds) *Istituzioni intermedie e sviluppo locale.* Rome: Donzelli, 3–24.

Latella, F (1996) 'Regioni in ritardo di sviluppo: verso il recupero di un ruolo transazionale della grande impresa?', *Rassegna Economica* 4, October–December, 1031–42.

Leach, R (1994) 'The missing regional dimension to the local government review', *Regional Studies* 28, 8, December, 797–802.

Lee, R and Wills, J (eds) (1997) *Geographies of Economies.* London: Edward Arnold.

Lefebvre, E and Lefebvre, LA (1998) 'Global strategic benchmarking, critical capabilities and performance of aerospace subcontractor', *Technovation* 18, 4, 223–34.

Linsu, K, Nugent, J and Seung-Jae, Y (1997) 'Transaction costs and export channels of small and medium-sized enterprises: the case of Korea', *Contemporary Economic Policy* XV, 104–20.

Lorraine, D (1996) *Embedding Inward Investors: Greenfield Barriers and Bridges.* Washington, Tyne and Wear: Training Department, Nissan.

Lovering, J (1999) 'Theory led by policy: the inadequacies of the "new regionalism" (illustrated from the case of Wales)', *International Journal of Urban and Regional Research*, 23, 379–95.

Luger, M and Goldstein, H (1990) *Technology in the Garden.* Chapel Hill: University of North Carolina.

Madgwick, A and James, M (1980) 'The Network of Consultative Government in Wales', in G Jones (ed.) *New Approaches to the Study of Central-Local Government Relationships.* Aldershot: Gower, 101–15.

Malmberg, A, Sövell, Ö and Zander, I (1996) 'Spatial clustering, Local accumulation of knowledge and firm competitiveness', *Geografiska Annaler* (B) 78, 85–97.

Markusen, A (1985) *Profit Cycles, Oligopoly and Regional Development.* Boston, MA: MIT Press.

Markusen, A (1994) 'Studying regions by studying firms', *Professional Geographer* 46, 477–90.

Markusen, A (1996a) 'Sticky places in slippery space: a typology of industrial districts', *Economic Geography* 72, 3, 293–313.

Markusen, A (1996b) 'Toronto's economic future: a rumination on comparisons with seven US cities', in JK Bell and S Webber (eds) *Urban Regions in a Global Context.* Toronto: Centre for Urban and Community Studies, University of Toronto, 47–68.

Markusen, A (1999) 'Fuzzy concepts, scanty evidence, policy distance: the case for rigor and policy relevance in critical regional studies', *Regional Studies* 33, 9 869–84.

Markusen, A and Park, SO (1993) 'The state as industrial locator and district builder: the case of Changwon, South Korea', *Economic Geography* 69, 2, 157–81.

Markusen, A, Hall, P, Deitrick, S and Campbell, S (1991) *The Rise of the Gunbelt.* New York: Oxford University Press.

Marques, MML (1992) *Subcontratação e autonomia empresarial. Um estudo sobre o caso português.* Oporto: Edições Afrontamento.

Martín, C (1993) 'Principales enfoques en el análisis de la competitividad', *Papeles de Economía Española*, no. 56.

Martin, R (1999) 'The new "geographical turn" in economics: some critical reflections', *Cambridge Journal of Economics* 23, 65–91.

Martin, R and Sunley, P (1996) 'Paul Krugman's geographical economics and its implications for regional-development theory – a critical-assessment', *Economic Geography* 72, 3, 259–92.

Martin, R and Sunley, P (1997) 'The post-Keynesian state and the space economy', in R Lee and J Wills (eds) *Geographies of Economies.* London: Edward Arnold, 278–89.

Martins, MB (1976) *As Multinacionais em Portugal.* Lisbon: Editorial Estampa.

Maskell, P (1999) 'Future challenges and institutional preconditions for regional development policy of economic globalisation', paper presented to the International Economic Conferences on 'Local developments in Europe: new paradigms and new schemes of economic policy', Varese, 1–2 October.

Maskell P and Malmberg, A (1999a) 'Localised Learning and Industrial Competitiveness', *Cambridge Journal of Economics* 23, 167–85.

Maskell, P and Malmberg, A (1999b) 'The competitiveness of firms and regions: ubiquification and the importance of localised learning', *European Urban and Regional Studies* 6(1), 9–26.

Massey, D (1995) *Spatial Divisions of Labour* (second edition). Basingstoke: Macmillan.

Matzner, E and Streeck, W (eds) (1991) *Beyond Keynesianism: The Socio-Economics of Production and Full Employment.* Aldershot: Edward Elgar.

Mayer, M (1996) 'Postfordistische Stadtpolitik. Neue Regulationsweisen in der lokalen Politik und Planung', *Zeitschrift für Wirtschaftsgeographie* 40(1–2), 20–7.

McDowell, L (1997) 'A tale of two cities? Embedded organisations and embodied workers in the City of London', in R Lee and J Wills (eds) *Geographies of Economies*. London: Edward Arnold, 118–29.

Miege, B (1987) 'The logics at work in the new cultural industries', *Media, Culture and Society* 9(3), 273–89.

Monitor Company (1991) 'La ventaja competitiva de Euskadi. FASE I. Indentificación del potencial de competitividad', *Ekonomiaz* 21, 156–209.

Monitor Company (1996) *Programa de competitividad. Resumen de conclusiones de los grupos de trabajo de los clusters.* Madrid: Monitor Consultancy.

Morgan, K (1994a) 'The fallible servant: making sense of the WDA', papers in *Planning Research,* Department of City and Regional Planning, University of Wales College of Cardiff, September.

Morgan, K (1994b) 'Development from within: economic renewal and a Welsh Parliament' in J Osmond (ed.) *A Parliament for Wales.* Llandysul, Dyfed: Gomer, 153–65.

Morgan, K (1995) 'Institutions, innovation and regional renewal: the development agency as animateur', paper prepared for the Regional Studies Association Conference 'Regional futures: past and present, East and West', Gothenburg, Sweden, 6–9 May.

Morgan, K (1997) 'The learning region: technology, institutions and regional renewal', *Regional Studies* 31, 5.

Morgan, K and Roberts, E (1993) *The Democratic Deficit: A Guide to Quangoland.* Cardiff: Department of City and Regional Planning, University of Wale.

Moye, M (1996) 'Financing the industrial cooperatives of the Mondragon Group', ERSC Centre for Business Research Working Paper 25, 1–55.

Müller, F (1995) 'Auslandsaktivitäeten der Bekleidungsindustrie. Strukturwandel und Anpassungsstrategien – unter Berücksichtigung von Erfahrungen deutscher Unternehmer in Portugal', PhD Thesis. Aachen: Rheinisch Westfaelische Technische Hochschule.

Murphy, P and Caborn, R (1995) Regional Government for England – An Economic Imperative. Sheffield Hallam University, Sheffield: PAVIC Publications.

MWMT (1993a) *Technologie-Handbuch Nordrhein-Westfalen.* Düesseldorf: MWMT.

MWMT (1993b) *Regionalization. New Approaches to Structural Policy in Nordrhein-Westfalen.* Düsseldorf: MWMT.

National Assembly for Wales, The (1999) *National Economic Development Strategy.* Cardiff: European Task Force, National Assembly for Wales.

National Research Council (1997) *Policy Issues in Aerospace Offsets.* Washington, DC: National Academy Press

Negroponte, N (1995) *Being Digital.* London: Hodder and Stoughton/Coronet.

Nelson, RR (1993) *National Innovation Systems: A Comparative Analysis.* Oxford: Oxford University Press.

Nordhause-Janz, J and Rehfeld, D (1991) *Umweltschutz made in NRW. Eine empirische Untersuchung der Umweltschutzwirtschaft in Nordrhein-Westfalen.* Munich: Rainer Hampp Verlag.

North, P (1991) 'Institutions', *Journal of Economic Perspectives* 5, 1, 97–112

O'Donnell, R (1996) 'The competitive advantage of peripheral regions' in B Fynes and S Ennis (eds) *Competing from the Periphery.* London: Dryden Press, 47–82.

OECD Working Party on the Information Economy (1998) *Content as a New Growth Industry.* Paris: OECD (DSTI/ICCP).

Oinas, P (1997) 'On the socio-spatial embeddedness of business firms', *Erdkunde* 51, 23–32.

Oinas, P (1998) *The Embedded Firm? Prelude for a Revived Geography of the Enterprise* (Series Acta Universitatis Oeconomicae Helsingienas, A-143). Helsinki: Helsinki School of Business and Business Administration.

Oinas, P, and Virkkala, S (1997) 'Learning, competitiveness and development. Reflections on the contemporary discourse on "Learning Regions"' in H Eskelinen (ed.) *Regional Specialisation and Local Environment.* Copenhagen: NordRefo, 263–77.

Okamuro, H (1995) 'Changing subcontracting relations and risk-sharing in Japan: an econometric analysis of the automobile industry', *Hitotsubashi Journal of Economics* 36, 207–18.

One North East (1999) *Unlocking our Potential: Regional Economic Strategy.* Newcastle upon Tyne: One North East.

Osmond, J (ed.) (1994) *A Parliament for Wales.* Llandysul, Dyfed: Gomer.

Painter J, Wood, M and Goodwin, M (1995) 'British local governance beyond Fordism: a regulationist perspective', paper presented at the ESRC Local Governance Programme Conference, Exeter, 19–20 September.

Painter, J and Goodwin, M (1995) 'Local governance and concrete research: investigating the uneven development of regulation', *Economy and Society* 24, 3, August, 334–56.

Paliwoda, S and Bonaccorsi, A (1994) 'Trends in procurement strategies within the European aircraft industry', *Industrial Marketing Management* 23, 235–44.

Park, SO (1995) 'Seoul (Korea): city and suburb', in G Clark and WB Kim (eds) *Asian NIEs and the Global Economy.* Baltimore: Johns Hopkins University Press, 143–67.

Park, SO and Markusen, A (1995) 'Generalizing new industrial districts: a theoretical agenda and an application from a non-western economy', *Environment and Planning* A27, 81–104.

Peck, F (1996) 'Regional development and the production of space: the role of infrastructure in the attraction of new inward investment', *Environment and Planning* A28, 327–39.

Peck, J and Tickell, A (1995) 'Business goes local: dissecting the "business agenda" in Manchester', *International Journal of Urban and Regional Research* 19(1), 55–78.

Peterson, RA and Berger, DG (1975) 'Cycles in symbol production: the case of popular music', *American Sociological Review* 40(2), 158–73.

Phelps, N (1993) 'Branch plants and the evolving spatial division of labour: a study of material linkage change in the northern region of England', *Regional Studies* 27, 2, 87–101.

Phelps, N, Lovering, J and Morgan, K (1998) 'Tying the firm to the region or tying the region to the firm?', *European Urban and Regional Studies* 5, 2, 119–37.

Picard, RG (1989) *Media Economics: Concepts and Issues.* Newbury Park, CA: Sage.

Pike, A (1994) 'New activities for old industrial spaces? Restructuring the global automotive industry and the old industrial regions of the UK', unpublished PhD thesis, Department of Geography, University of Liverpool.

Pike, A (1998a) 'Making performance plants from branch plants? In-situ restructuring in the automobile industry in UK Region', *Environment and Planning* A30, 881–900.

Pike, A (1998b) Developing the Automotive Industry in the North-East of England (report for the 'Competitiveness Project'). Newcastle upon Tyne: Centre for Urban and Regional Development Studies (CURDS).

Pike, A and Tomaney, J (1999) 'The limits to localisation in declining industrial regions? Trans-national corporations and economic development in Sedgefield Borough', *European Planning Studies* 7, 4, 407–28.

Pike, A. (1999) 'The politics of factory closures and task forces in the North-East of England', *Regional Studies* 33, 6, 567–75.

Piore, MJ. and Sabel, CF (1984) *The Second Industrial Divide: Possibilities for Prosperity.* New York: Basic Books.

Pires, I (1994) 'A teia e a trama na geografia das indústrias têxtil e do vestuário', PhD thesis, Universidade de Lisboa.

Pires, I (1998) 'The restructuring of textile and clothing firms in Portugal', in J Gaspar, E Kulke and L Schatzl (eds) *Effects of the European Integration Process on the Spatial Economic Development in Portugal* (EPRU no. 46). Lisbon: CEG.

Port of Tyne Authority (1996) *Current*, April, 1, Port of Tyne Authority: Newcastle upon Tyne.

Porter, ME (1990) *The Competitive Advantage of Nations*. London: Macmillan.

Pratt, AC (1997) 'The cultural industries' production system: a case study of employment change in Britain, 1984–1991', *Environment and Planning* A29(11), 1953–74.

Putnam, R (1995) 'Bowling alone: America's declining social capital', *Journal of Democracy* 6, 1, 65–78.

Quaternaire Portugal (1995) *Plano estratégico do sistema urbano do Vale do Ave*. Porto: unpublished.

Reich, R (1993) *The Work of Nations: Preparing Ourselves for the 21st Century*. London: Simon & Schuster.

Reis, J (1998) 'Os sistemas produtivos locais em Portugal: uma transição difícil', in J Gaspar, and M Vale (eds) *Industrial Development and Territory*. Coimbra: CCRC, 35–58.

REK DO (1993) Regionales Entwicklungskonzept Dortmund/Kreis Unna/Hamm. Dortmund: Regional Konferenz.

Reynolds, P (1989) 'New firms: enhancing their growth', *Economic Development Commentary* 13(2), 4–11.

Rhodes, M (1995) 'Regional development and employment in Europe's southern and western peripheries', in M Rhodes (ed.) *The Regions and the New Europe: Patterns in Core and Periphery Development* (European Policy Research Unit Series). Manchester and New York: Manchester University Press, 273–328.

Robins, K and Cornford, J (1992) 'What is flexible about independent producers?' *Screen* 33(2), 190–200.

Robins, K and Cornford, J (1994) 'Local and regional broadcasting in the new media order', in A Amin and N Thrift (eds) *Globalisation, Institutions and Regional Development in Europe*. Oxford: Oxford University Press, 217–38.

Rogers-Hollingsworth, J, Schmitter, PC and Streeck, W (eds) (1994) *Governing Capitalist Economies*. Oxford: Oxford University Press.

Rullani, E (1997) 'L'evoluzione dei distretti industriali: un percorso tra deconstuzione e internazionalizzazone', in R Varaldo and L Ferrucci (eds) *Il distretto industriale tra logiche di impresa e logiche di sistema*. Milan: Angeli, 54–85.

Sá Marques, T (1986) 'Sistema produtivo industrial e território. Um estudo da têxtil em Guimarães', MA thesis, Universidade de Lisboa.

Sabel, CF (1992) 'Studied trust: building new forms of co-operation', in F Pyke and W Senenberger (eds) *Industrial Districts and Local Economic Regeneration*. Geneva: International Institute for Labour Studies, 215–50.

Sachs, JD and Warner, A (1995) 'Economic reform and the process of global integration', *Brookings Papers on Economic Activity* 1, 1–118.

Sadler, D (1992) *The Global Region*. London: Pergamon.

Sadler, D (1997) 'The role of supply chain management strategies in the "Europeanization" of the automobile production system', in R Lee and J Wills (eds) *Geographies of Economies*. London: Edward Arnold, 311–20.

Sako, M (1992) *Prices, Quality and Trust: Interfirms Relations in Britain and Japan*. Cambridge: Cambridge University Press.

Sally, R (1994) 'Multinational enterprises, political economy and institutional theory: domestic embeddedness in the context of internationalisation', *Review of International Political Economy* 1, 161–92.

Savy, M, and Veltz, P (eds) (1995) *Économie Globale et Réinvention du Local*. Paris: Datar/Éditions de l'Aube.

Saxenian, AL (1983) 'The Urban Contradictions of Silicon Valley', *International Journal of Urban and Regional Research* 17(2), 236–57.

Saxenian, AL (1991) 'Contrasting Patterns of Business Organisations in Silicon Valley,' *Working Paper 535*, Institute of Urban and Regional Development, University of California at Berkeley, April.

Saxenian, AL (1994) *Regional Advantage: Culture and Competition in Silicon Valley and Route 128*. Cambridge, MA: Harvard University Press.

Saxenian, AL (1999) *The New Immigrants*. San Francisco: Public Policy Institute of California.

Sayer, A (1997) 'The dialectic of culture and economy', in R Lee and J Wills (eds) *Geographies of Economies*. London: Edward Arnold, 16–26.

Sayer, A and Walker, R (1992) *The New Social Economy*. Oxford: Blackwell.

Scheffer, M (1994) *The Changing Map of European Textiles. Production and Sourcing Stategies of Textile and Clothing Firms*. Brussels: OETH.

Schoeneberger, E (1996) *The Cultural Crisis of the Firm*. Oxford: Blackwell.

Schuyler, N (1995) *The Business of Multimedia*. New York: Allworth Press.

Scott, A (1997) 'The cultural economy of cities', *International Journal of Urban and Regional Research* 21(2), 323–39.

Scott, AJ (1995) 'From Silicon Valley to Hollywood: growth and development of the multimedia industry in California', *Working Paper No. 13*. Los Angeles: Lewis Centre for Regional Policy Studies.

Scott, AJ (1996) 'The craft, fashion and cultural products industries of Los Angeles: competitive dynamics and policy dilemmas in a multisectoral image-producing complex', *Annals of the Association of American Geographers* 86(2), 306–23.

Scott, AJ (1998) 'From Silicon Valley to Hollywood: growth and development of the multimedia industry in California', in HJ Braczyk, P Cooke and M Heidenreich (eds) *Regional Innovation Systems: The Role of Governance in a Globalized World*. London: UCL Press, 136–62.

Scott, P and Creighton, K (1994) 'Possible directions of the Asia aircraft manufacturing industry', *Journal of Asia Business* 10, 3, 49–72.

Screen Digest (1997) 'Interactive entertainment software: rapidly maturing market', *Screen Digest*, June, 129–136.

Screen Digest (1998) 'Interactive software spending matches other media', *Screen Digest*, July, 153–60.

Screen Digest (1999) 'Interactive leisure software: UK and European market assessment and forecast.' Screen Digest Ltd: London.

Sheff, D (1993) *Game Over: How Nintendo Zapped an American Industry, Captured Your Dollars and Enslaved Your Children*. New York: Random House.

Siegel, L (1998) 'New chips in old skins: work and labour in Silicon Valley', in G Sussman and J Lent (eds) *Global Productions: Labour in the Making of the 'Information Society'*. Cresskill, NJ: Hampton Press, 91–110.

Smelser, NJ and Swedberg, R (eds) (1994) *The Handbook of Economic Sociology*. Princeton, NJ: Princeton University Press.

SPRI (1998) *Gestión tecnológica de las empresas vascas*. Bilbao: SPRI.

Staiger, J (1983) 'Individualism versus collectivism', *Screen* 24(4–5), 68–79.

Storper, M (1989) 'The transition to flexible specialisation in the US film industry: external economies, the division of labour, and the crossing of industrial divides', *Cambridge Journal of Economics* 13, 273–305.

Storper, M (1995) 'The resurgence of regional economies ten years later', *European Urban and Regional Studies* 2(3), 191–221.

Storper, M (1997) *The Regional World*. New York: Guildford Press.

Storper, M (1999) 'Regional economies as relational assets', paper presented to the International Economic Conferences on 'Local Developments in Europe: New Paradigms and New Schemes of Economic Policy', Varese, 1–2 October.

Storper, M and Harrison, B (1991) 'Flexibility, hierarchy and regional development: the changing structures of production systems and their forms of governance,' *Research Policy*, 21, 407–22.

Storper, M and Scott, AJ (eds) (1992) *Pathways to Industrialization and Regional Development*. London: Routledge.

Storper, M and Scott, AJ (1995) 'The wealth of regions – market forces and policy imperatives in local and global context', *Futures* 27, 5, 505–26.

Strange, S (1988) *States and Markets*. London: Pinter.

Sträter, D (1997) 'Multimedia profiling and the regional restructuring of Munich as an industrial location', paper presented at the International Workshop on Regional Economic Restructuring and Multimedia, Stuttgart, Germany, 8–11 October.

Sugar, R (1993) 'Industry role in US aerospace superiority: some policy recommendations', *Comparative Strategy* 12, 289–93.

Sunley, P (1996) 'Context in economic geography – the relevance of pragmatism', *Progress in Human Geography* 20, 3, 338–55.

Swann, GMP, Prevezder, M and Stout, D (1998) *The Dynamics of Industrial Clustering*. Oxford: Oxford University Press.

Swyngedouw, E (1997) 'Neither global nor local: "globalisation" and the politics of scale', in K Cox (ed.) *Spaces of Globalisation: Reasserting the Power of the Local*. New York: Guildford Press, 137–66.

Taveira, E and De Sousa, FF (1990) 'Industrialização Rural num quadro de economia aberta – o caso do vale do Ave', in CCRC (ed.) *Industrialização em Meios Rurais e Competitividade Internacional*. Coimbra: CCRC.

Taylor, CR and Wiggins, ST (1997) 'Competition or compensation: supplier incentives under the American and Japanese subcontracting systems', *American Economic Review* 87, 4, 598–618.

Thorne, L (1996) 'Local exchange trading systems in the United Kingdom: a case for re-embedding?', *Environment and Planning* A28, 1361–76.

Tighe, C (1988) 'Jewel of Wearside', *Daily Telegraph*, 20 September,

Tighe, C (1996) 'Nissan prompted revival of North East's fortunes', *Financial Times*, 23 February.

Todd, D and Simpson, J (1986) *The World Aircraft Industry*. Cambridge, MA: Auburn House.

Tomaney, J (1996) 'Regional government and economic development: possibilities and limits', *Local Economy* 11 (1), 27–38.

Tomaney, J (1998) 'Globalisation and the North East', *The Journal*, 12 August, Newcastle Chronicle and Journal: Newcastle upon Tyne.

Tomaney, J, Pike, A and Cornford, J (1999) 'Plant closure and the local economy: the case of Swan Hunter on Tyneside', *Regional Studies* 33, 5, 401–11.

Torres, MC (1995) *Industria y territorio en Bizkaia*. Vitoria-Gasteiz: IVAP.

Truel, J (1983) 'Structuration en filière et politique industrielle dans l'électronique: un comparison internationale', *Revue d'Economie Industrielle* 23(1), 293–303.

Turok, I (1993) 'Inward investment and local linkages: how deeply embedded is 'Silicon Glen?', *Regional Studies* 27, 5, 401–17.

Uranga, G and Ozerin, L (1997) 'Comparing regional innovation systems in transition: the case of three Regional Development Agencies', paper presented to the EUNIT Conference on Industry, Innovation and Territory, Lisbon, 20–22 March.

Varaldo, R and Ferrucci, L (1997) 'La natura e la dinamica dell'impresa distrettuale', in R Varaldo and L Ferrucci (eds) *Il distretto industriale tra logiche di impresa e logiche di sistema.* Milan: Angeli, 26–53.

Velasco, R, Landabaso, M and Díez, MA (1990) 'El apoyo a la innovación en el País Vasco: instrumentos, métodos y experiencias (1982–1989)', *Papeles de Economía Española*, no. 9.

Vogel, HL (1990) *Entertainment Industry Economics.* Cambridge: Cambridge University Press.

Watson, S (1996) *Clusters of Competitiveness Evidence: Automotive Sector* (internal report). Newcastle upon Tyne: NDC.

WDA (1996) *Wales Regional Technology Plan: An Innovation and Technology Strategy for Wales.* Action Plan, Welsh Development Agency

Weiss, L (1998) *State Capacity: Governing the Economy in the Global Era.* Cambridge: Polity Press.

Williamson, OE (1975) *Markets and Hierarchies: Analysis and Antitrust Implications.* New York: Free Press and London: Macmillan.

Williamson, OE (1985) *The Economic Institution of Capitalism: Firms, Markets, Relational Contracting.* London: Macmillan.

Womack, J, Jones, D and Roos, J (1990) *The Machine that Changed the World.* New York: Rawson Associates.

Yeung, H (1997) 'Business networks and transnational corporations: a study of Hong Kong firms in the ASEAN region', *Economic Geography* 73, 1, 1–25.

Zukin, S and DiMaggio, P (eds) (1990) *Structures of Capital: The Social Organisation of the Economy.* Cambridge: Cambridge University Press.

Zysman, J (1994) 'How institutions create historically rooted trajectories of growth', *Industrial and Corporate Change* 3(1), 243–83.

Zysman, J (1996) 'The myth of the "global" economy: enduring national foundations and emerging regional realities', *New Political Economy* 1(2), 157–84.

INDEX

*For Product Safety Concerns and Information please contact
our EU representative GPSR@taylorandfrancis.com Taylor & Francis
Verlag GmbH, Kaufingerstraße 24, 80331 München, Germany*

T - #0148 - 160425 - C0 - 246/154/12 - PB - 9780117023802 - Gloss Lamination